9/24/02

Dave

And you were there!
To the greatest jazz enthusiast
of all time

John F.

QUINTET OF THE YEAR

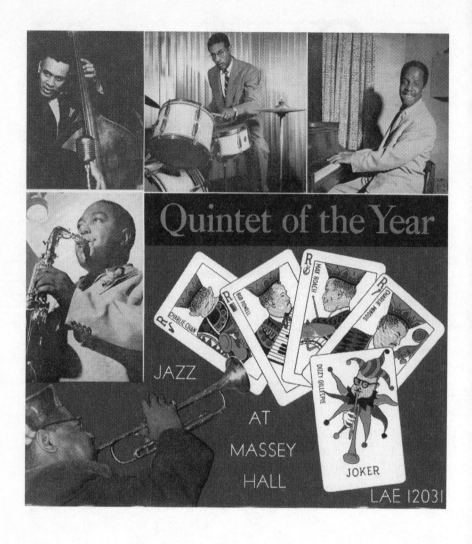

Quintet of the Year

JAZZ

AT

MASSEY

HALL

CHARLIE CHAN
BUD POWELL
MAX ROACH
CHARLIE MINGUS
DIZZY GILLESPIE
JOKER

LAE 12031

Quintet of the Year

Geoffrey Haydon

MACFARLANE WALTER & ROSS
TORONTO

Macfarlane Walter & Ross
An Affiliate of McClelland & Stewart Ltd.
37A Hazelton Avenue
Toronto, Canada M5R 2E3
www.mwandr.com

National Library of Canada Cataloguing in Publication

Haydon, Geoffrey
    Quintet of the year / Geoffrey Haydon.

Includes bibliographical references and index.
ISBN 1–55199–110–1

    1. Jazz musicians—United States—Biography.   2. Jazz—Ontario—
Toronto—1951–1960—History and criticism.   I. Title.

ML395.H416 2002   781.65′092′273   C2002–902587–7

Design by Geoff Green
Published by arrangement with Aurum Press Ltd., London
Printed in Great Britain

CONTENTS

For Max Roach,
a great artist and kind friend.

PREFACE

1958. Roaming among the jazz racks in Miller's music shop in Cambridge, I came upon an object with a sacred aura. Even in its silence, the 12-inch Microgroove LP called *Quintet of the Year* exercised a mighty pull. The heraldry of its sleeve combined plain photographs of the five modern masters with artful caricatures of them as playing cards. That Dizzy Gillespie should be shown as the joker was no surprise, but why did Charlie Parker's picture have its back to us, and why the caption 'Charlie Chan'? And why was the reverse side headed 'Charles Mingus presents'? The sleeve note (written by Alun Morgan for this British repackaging of the American original) thickened the plot by warning that, in spite of the billing, not all the music within had been recorded at Massey Hall in Toronto five years earlier.

I parted with a sizeable chunk of my student grant, hurried the LP back to my room in college, disrobed the vinyl and placed it on the Dansette turntable. Before lowering the needle, filled with proselytizing zeal I opened the mullioned window on to the Tudor courtyard. It was a warm day, and everyone in the ivory tower should share my experience.

The hectic brilliance of the music surpassed all imaginings, and nearly half a century later the need to communicate my excitement remains pressing. So the Massey Hall concert and the myths and mysteries surrounding it are at the centre of this book.

The five African-Americans who took part were all in the prime of life, yet one of them would be dead within two years, and another was already enduring long spells of confinement in mental hospitals. The first five chapters will examine the struggles, the creative achievements and the interlocking lives of the players, up to the moment when the recorder at Massey Hall was switched on. The last five will follow each participant after the event.

During the 1960s and 1970s I met Dizzy Gillespie, Charles Mingus and Max Roach when they brought their bands to Europe. I also hunted for Bud Powell, but my visit to Paris coincided with one of his bouts of illness, and the closest I came was watching videos of him in performance.

In the 1980s when I was making a documentary film about Max Roach, he insisted I should stay at his home and looked after me royally. I was taken to meet his friends and family in Brooklyn, and given a guided tour of the hallowed spots in Harlem. We also travelled with the film crew down to North Carolina, and here I received a nasty surprise. En route from Norfolk airport to Max's birthplace in Dismal Swamp, we stopped for the night at a motel outside Elizabeth City. After we had checked in, I went to investigate the establishment's refreshment room, described in its literature as 'the English Pub'. I was met by a wall of white staring faces and a spokesman who announced, 'We don't like your friend, and we don't want people like that coming around here.' When I realized they meant Max, I pointed out indignantly that the gentleman to whom they were referring was America's greatest drummer, and I had journeyed 3000 miles for the privilege of filming him. Stony silence. I went to see Max in his cabin and found him preparing to leave. Nothing had been said to him but he had recognized what kind of place this was. 'I think I'll drive on and stay with my folks tonight,' he told me casually. I persuaded him to stay, then spent a sleepless night. I was the one who had brought him here, and I was mortified and outraged. Max urged me not to take it so hard.

By the time I started on the book, Max Roach was the only survivor of the Massey Hall five. Without his encouragement this quintet of linked biographies would not have been undertaken. I offer it as my homage to the glory of African-American music, and in recognition of the often harsh circumstances of its creation.

*

Others who kindly helped me along the way are listed below:

Ian Carr, Brian Dale, Mark Gardner, Bob Glass, the late Norman Granz, Dave Green, Anne Higgins, Mark Miller, Alun Morgan, the late Francis Paudras, Brian Priestley, Peter Pullman, Mildred Roach, Alyn Shipton, Ken Vail, Paul Wilson and Celia Mingus Zaentz.

I am grateful to Alan Scharf and Tony Williams for the use of some previously unpublished photographs.

I should also like to thank my editor Graham Coster and my wife Mary for their saintly forbearance during this book's mammoth gestation.

Geoffrey Haydon. London, England. 2002

ONE

COSMIC RAYS

'Charlie Parker was like the sun, giving off the energy we drew from him.'
Max Roach[1]

ORSON WELLES, playing devil's advocate in the film *The Third Man*, justifies corrupt government by pointing out that under the Borgias the Italians grew used to terror and murder, 'but they produced Michelangelo, Leonardo and the Renaissance'.

He might have chosen as his example the ruffian regime of Tom Pendergast, mayor of Kansas City from 1928 to 1939. During the Pendergast era, gambling, prostitution, and narcotics thrived; Prohibition was ignored and the nightspots were crammed. The best black musicians in the land were drawn here by the abundance of jobs. In particular, Kansas became the city of great saxophonists. By 1935 the resident masters of the instrument included Ben Webster, Herschel Evans and Lester Young. This was the hothouse where Charlie Parker metamorphosed from unexceptional schoolboy into one of the greatest American artists of the twentieth century. It was also where he contracted his heroin habit.

He was born in Kansas City, Kansas, on 29 August 1920. His father, Charles Parker, Senr., had perched here at the end of a tour singing and dancing on the TOBA circuit. (TOBA was the Theatre Owners Booking

1

Association, the mean cartel that controlled black vaudeville. Its performer-victims liked to say the initials stood for Tough On Black Artists.) Charlie's mother, Addie, was a local girl, part Choctaw Indian, who married the roving entertainer when she was sixteen years old.

By the time Charlie was ten his hard-drinking father had left home and left town. Mother and son moved across the river to the more populous Kansas City, Missouri. Their new address, a two-storey frame house on Olive Street in the black ghetto, was a short walk from the entertainment district.

In 1932 Charlie entered Lincoln High School, whose marching band was a source of civic pride. He signed up for band practice and was granted the use of a cumbersome baritone horn. His mother bought a piano for the home and an ancient alto saxophone for her son, and since the sax came without a case, she sewed a bag for it. Tutty Clarkin, a nightclub operator in Kansas City at the time the instrument was in service, remembers it with 'rubber bands and cellophane all over it. He had to hold it sideways to make it blow.'[2]

Charlie was big for his age. He joined a group of older boys who played for dances and called themselves the Deans of Swing. And since his mother worked at night cleaning the offices of Western Union, there was no one to stop him sampling the fruits of Tom Pendergast's town.

The Sunset Club on Twelfth Street was a good place to start. Thanks to the loudspeaker rigged up outside, you could enjoy the action without paying admission. The piano player in there was Pete Johnson, known as 'Roll 'em Pete' because of his boogie-woogie left hand. The other feature was the giant-voiced bartender, Big Joe Turner, who belted out the blues when the spirit moved him. Sometimes Big Joe would start his serenade behind the bar in the Sunset, then lumber across the street and finish it in the Lone Star opposite.

Rivalling the Sunset and the Lone Star were the Boulevard Lounge, the Cherry Blossom, the Subway and many more, and topping them all was the Reno, with its elaborate floor show plus 'Music for Your Dancing Pleasure by the Count Basie–Prof Smith Band of Rhythm'. Prof Smith, also known as Buster, led the peerless saxophone section. He would become young Charlie's friend and mentor. The most original soloist was Lester Young, and he would serve as Parker's role model. Jam sessions at the Reno began after the last floorshow, at around 5.00 in the morning. If you were a schoolboy and you managed to sneak in the back door, you were unlikely to be at your desk for the start of lessons at Lincoln High.

Up to here, Charlie knew nothing about the theory of harmony, and thought all music was played in one key. The tunes he knew best were 'Up a Lazy River' and 'Honeysuckle Rose'. However, inspired by what he witnessed at the Reno, he tried to make his mark during a minor-league jam session at the Hi Hat club. The episode left a painful memory: 'I was doing all right until I tried doing double tempo on *Body and Soul.* Everybody fell out laughing. I went home and cried.'[3]

*

He also practised up to fifteen hours a day: 'I took the scales a half step at a time. After I learned the scales, I taught myself to play the blues in all the twelve keys. Then I learned *I Got Rhythm* in all the twelve keys.'[4] Next he joined the musicians' union, giving his age as eighteen and putting Lincoln High School entirely behind him.

In July 1936, against his mother's advice, Charlie married his steady girlfriend, the shy but stunningly beautiful Rebecca Ruffin. He was fifteen, his bride was sixteen (although Rebecca put herself down as eighteen on the marriage licence). Charlie's mother accepted Rebecca into her house and was pleased when her daughter-in-law turned out to be a homebody with no interest in Kansas City nightlife. But Rebecca's warm presence failed to lure Charlie into domesticity.

His longest spell indoors followed a car crash that broke some ribs and damaged his spine. For two months he lay upstairs recuperating and consoling himself with his stash of marijuana (not illegal in those days). The silver lining was a brand new Selmer saxophone, bought with the insurance money.

According to Tutty Clarkin, Charlie's earliest experiments with drugs involved getting high on nutmeg. From there he graduated to Benzedrine inhalers. 'He'd break them open and soak them in wine. Then he smoked tea [marijuana] and finally got hooked on heroin.'[5] In the account Parker himself gave, his dissipation began when he was only twelve years old; three years later a friend introduced him to heroin. He woke up one morning soon after that feeling terribly sick and not knowing why.[6]

The parlour of the Parker home was furnished with a Victrola alongside the piano, and Rebecca has said that Charlie made assiduous use of both. But as his musicianship grew, so did his reputation for overreaching himself. He suffered his greatest humiliation when he dared to join a jam session at the Reno club involving members of the Count Basie orchestra. The tempo was brisk and when Charlie's turn came he seemed not to go with the flow. Basie's drummer, Jo Jones, became so vexed that he hurled a cymbal at Charlie's feet.

Charlie's considered response was to take a three-month engagement at a lakeside resort in the Ozark Mountains, with a band that played for dancing every night. He had not come here to hide, he had come to learn. The band's guitarist, Efferge Ware, was a refined harmonist, happy to share his knowledge. Charlie's other educator was his set of Count Basie phonograph records. From these he memorized, note for note and nuance for nuance, the ground-breaking solos by Lester Young.

*

Mission accomplished, Parker came down from the mountain. The musicians of Kansas City marvelled at the transformation. One who bore witness was the pianist Jay McShann, who was playing in a jam session when Parker pushed his way on stage. 'He'd get off on a line of his own and I would think he was headed for trouble, but he was like a cat landing on all four feet. He was a strange kid, very aggressive and wise.'[7]

Parker's next regular job was in the 12-piece band newly formed by Buster ('Prof') Smith, previously with Count Basie. Playing second alto to Smith was a position Parker valued highly, and Smith was confident enough in the young man to share the solo space with him. This happy period for Parker ended in September 1938, when Buster Smith went to rejoin Basie, who had moved to New York.

By now Parker was a father, but the arrival of the baby boy did not cement relations with Rebecca. Things at home were going badly. Jewellery and household items, including his mother's iron, were converted into cash to feed his drug habit.

Things were also going badly in the music business. The Federal tax net was tightening around Mayor Pendergast and nightclubs were losing their favoured status. Parker took to jamming with his friends under the stars in the city park. At the start of 1939 he pawned his saxophone and jumped a freight train going north.

*

When Buster Smith opened the door of his New York apartment and found Parker standing there – on painfully swollen legs, in shoes that had been worn too long – he was not greatly surprised. Parker moved in. Smith's wife had a day job, so after she went off to work in the mornings, Parker would sleep in the matrimonial bed. When she came home he got up and stayed out all night.

The musicians' union decided who was eligible to work in New York, so for an outsider to find paid employment as a performer was almost impossible. Parker played in jam sessions in Harlem (presumably using Buster Smith's saxophone) and took a job washing dishes at Jimmy's Chicken Shack, where the resident attraction was the blind pianist Art Tatum, one of the world's great musicians. Tatum's noble keyboard style possessed the qualities that Parker was seeking for himself: rhythmic variety, harmonic richness, precision of touch, and mastery in all the keys, at any speed. Parker stuck his lousy job at the Chicken Shack for the full three months of Tatum's residency.

Back on the jam session circuit he made friends with the astute guitarist Biddy Fleet. The two of them would practise in the back room of Dan Wall's Chili House up in Harlem, exploring the exciting melodic possibilities of the upper intervals (ninths, elevenths, thirteenths) of chords. New York was encouraging Parker to spread his artistic wings. He would have stayed, and would have been bound to bump into Dizzy Gillespie, had he not received an urgent telegram from his mother.

*

The shock news from Kansas City concerned his father. The roaming Charles Parker, Senr. had been stabbed to death by a woman rumoured to be a prostitute.

After the funeral, Parker stayed with his family, but he could not settle. Within months he was asking Rebecca for a divorce. From this unhappy time comes the first recording Charlie Parker ever made. This sensational treasure (an amateur disc, rough hewn and simply labelled *Honey and Body*) lay buried until the 1980s, when Parker sleuths visiting Kansas City hauled it into the light. On it we hear Parker, entirely alone, playing variations on 'Honeysuckle Rose' and 'Body and Soul'. His tone is unformed and the architecture is fairly conservative, but the Parker lineaments are there: the double time flurry, the chromaticism, the quotation from popular song and the profound sense of swing.

His first job back in Kansas City was with the band of Harlan Leonard (a snooty fellow by all accounts). The happy part of it for Parker was the friendship he formed with the composer and arranger Tadd Dameron, with whom he shared adventures in harmony and drug taking. Dameron will crop up again, and one of his compositions will be performed at Massey Hall, but this first communion with Parker was brief, because Parker was fired. He was snapped up by the pianist Jay McShann, who was forming a big band.

Strangely, it was not in heady New York but during this Kansas City lull that Parker first met Dizzy Gillespie, the co-revolutionary whose musical thinking was closest to his own. Historians agree that their paths crossed when Gillespie came to Parker's home town with the famous Cab Calloway Orchestra, but the exact date has been the subject of scholarly debate. In his 1999 biography of Gillespie, Alyn Shipton argues convincingly for 24 June 1940. This was during Gillespie's second visit to Kansas City with Calloway, when both the Calloway Orchestra and Jay McShann's band were playing at Fairyland Park, the city's summertime pleasure gardens. Word had reached McShann's trumpeters that Gillespie was a talent they must hear, so they attended the Calloway show on

23 June. Afterwards they cornered the young trumpet star and boasted about their local hero, Charlie Parker. That night Parker could not be found, but next day, in the upstairs room at the HQ of the coloured (seg-regated) musicians' union, he and Gillespie were brought together. Parker played, Gillespie accompanied him on the piano, and left Kansas City deeply impressed, as he later recalled:

> I was astounded by what the guy could do. The way that he assembled notes together. That was one of the greatest thrills because I had been a Roy Eldridge fan up to then, but I was moving on. Charlie Parker and I were moving in practically the same direction.[8]

*

Parker and Gillespie would not meet again to experiment for two years. During that time, the McShann band was Charlie Parker's home. Although he was the youngest member – still not twenty when he joined – McShann put him in charge of the saxophone section.

It was while he was on the road with McShann that Parker acquired his nickname. McShann himself liked to tell the story. According to him, Parker's favourite dish was chicken, or 'yardbird'. One day the band bus hit a luckless fowl, and Parker jumped out and collected the corpse. At the hotel he rushed this 'yardbird' to the kitchen and called for it to be cooked and served. So he became 'Yardbird', or just 'Yard', or, to most people, just 'Bird'.

In November 1940 the McShann band made a set of discs at radio sta-tion KFBI in Wichita, Kansas, and from these we can hear just how good twenty-year-old Parker was sounding. His tone is still not fully formed, but his invention and poise, particularly on the fast-moving 'Honeysuckle Rose', place him far ahead of his companions.

The commercial breakthrough for the McShann band came in April 1941, when the Decca recording company called them to its studios in Dallas, Texas, to record some bluesy material for its 'Sepia Series'. The big hit from the session was 'Confessin' the Blues', featuring the manly, insinuating voice of Walter Brown, backed only by the McShann rhythm section. This jukebox favourite eventually sold more than 500,000 copies. On the

B-side, generally ignored, was the easy-paced 'Hootie Blues'. Here Walter Brown is backed by the full orchestra, and before he sings there is a 12-bar solo by Charlie Parker. This was the first time the Parker message had slipped out to the world at large, and musicians who chanced upon it, like young Miles Davis in St Louis, were thrilled. The message read: you can preserve the essence of the blues while creating something freshly beautiful.

*

In January 1942, promoted by Decca as 'the band that plays the blues', McShann's men opened at the famed Savoy Ballroom in New York's Harlem. Sessions at the Savoy were regularly broadcast, so musicians all over the country became aware that something extraordinary was happening. Those in the New York area hurried to the Savoy to meet the alto saxophonist they had heard reeling off chorus after high-speed chorus on the chord sequence of 'Cherokee'. A snatch of what inspired them has come down to us on an amateur disc-recording, probably taken from the radio. Although stuck with a chugging rhythm section, Parker manages to sound free as a bird.

His fondness for 'Cherokee' went back to his first visit to New York, in 1939, when he and Biddy Fleet adopted it as their practice piece. The romantic song (addressed by English composer Ray Noble to an imaginary Native American maiden) has a melody that floats lazily, all long notes, over a racing pulse. By taking this melody a little faster than Noble intended, you hit a febrile metronome reading of 300 beats per minute. But the crucial quality of 'Cherokee' for Parker was its harmonic design. Its A section never strays far from the home key of B flat, but section B comes as a delightful shock – plunging us into the outlandish key of B, then leading us through the keys of A and G on the journey home. Negotiating this tricky route at high speed, with extra diversions of his own, evidently gave Parker huge satisfaction.

*

Dizzy Gillespie came regularly to sit in with the McShann band at the Savoy, and after the show he and Parker would head for Harlem's musical test-beds. First stop Minton's Playhouse on 118th Street, where they were likely to find Thelonious Monk and his brilliant pupil Bud Powell. When Minton's closed they'd move on to an after-hours spot such as Clark Monroe's Uptown House, where the drummer was a teenager from Brooklyn called Max Roach. At Monroe's, they could jam from 4.00 until 8.00 in the morning. Looking back on those heady days, Gillespie offered this appreciation of Charlie Parker's part in the musical upheaval:

> When Charlie Parker came to New York in 1942 the new style of music had already begun, but he made a gigantic contribution . . . His modus operandi was different, how he attacked and how he swung . . . I'd show Yardbird things on the piano and how our music was structured. But he played very syncopated and sanctified . . . And the notes! Bird has some notes in his melodies that are deep, as deep as anything Beethoven ever wrote . . . [9]

In July 1942 the McShann band made some records for Decca in New York. Parker's solo on one of them, *The Jumpin' Blues*, opens with a catchy phrase that became the basis of a favourite theme used by the modernists. In his honour they called it 'Ornithology'.

When McShann and his orchestra resumed their travels, Parker dropped out. To survive in New York he took a job at Clark Monroe's Uptown House, where he joined young Max Roach as a member of the (non-union) house band. The nightly reward was a meal and a share of the sometimes-meagre kitty. Musicians visiting New York were taken to marvel at the Parker phenomenon, but his friends became alarmed by Parker's declining health. His life revolved around music, drugs and alcohol. Something had to be done. A deputation of Parker admirers approached the bandleader Earl 'Fatha' Hines and told him they knew just the candidate to fill the vacancy in his saxophone section. They took Hines to hear Parker at Monroe's, and Hines was impressed, but what he needed was someone to play the *tenor* saxophone. Parker said he could do it, so Hines advanced him the money to buy the larger instrument.

The sound of that seminal Earl Hines orchestra (it also included Gillespie and several more free-thinkers) was not saved for posterity, because in August 1942 the powerful musicians' union, the AFM

(American Federation of Musicians), imposed a nation-wide recording ban. What we are lucky to have (uncovered in 1986) is a private recording, made in a Chicago hotel room on 15 February 1943, of Parker and Gillespie playing together to please themselves.

The owner-operator of the disc recorder is jazz enthusiast Bob Redcross. The third musician taking part is Oscar Pettiford, who lays down a sinewy, propulsive bass line. The chosen tune is 'Sweet Georgia Brown', and Parker takes the first solo. He is playing tenor, of course, and the richness of his tone comes as a delight: the mingled shades of Coleman Hawkins and Lester Young. The intricate phraseology and rapid delivery, though, are Parker's own. After three eloquent and ingenious choruses, he hands over to Gillespie who fires off some riffs then surges forward. Now it's Parker again, urged on by Gillespie's shouts of 'Come on Yard!' There's just room on the disc for a second burst from Gillespie, before the two horns entwine to grace 'Sweet Georgia Brown' with an impromptu polyphonic ending.

This Tru-Tone 78 cut by Bob Redcross opens the short list of recordings made by these two great artists in tandem: a list in which the Massey Hall concert will loom very large.

*

In April 1943, while the Hines band was in Washington, DC, Parker wed wife number two, the dancer Geraldine Scott. Their short relationship was a calamity for Geraldine, who was left with a heroin habit. Nor could Parker make a go of his job with Earl Hines. He was often late. Sometimes he failed to appear. In August he left. So, too, did Gillespie.

During the next six months Parker worked obscurely in Chicago and Kansas City. Private recordings he made in his home town with the guitarist Efferge Ware did not surface until the 1990s. On these we hear him patiently refining his art, working through favourite test pieces like 'Body and Soul' and 'Cherokee'.

During his absence the modernist tendency moved downtown from Harlem and gained a footing on 52nd Street in white New York. The group that made the breakthrough was co-led by Dizzy Gillespie and

Oscar Pettiford, and had Max Roach on drums. They sent Parker a telegram urging him to join them. No reply.

The good shepherd who returned Parker to the fold was the singer Billy Eckstine, who had left Earl Hines and was forming a big band of his own. Eckstine had star appeal. He was also a fervent apostle of the new music. He made Gillespie his musical director, then tracked down Parker and put him in charge of the saxophone section. Gillespie and Parker (now back on alto) were the featured soloists.

'Listen. The greatest feeling I ever had in my life – with my clothes on – was when I first heard Diz and Bird together in St Louis, Missouri, back in 1944. I was eighteen years old.'[10] So begins the autobiography of Miles Davis, recalling the time the touring Eckstine band reached his home town.

As soon as they arrived in St Louis, Eckstine and his men showed an attitude that thrilled the black population. They had been booked to appear at the Plantation, a club for white folks, run by gangsters, where Negro musicians were expected to use the back door. The Eckstine crew marched straight in at the front, shocking the hoodlums with their lack of servility. Then during the intermission, in spite of warnings, they sat among the audience. Parker's old friend and fellow prankster from Kansas City, Tadd Dameron (now with Eckstine as an arranger) poured himself a glass of water. What happened next stuck in the mind of the band's drummer, Art Blakey:

> Tadd was drinking out of one of the beautiful glasses they had to serve the customers. Bird walked over to him saying, 'Did you drink out of this glass, Tadd?' 'Yeah,' Tadd says. Bam! Bird smashes it. 'Then it's contaminated. Did you drink out of this one?' 'Yeah,' Tadd says. Bam! 'It's contaminated.'[11]

The band moved across town and played instead at the all-black Riviera club. Miles Davis went down there with his trumpet, hoping he might be allowed to sit in. As soon as he got inside, Gillespie (whom he had never met) rushed up to him shouting, 'Come on. We need a trumpet player. One of ours got sick!' Miles was a proficient sight-reader but he had trouble concentrating on his part that night, 'because the whole band would have an orgasm every time Diz or Bird played – especially Bird. I mean Bird was unbelievable.'[12]

*

When the Eckstine band returned to New York and prepared for the next leg of its tour, Parker announced he would travel no further. Instead he would work on 52nd Street, where top black talent was now performing nightly for a white clientele. He took a job with Ben Webster's group but often strayed from club to club along The Street, sitting in with other bands Kansas City fashion. One of his stopping places was Tondelayo's, where he would jam with the trio of guitarist Tiny Grimes, and this was fortunate for posterity, because Grimes then recruited Parker to help him make some records on 15 September 1944.

The Savoy company was hoping to market Grimes as a singer, so for most of the three-hour session Grimes did his best with his voice. Two songs emerged at last, 'Romance without Finance' and 'I'll Always Love You'. Their value resides almost entirely in Parker's exquisite obbligatos. To fill the B-sides the musicians recorded two instrumentals. One was 'Tiny's Tempo', a bouncy 12-bar blues with a commanding solo from Parker. The other went down as a Parker original, which he called 'Red Cross'.

The reference is to Bob Redcross, the man who recorded Parker and Gillespie playing 'Sweet Georgia Brown'. In that same Chicago hotel room, the Redcross machinery captured Parker toying with a popular two-bar riff that fits the 'I Got Rhythm' chord sequence. 'Red Cross' is an outgrowth of that riff. (So too, by the way, is the number Gillespie sold to the bandleader Jimmy Dorsey as 'Grand Central Getaway'.)

During Parker's solo on 'Red Cross' his flexible, daring way with time is flatly contradicted by the chugging Grimes rhythm section. However, the convergence of Parker, Gillespie and a sympathetic rhythm team was imminent.

*

Early in 1945, when Gillespie was invited by the Three Deuces club on 52nd Street to form a quintet representing the best of the modern movement, he began with Parker. The rest of his dream team was to be Bud Powell on piano, Curley Russell on bass and Max Roach on drums. Roach was not immediately available and Powell could not come at all, so two young white musicians deputized: pianist Al Haig and drummer Stan Levey. These were worthy substitutes, and judging from contemporary accounts the result was sensational.

The commercial recordings Parker and Gillespie made together in February 1945 do not quite represent the state of the art (the record company, Guild, booked a swing-style rhythm section), but *Groovin' High* and *Dizzy Atmosphere* are new-music landmarks just the same. The next session, in May, came closer to simulating the action at the Three Deuces, because this time Al Haig and Curley Russell were included. The quintet recorded 'Hot House' (an intensely chromatic line by Tadd Dameron on the chords of 'What Is This Thing Called Love') and two compositions by Gillespie: 'Shaw 'Nuff' and 'Salt Peanuts'. All the new pieces became classics of the modern repertoire, and will crop up again and again in these pages. Two of them will feature at Massey Hall. The main point here, though, is the performance of the principals on these premier recordings. Their unison renditions of the fiendishly intricate themes are a marvel. When it comes to playing solos in the new language, Parker is the more confident. As Gillespie put it, 'he set the standard for phrasing our music, the enunciation of the notes'.[13]

At the Three Deuces, however, to Gillespie's frustration and sadness, Parker's drug habit was deflecting him from his professional responsibilities. He often came late, and on some evenings he was not there at all. One night in the dressing room after the show, Gillespie and the others in the band put it to Parker that he was throwing his life away and they could not afford to lose him. His dumbfounding reply was that maybe God had put him on earth not primarily as a musician, but as an example to others of the harm drugs can do.

By July, Gillespie had had enough. He shocked disciples of the new music by dissolving the quintet.

*

There had been other recording sessions in 1945 where Parker and Gillespie had been confined to supporting roles. On one such occasion the consequences were sublime, on another they were hilarious. The central figure in the comedy was Henry 'Rubberlegs' Williams, a big personality from the world of vaudeville, cutting his first discs as a blues singer. Before the singing began, Williams accidentally drank Parker's coffee instead of his own. To brighten himself up Parker had dosed his drink with Benzedrine – for him a moderate stimulant, but for the unprepared Williams a fuel that rocketed his performances from the vigorous to the demented.

The occasion of the sublime music was the session led by the vibraphonist Red Norvo, who added Parker and Gillespie to his group of swing musicians and called the ensemble 'Red Norvo and his Selected Sextet'. The *chef d'oeuvre* from this intriguing date is 'Slam Slam Blues', an ultra-slow 12-bar, named after bassist Slam Stewart, but immortalized by the searing, blues-drenched personal statement from Parker.

In September there was a session under the command of the pianist Sir Charles Thompson, but for Parker chronologists the next crucially important date in 1945 is Monday 26 November. That was when, in response to an invitation from Savoy records, he made his first recordings as leader, having picked his own team.

The chosen trumpeter was nineteen-year-old Miles Davis, who had left his home in St Louis and followed his idols to New York. Miles had been playing with Parker on 52nd Street – filling the gap left when Gillespie took his big band on tour. The preferred pianist for this record date was Bud Powell. Curley Russell would play bass, Max Roach the drums.

The man responsible for the smooth running of the session, Savoy's Teddy Reig, took the precaution of riding up to Harlem several hours ahead of time to locate Parker and the others and remind them of their duties. Of Bud Powell there was no trace. Instead, Parker announced that his old friend Dizzy Gillespie, back in town after his tour, would play the piano. The startled Reig was also introduced to the back-up pianist, Argonne Thornton, otherwise known as Sadik Hakim.

As part of his deal with Savoy, Parker had undertaken to provide four original compositions, but he committed no music to paper until just before the session started. The scene in the studio was further confused by hangers-on and dope peddlers, but we know exactly how the session unfolded musically because after Parker's death Savoy issued every note that had been recorded, including false starts and rejected takes.

   The first number was an easy-paced 12-bar blues in F called 'Billie's Bounce'. Parker's written theme is a strong one, both funky and intricate, but when it came to his solo his reed had a tendency to squeak. After three takes, he insisted his mouthpiece needed attention, and the nervous Teddy Reig accompanied him to a saxophone repair shop.

   Back in the studio, Parker tested the instrument before tackling 'Billie's Bounce' again. Unknown to him, the Savoy engineer recorded the test. It has come down to us as 'Warming Up a Riff'. The tempo is quick, the rhythm section sure; Gillespie at the piano lays down the chords of 'Cherokee', and Parker takes wing. Borne aloft on the warm currents of this favourite harmonic pattern, he displays a musical daring that makes Gillespie laugh out loud. Then he stops in mid-flight and pronounces his mouthpiece OK. Back to 'Billie's Bounce', which needed two more takes before Parker was satisfied.

   Next came another, slower 12-bar blues in F, with an earthy, riffing theme. Parker called it 'Now's the Time'. Gillespie's piano introduction hits exactly the right groove, but, largely on account of the nervousness of Miles Davis, there are several false starts and two complete takes. Parker creates exemplary but distinctly different solos on both takes. He is the absolute master of the blues idiom, able to convey its sorrowing essence while turning it to his own, intensely expressive purposes.

   The third piece was logged by Savoy as 'Thriving on a Riff' (composer: Parker). This dashing line above the 'I Got Rhythm' chords is usually known as 'Anthropology', and credited to Parker and Gillespie jointly, but in the studio on that day Gillespie ceded the piano stool to Argonne Thornton.

   Before embarking on the final number, still bothered by his reed, Parker called for another off-the-record work-out. Again the result was unofficially recorded. This time it's an improvisation on the chords of the Gershwin ballad 'Embraceable You', although Gershwin's melody is not stated or even referred to. Savoy labelled this fantastical invention 'Meandering', a title that fails to recognize the unity imposed by Parker's genius on the diversity of his ideas.

And now for the pièce de résistance. The chord sequence yet again is 'Cherokee', and the pace is a scorching 300 beats per minute. To make it work, Gillespie not only plays the piano, he also takes over the trumpet part from a defeated Miles Davis. The outstanding opening routine includes a crucial role for Max Roach. According to Max, Parker created it in response to his complaint that the drummer is always taken for granted. So at the beginning the double bass stays silent, and Parker and Gillespie perform death-defying feats above the drums alone. Next, on Take 1, Parker and Gillespie start to cruise through Ray Noble's melody. They have not gone far before they are interrupted by whistling and clapping and panicky shouts of 'Hey! Hold it!!' from Teddy Reig, acting on behalf of his boss, Herman Lubinsky, who expects four *original* (i.e. copyrightable) tunes for his money. So the musicians start again, and this time the introduction leads straight to Parker's solo, with Gillespie moving smartly from trumpet to piano. Parker's two 64-bar choruses are an awesome demonstration of virtuosity at the service of invention. Subverting the obvious cyclical repeats of the 'Cherokee' chord sequence, he erects instead a stately new edifice of symmetries and asymmetries. Then a short Max Roach solo leads to a recapitulation of the introductory framework, where Gillespie and Parker trace yet more delicate arabesques. The 2 minute 50 second masterpiece was given the title 'Koko'.

The unexpurgated Savoy recordings are a monument to the twenty-five-year-old Parker's mature style. One of the virtues so far unmentioned is his instrumental tone, which, in spite of the reed problems, has achieved that unsentimental, instantly recognizable quality he was seeking. It triumphs by combining a keen cutting edge (sometimes verging on the squeak) with massive, vibrato-free strength in depth.

The other point to note is Parker's choice of drummer. The importance of Max Roach's speed and musicality to the artistic success of these recordings cannot be overstated. For the rest of Parker's short life his playing would peak whenever Roach was behind the drums.

*

A fortnight after the Savoy session, Parker left New York and travelled to California with Gillespie for an eight-week engagement. In Parker's case the eight weeks would stretch painfully to sixteen months.

The package sold by Gillespie's agent Billy Shaw to Billy Berg's club in Hollywood was the Dizzy Gillespie Sextet, with the young vibraphone player Milt Jackson bolstering the front line. The snag, not admitted to Berg, was Parker's addiction-related unreliability. The sextet's drummer Stan Levey recalled the tensions of that California trip:

> Charlie was really ill; he was strung out. But his ability, his gift, just made up for anything. So the attitude Dizzy had toward Charlie was, well, we have a child here who has a great talent. Dizzy was voracious in his drive to succeed, and Charlie was oriented to drugs. So there was the problem.[14]

On opening night, 10 December 1945, those in the know turned up at Billy Berg's; but these cognoscenti could not afford to come regularly, and Berg's usual crowd gave the music the thumbs down. Berg complained that Parker rarely appeared. He felt entitled to a saxophonist, so Gillespie hired the tenor player Lucky Thompson as Parker's permanent understudy. Berg also required the music to be more commercial. He wanted the sextet to add a vocalist or sing themselves. Gillespie was outraged but Parker said why not? and amazed young Ray Brown, the bassist, by dreaming up some vocal arrangements.

On 29 December, Parker and Gillespie played the straight men at an off-beat recording session programmed around the talents of Slim Gaillard, purveyor of novelty and nonsense songs. They gamely entered into the spirit, adding bright solos to such jolly fare as 'Flat Foot Floogie' and exchanging verbal pleasantries with Gaillard on 'Slim's Jam'.

Of greater moment was their second playing engagement on that same day – together with the rest of the sextet – on the Armed Forces Radio Service *Jubilee* programme. Thirty years later a recording of the event was uncovered in the AFRS vault. This vital find allows us to hear three core items from the Parker–Gillespie repertoire – 'Shaw 'Nuff', 'Groovin' High' and 'Dizzy Atmosphere' – as they would have been played at the Three Deuces. (The commercial discs made by Guild had been handicapped by unaccustomed rhythm men and limited playing time.) Here, in plenty of space and with the right support, Parker and Gillespie extend their magnificent wings. The only bum note is struck by the mindless MC, Bubbles 'The Stomach' Whitman, who raves about Dizzy, 'the professor of Rebop', and ignores Parker entirely.

On 28 January 1946 Parker and Gillespie took part in a big jazz bash promoted by Norman Granz at the Los Angeles Philharmonic Auditorium. Since they were also due at Billy Berg's that night, Granz had agreed that they should play the first half of his programme only. Gillespie came early, but Parker needed to scour the sprawling city for drugs and did not arrive until just before the interval. So while Gillespie left for Billy Berg's as promised, Parker stayed for the Jazz at the Philharmonic second half. The most potent consequence was the solo he played on 'Lady Be Good'. This magic mix of high sophistication and downright earthiness astonished those present and, thanks to the concert recording, has been a source of wonder ever since. John Lewis (future director of the Modern Jazz Quartet) described it thus: 'Bird made a blues out of "Lady Be Good". That solo made old men out of everyone on stage that night.'[15]

The engagement at Billy Berg's ended on 4 February. Next evening, local record-shop owner Ross Russell made his first, fraught attempt to be a record producer. His ambition was to bring together Gillespie, Parker and Lester Young. The studio overflowed with hangers-on, but Lester Young never came. All that could be recorded was a Lester-less rehearsal on the chords of 'Lover', with a short solo by Parker, eventually issued as 'Diggin' Diz'. The following night Russell tried again, but this time Parker joined Young on the list of absentees.

At the end of that week the Gillespie Sextet flew back to New York. All except Parker, who traded his ticket for drug money and stayed behind.

*

When news spread that the great Charlie Parker had found himself a job at the Finale club, this unglamorous location became the Mecca for all the young jazz musicians on the West Coast. Miles Davis hitched a ride to Los Angeles with Benny Carter's band and soon was playing at the club regularly. According to him, the most passionate among the host of locals who came to worship Bird was Charles Mingus. Mingus's own vivid account of how he fell under Parker's spell belongs to a future chapter.

Another regular at the Finale club was Ross Russell. Undaunted by the 'Diggin' Diz' shambles, he was wooing Parker towards a one-year recording contract. According to Russell's account, when Parker learned that Igor Stravinsky and Arnold Schoenberg had made their homes in Southern California, he saw the region in a new light. He wanted a residence of his own, with a library of music by the great composers and a swimming pool. When Russell brought up the subject of segregation, Parker told him, 'That's uncool, but you and I don't have to talk about that.'[16]

On 28 March 1946 Parker made his first records for Russell's Dial label, supported by Miles Davis, tenor saxophonist Lucky Thompson and a rhythm section from the Finale club.

The first piece they recorded was a Parker original he called 'Moose the Mooche', in honour of the gentleman in Los Angeles who was supplying him with heroin. It's an elusive, superbly crafted theme, and it gave Parker's colleagues a good deal of trouble. Next they recorded 'Yardbird Suite' (a catchy Parker theme, named after Stravinsky's *Firebird Suite*) and 'Ornithology'. These went through smoothly, leaving plenty of time for the taxing final item: Dizzy Gillespie's 'A Night in Tunisia'.

Parker had known this composition since 1942, when he used to play his part in its performance by the Earl Hines Orchestra. It was probably in the sextet's repertoire at Billy Berg's, but wider interest had been stimulated by Gillespie's commercial disc of it – recently made in New York. Parker follows the Gillespie arrangement closely until the first solo. On the Gillespie record Dizzy takes this solo himself, beginning with a two-bar unaccompanied break. Here the first solo is Parker's, after a four-bar break as astonishing as any in jazz: an orderly and beautiful torrent of notes, gushing forth at the rate of twelve per second.

The difficulties the other musicians were having with the intricate exposition of 'Tunisia' meant that five takes were needed. Parker's break on Take 1 was exceptionally brilliant. His break on Take 5 (the issued take) was almost identical. Ross Russell eventually released the inspired outpouring from Take 1 as a separate item, labelled 'Famous Alto Break'. In the years to come Gillespie's 'A Night in Tunisia', crowned with this spectacular Parker feature, would stop the show whenever the two of them met on concert stages (including the stage at Massey Hall).

*

A month after the recording session, Ross Russell was astonished to receive a letter, signed by Parker and stamped by a notary public, authorizing him to pay half of all royalties to one Emery Byrd, better known by his nickname of Moose the Mooche. Another letter followed, this time from Byrd himself, helpfully advising Russell that all benefits should be sent to him at his new address: the prison at San Quentin.

The imprisonment of his heroin supplier was the start of a nightmare for Parker, far from the swimming pools and the libraries of his dreams. In the ghetto the heat was on. Drugs were impossible to obtain. The police were harassing the Finale Club. Parker tried to douse his heroin habit with alcohol. Badly needing money, he pressed Russell to set up another recording session.

On 29 July he joined trumpeter Howard McGhee and a local rhythm section in a studio hired by Russell. The contrast between the Parker of the 'Night in Tunisia' session and Parker now was deeply shocking. Russell had a doctor standing by. The first number was fast, and Parker fumbled it. The doctor dosed him with Phenobarbital. Parker said he would try 'Lover Man'. The way he played this torch song was deeply, deeply affecting – a sequence of painful but defiantly musical gasps from a drowning genius. Devotees like Charles Mingus loved this record for its emotional power, but Parker hated it and said it 'should be stomped into the ground'.[17]

After the recording session, he was put into a taxi and sent back to his third-rate hotel. Here he caused outrage by appearing naked in the lobby, asking for change for the payphone. Persuaded back to his room, he lit a cigarette and contrived, under the influence of alcohol and Phenobarbital, to set fire to his bed. The police were called.

Racism in the Los Angeles Police Department remains an issue today, so how its officers handled a troublesome, naked, burly black man in a Chinese-run hotel in 1946 hardly bears thinking about. What we know is that, because of police contempt for the black people in their custody, Russell was unable to discover Parker's whereabouts for several days. He found him eventually, handcuffed to the iron bedstead in a tiny cell in the Psychopathic Ward at the county jail. Parker cursed the LAPD and called on Russell to arrange his immediate release. Not so easy. The charges were indecent exposure and resisting arrest. He was also suspected of arson and there was a suggestion of insanity. He might well be committed to a maximum-security institution for the criminally insane. The best Russell and his lawyer could achieve for him was six months confinement in Camarillo State Hospital, which offered a rehabilitation programme for alcoholics and drug addicts.

When she learned what had happened, Parker's girlfriend Doris Sydnor flew from New York and stayed in Los Angeles so she could visit him regularly.

According to Miles Davis, the course of electric shock treatments applied to Parker at Camarillo was so severe he almost bit off his tongue.

*

When the six months were up, Parker could not be released until an approved resident of California accepted responsibility for him. Russell agreed to be that person, but he wanted Parker, in exchange, to sign a new recording contract. Parker signed and was released into Russell's care at the end of January 1947.

On 19 February he recorded for Russell again, using the Errol Garner trio as his rhythm section. The nasty surprise for Russell was a young baritone called Earl Coleman, whom Parker had befriended and insisted on including. Most of the session was taken up with Coleman's vocal efforts, patiently supported by Parker's lyrical saxophone. Their finished version of the ballad 'This Is Always' confounded Russell by outselling every other item in his catalogue. In the session's dying moments Parker and the Garner trio ad-libbed two upbeat instrumentals. One of these, a 12-bar blues in C that Russell labelled 'Cool Blues', won the Grand Prix du Disque in France.

In return for tolerating Coleman, Russell asked for and was granted one more recording session before Parker left California. It took place on 26 February and this time Parker was supported by trumpeter Howard McGhee, tenorist Wardell Gray, and a West Coast rhythm section. One of the numbers they recorded was a Parker original: a tantalizing 12-bar blues, seemingly simple but rhythmically fiendish. It perplexed the other musicians and required five takes. Parker delivered a fine solo on each. Russell issued Take 5 under the benign title 'Relaxin' at Camarillo'.

For the next two weeks Parker drank colossal quantities of whisky and played as a member of Howard McGhee's band at the Hi-de-Ho club. A Parker devotee called Dean Benedetti was there too, with his disc-recorder, which he switched on whenever his hero took a solo. Forty years would pass before the Benedetti family handed this priceless hoard to expert restorers. Of particular interest to us is what it reveals about the provenance of one of the pieces played at Massey Hall. We shall return to it.

*

Early in April 1947 Parker and Doris went back to New York. Pursuing his biggest asset, Ross Russell transferred his company, Dial, from the West Coast to the East. Dean Benedetti, too, felt compelled to make the move.

The Dial recordings, together with stories of his crazy Californian adventures, had preceded Parker to New York, so Bird-worshippers gathered with their hosannas. The idolatrous drew meaning from the fact that he reappeared on Easter Monday.

Small's Paradise in Harlem threw a homecoming party. He arrived late, borrowed an instrument and created a sensation. The next night he popped up magically at the Savoy Ballroom, where the Gillespie big band was playing. The first anyone knew of his presence was when he materialized among the dancers on the ballroom floor, music spouting from his horn. There was talk of him becoming a regular with the Gillespie band, but when he joined them for one night at the McKinley Theatre in the Bronx, Gillespie spotted he was back on drugs, so that was that.

Max Roach arranged and advertised a musical evening at a social club in Brooklyn, with Parker as the star, but by the time the great man arrived, the evening was almost over. He played one tune, then led Roach into the owner's office and said in a fierce deep voice, 'Max, give me my $100.' When Roach demurred, Parker ordered the owner to leave them, barred the door, rearranged the furniture to form a boxing ring, and put up his fists. Roach couldn't help laughing. 'I gave Bird $50, and he accepted.'

Parker and Doris Sydnor moved into Harlem's Dewey Square Hotel (just around the corner from Minton's), although Parker's place of work was to be downtown on 52nd Street. The manager of the Three Deuces offered him good money to come down there with a band, so he gathered a quintet. Roach was the drummer. Miles Davis was poached from the Gillespie orchestra. Tommy Potter (ex-Billy Eckstine orchestra) played bass. The little-known pianist was New Yorker Duke Jordan. Davis and Roach told Parker they would have preferred Bud Powell on piano, and savoured the irony when their harum-scarum leader ruled that Bud could not be relied upon.

Unreliable or not, Powell was the pianist at Parker's first New York recording date for eighteen months. To Ross Russell's chagrin, this session (on 8 May) was not for him, but for the rival Savoy company.

The first piece they recorded was 'Donna Lee' – claimed by Miles Davis but built from phrases we know (from the Benedetti recordings) to have originated with Parker. The other three pieces are all Parker compositions. 'Chasing the Bird' has twin themes, performed by Parker and

Davis in counterpoint. (According to Max Roach, Parker enjoyed playing Bach's two-part inventions on the piano.) 'Cheryl' (intricate melodic
line) and 'Buzzy' (pithy phrase, stated thrice) are contrasting additions to
the literature of the 12-bar blues. Parker's playing throughout is massively
assured, and with Roach behind him his huge capacity to *swing* is made
fully manifest. The presence of Powell, too, dramatically raises the stakes.
Here is that rarest of artists: a soloist, besides Gillespie, who can compete
with Parker on his own terms.

At the Three Deuces, however, the pianist was still Duke Jordan. Max
Roach told me about the band's routine:

> Miles and I would practise all day to get ready for this gentleman. And
> he'd come on the stage and his first piece, his *warm up* piece, would be
> the fastest thing we'd play all night. And it would destroy Miles and
> myself; just reduce us to nothing. I would be scuffling, Miles would be
> puffing, and he'd just breeze through it, and the rest of the evening he
> would deal with 'Slow Boat to China' or 'A Pretty Girl Is Like a Smile' –
> if a nice lady was in the club he'd fit that in.

*

On 29 September 1947, when the Dizzy Gillespie Orchestra with Ella
Fitzgerald played a sell-out concert at New York's Carnegie Hall, an
added attraction, in small letters on the posters, was 'Yardbird Parker'.

Parker was scheduled to join Gillespie for a set accompanied only by
the rhythm section, and according to Teddy Reig, producer of the concert and the recording, the reunion nearly didn't happen. Hunting for
Parker shortly before curtain up, Reig found he had passed out in his
bath. He had to be dried, dressed and rushed to Carnegie Hall in a taxi
cab.

Each of the pieces Parker and Gillespie chose to play was a classic of
the new music. First, 'A Night in Tunisia', incorporating for the first time
in a joint performance Parker's stunning alto break. This double-time
derring-do, part memorized and part off-the-cuff, was a guaranteed sensation in itself, as well as the perfect launch pad for Parker's solo. Tonight,
with Gillespie shouting encouragement, the solo is almost frightening in

its intensity. Undaunted, Gillespie adds a brilliant improvisation of his own.

'A Night in Tunisia' is followed by other familiar Gillespie compositions: 'Groovin' High' and 'Dizzy Atmosphere' (so fast that the drummer sounds distressed). Then come two by Parker. First the gloriously melodic 'Confirmation', and finally 'Koko': the ultimate challenge for virtuosi. Here the rhythm section copes as best it can, while Parker turns in a solo that brings the audience to its feet.

Some commentators insist the set Parker played with Gillespie was a grudge match. As they would have it, Parker (the true genius of the new music) was out to nail Gillespie (touted by publicists as 'Mr Bebop'). Gillespie did not see it that way at all:

> People try to create dissension between Charlie Parker and me. They
> don't know how warm a relationship we had. After one of the numbers,
> he walked out on the stage with one long rose and gave it to me. And he
> kissed me on the mouth. I get a warm feeling every time I think about
> Charlie Parker.[18]

However, during all his solos on this evening, Parker made aggressive use of his instrument's upper reaches. He and Gillespie loved each other – no reason to doubt Gillespie on that – but, as their friend the trombonist Trummy Young has pointed out, 'every time they got on the stand it was competitive. They had blood in their eyes.'[19]

*

On 25 October 1947 Ross Russell convened his first New York recording session. This was also the first time the working quintet, with Duke Jordan on piano, had come to the studio.

The evening did not begin well. Parker startled Russell by arriving extremely early, looking grim, and demanding $50. He used the cash to buy heroin from a loitering supplier, and retired to the men's room with his purchase. After that, everything went swimmingly. Russell was impressed by the group's togetherness and the fleetness and buoyancy of the rhythm section. A special microphone was installed to catch the regal shimmer of Max Roach's cymbal. California seemed long ago and far away.

Three Parker originals were recorded. Then, in response to Russell's request for something similar to 'Koko', Parker produced 'The Hymn': an ultra-fast blues whose theme, like Ray Noble's 'Cherokee', moves sedately, all long-held notes over the furious pulse. (This blues used to be played, much more slowly, by the Jay McShann Orchestra.)

The session ended with stunning performances of two ballads: Jerome Kern's 'All the Things You Are' and George Gershwin's 'Embraceable You'. On the chosen take of 'All the Things', Parker never makes the Kern melody explicit, so Russell issued it as an original composition, labelled 'Bird of Paradise'.

The first take of 'Embraceable You' is an extemporized masterpiece. After a shy but lovely introduction by Duke Jordan, the master proclaims his arrival with a tantalizing 6-note phrase, remote and yet not remote from the Gershwin melody. The phrase comes again, gently modified, and then again, raised in pitch to suit the harmonic contour. Thrice more it sounds, trailing clouds of glory, before releasing a flood of gorgeous song. The discovery (made by jazz writer Gary Giddins in the 1980s) that Parker lifted his key phrase from an obscure ballad called 'A Table in the Corner' detracts not a jot from his compositional genius.

A week later, mindful of a looming musicians' union ban on recordings, Ross Russell hurried the quintet back into the studio. They recorded six more items: three meditations on popular love songs ('Out of Nowhere', 'My Old Flame' and 'Don't Blame Me') and three Parker originals.

'Bird Feathers' is a fast blues with a fiercely percussive theme, complex and dense within a narrow compass, like African drumming. 'Scrapple from the Apple' (using the 'Honeysuckle Rose' harmonies) is another rhythmic treat. The bubbly 'Klact-oveeseds-tene' gives rise to a magician's improvisation, wherein Parker fires a seemingly random burst of notes, then, with Max Roach's devoted assistance, sweeps them up and conjures them into a wondrous pattern. And what about that title? Parker often neglected to christen his compositions, but the name for this one was handed to Ross Russell, precisely inscribed on the back of a Three Deuces business card. When Russell tried to establish what the strange word meant, Parker walked away. Some think it derives from *auf Wiedersehen*: the German for goodbye, or perhaps 'get lost'.

After the second Dial session, agent Billy Shaw found work for the quintet in the El Sino lounge in Detroit, but the engagement ended prematurely when Parker quarrelled with the owner, went back to the hotel and hurled his saxophone from a high window. According to Miles Davis, Parker often had difficulty finding heroin when he was out of town, 'and then he would drink a lot, which was what he did this night'.[20] Back in New York, Billy Shaw read Parker the riot act, then advanced him the money to buy a new, Paris-made Selmer alto.

Armed with this top-of-the-range instrument, on 17 December 1947 Parker made his last records for Ross Russell. Four of them were new Parker compositions, including a gem called 'Quasimado' (*sic*). This complex, tragi-comic theme on the harmonies of 'Embraceable You' bobs along world's away from Parker's hallowed 1945 improvisation on the same chords.

Billy Shaw must have patched things up with El Sino's, because the quintet returned there for a Christmas engagement. While they were in Detroit, the Savoy company (like Ross Russell, anxious to beat an impending AFM ban) rushed them into a studio. Four sides were cut: two themeless, breakneck improvisations on standard chord sequences; and two easy-paced 12-bar blues with themes by Parker. One of these, 'Bluebird', is a simple, repeated phrase in the refreshing key of E flat. From this kernel emerges one of Parker's profoundest solos, elaborately woven, and deep-dyed in blues feeling.

'Bluebird' crowned a year of magnificent recordings and new compositions, a body of work equal to Louis Armstrong's in the 1920s, and unsurpassed in the history of jazz. But, in the piercing phrase of the African-American musician and dramatist Archie Shepp, 'a black man is always black'.[21] Duke Jordan has given us an idea of how it felt to be Charlie Parker at the end of 1947:

Though he was the idol of all musicians, Bird knew the limitations of his success. Being a Negro he could go just so far and no further. Once, he finished a set [at the Three Deuces] to great acclaim, and went quietly to a bar around the corner called McGuire's. The bartender addressed him as a nigger. Parker vaulted over the bar to teach the fellow manners. The man picked up a bottle and broke it over Bird's head. It cut his dome and he always had a little scar.[22]

*

On 1 January 1948 the second AFM recording ban came into force, so to hear how Parker sounded during the first part of that year we have to turn to the pirates. For example, when the quintet opened at the Three Deuces on 30 March, Dean Benedetti was there with a primitive tape recorder. His tapes allow us to hear a free-wheeling, risk-taking Parker, challenging his band to keep pace with his speed of thought, soaring beyond pulse and chords towards the realm of total freedom.

Max Roach told me that one night, when they asked Parker how they could be like him, he offered his disciples this analogy:

He said, 'My cup runneth over. You take this glass of water here. The empty glass is you. Water is musical knowledge. When the glass is full, to the very top, all you have to do is just blow at it and it runneth over. Ideas just gush out of you. But it takes time to fill your cup.'

For one week in July, when the quintet was playing at the Onyx club on 52nd Street, Dean Benedetti secreted his machinery under the stage and recorded every night. Sometimes Parker's playing here takes on a violent and abstract quality, like action painting – particularly when he forces his saxophone up beyond its range until it shrieks in protest.

Thelonious Monk's furiously fast '52nd Street Theme' was the quintet's signature tune. Another trademark – most unlikely on the face of it – was Percy Grainger's oh-so-English 'Country Gardens', which Parker made a point of gluing to the end of even his most tender ballad performances. We know from Miles Davis, who found it infuriating, that Parker liked to affect a posh English accent. Both the Grainger quotation and the plummy tones seem to have been devices for keeping the world at arm's length. As Miles put it, 'Bird always wore a mask over his feelings, one of the best masks I have ever seen.'[23]

*

During September 1948 Savoy twice flouted the AFM ban and sneaked Parker and the quintet into a New York recording studio. At these fertile sessions John Lewis, not Duke Jordan, was the pianist, so it was Lewis who found himself supporting one of the most moving blues improvisations ever recorded. Miles Davis did not play on this one. They named it 'Parker's Mood'. It begins with an unaccompanied fanfare from Parker, hugely authoritative, a fitting summons to a great event. This is followed by a short interlude of cool piano playing from Lewis, which teases our expectations. Then Parker creates, out of two 12-bar choruses, a flawless piece of architecture, where elaborately graceful call-and-response patterns rise from deep blues foundations. Lewis inserts a dainty sliver, and then, encouraged by Roach's subtle suggestion of double time, Parker tops the stately edifice with one more chorus of breathtaking radiance.

*

While the Parker Quintet was stuck at the Onyx, the Gillespie Big Band was on the move. It began 1948 with concerts in Europe, and now it was touring America. On 26 September, for one night only, Parker played as the guest of the band at the Pershing Ballroom in Chicago. According to band member Elmon Wright, Gillespie and Parker 'both took off with the big band arrangements behind them. It sent chills up my spine.'[24]

Parker again absented himself from his quintet for three weeks in November, playing a string of well-paid concerts with Norman Granz's Jazz at the Philharmonic, which had outgrown its Los Angeles origins and gone on tour.

Granz told me of his struggles to keep Parker on board as the show moved from town to town. In most places he found a doctor to take care of his star's heroin needs, but when the tour reached Los Angeles he took extra precautions. He lodged Parker in an out-of town motel and hired an off-duty detective from the narcotics bureau to watch over him. Parker slipped out the back door and found his minder had foolishly left his keys in his car. So at curtain up no Charlie Parker. Granz offered $100 to the local musicians hanging around backstage if they could bring him in. While they hunted, Coleman Hawkins played an epic version of 'Body and Soul'. When at last Parker was delivered, he was in a stupor. Granz shoved his head under the tap:

> And finally he revived enough for me to say, 'Charlie, if you don't get out on that stage I'm gonna kill you'. I think he believed me because he staggered out – his hair was all wet – and somebody stuck a saxophone in his hands and he played one number. And that was the end of the concert. And in fact the end of the tour.[25]

But not the end of the Parker–Granz relationship. Shortly afterwards, when the AFM ban was lifted, agent Billy Shaw negotiated a contract for Parker with Mercury, a major record label where Granz was jazz supremo.

*

On 9 December 1948 the Parker Quintet (now with Al Haig on piano) began a troubled engagement at the Royal Roost, the first of the new-style 'jazz palaces' on New York's Broadway. The problem (unconnected with the location) was the slump in morale within the quintet. Miles Davis, in particular, had become outraged by Parker's long absences and persistent attempts to dodge paying his musicians their wages. Even the ultra-loyal Max Roach was tiring of Parker's claim that they owed him everything because he taught them all they knew. Breaking point at the Royal Roost came on Christmas Eve. Parker delayed the performance while he languorously smoked a cigarette, suggestively squeezed air from a toy balloon into the microphone, then shot Al Haig with a cap pistol. Miles stormed off the bandstand protesting, 'Bird makes you feel one foot high.'[26] A new trumpeter, Kenny Dorham, started the next night. Max Roach, too, protested that enough was enough. Parker had to use a substitute drummer until Max could be coaxed back.

Why did Parker behave as he did? Part of the problem was the pressure he felt was on him to deliver instant art every night. When his friend the painter Harvey Cropper asked him why he disappointed people by not playing when he was scheduled, he replied, 'You're an artist. Paint a picture for me *right now*.'[27] The strange thing is, Parker could do just that. On Christmas Day 1948, during a broadcast from the Royal Roost, a listener phoned to say he wanted to hear Irving Berlin's 'White Christmas'. Someone was recording from their radio, so we have Parker's response. Steering clear of the dolefulness of Bing Crosby's hit version, he chooses a medium-bright tempo and plays the theme with warmth and good humour. Then he takes two ad lib choruses, beautifully balanced, sparkling with Christmas cheer, incorporating a snatch of 'Jingle Bells' and some double-tempo prestidigitation. A small jewel, offered as a gesture of seasonal goodwill.

*

The big news for Parker at the start of 1949 was that he would be going abroad for the first time, to the International Jazz Festival in Paris. In celebration, he wrote a blues called 'Visa', which his quintet recorded in April for Norman Granz.

On 5 May, in the midst of preparations for the journey, the quintet recorded for Granz again: three more Parker originals, including two that in the excitement were both called 'Passport'. Two days later the quintet was in Paris. (Incidentally, Parker's passport gave his height as 5 feet 10½ inches and his weight as 214 pounds.)

According to Kenny Dorham, 'Bird had all Paris at his feet. In all his life, he never witnessed such enthusiasm. He just stood there with an expression of exuberance on his face.'[28] The concerts were in the Salle Pleyel, where Gillespie had played the previous year. A rough recording was made, on which we hear Parker adding continental touches to a Gillespie party piece. During the vocal chorus, instead of constantly hollering 'Salt Peanuts! Salt Peanuts!', he sends his French fans wild by suddenly switching to 'La Même Chose! La Même Chose!' And at the start of his solo he again acknowledges his Gallic surroundings by quoting from the bassoon

solo that opens Stravinsky's *The Rite of Spring*, the ballet that had scan-
dalized the French capital in 1913.

The late-night jam sessions, in the cabarets on the Left Bank of the
Seine, were blessed by the existentialist philosopher Jean-Paul Sartre.
Pilgrims flocked across Europe to engage Parker in intellectual debate.
Champagne was the all-day drink. Obtaining drugs was no problem. A
critic from the *Melody Maker*, bible for Great Britain's syncopated music
fans, hastened from London bearing a questionnaire he had compiled on
behalf of his readers. Parker, no doubt charmed by the English accent,
rewarded each question with a quotation from the Rubáiyát of Omar
Khayyám.

*

The Paris idyll lasted just ten days. Back in America the sense of anti-
climax was palpable. Parker and the quintet marked time, mainly in the
stale cellars of 52nd Street. Kenny Dorham left and was replaced by the
Jewish trumpeter Red Rodney (born Robert Chudnick). Max Roach
handed over to Roy Haynes.

In November 1949 Norman Granz came up with something new. He
called Parker to the studio to record a selection of popular tunes ('Just
Friends', 'April in Paris' and so on), accompanied by a small ensemble of
strings and woodwind. The bassist at the session was Ray Brown, who
had been in California with the Gillespie–Parker sextet. Asked to sum up
Parker with Strings in an interview nearly fifty years later, Brown did so
pithily:

> That's not a very good orchestra. I don't think those are very good
> arrangements. But he makes them something wonderful. You can play it
> right now and he just jumps off that record . . . He could play *anything*
> and make you like it.[29]

The first records sold well, so more were made. Bird with Strings could
also be booked as a live act, and Parker in a white suit in front of his little
orchestra became a familiar sight. Hemmed in by the gooey arrangements, he embroidered familiar tunes rather than recomposing them.

Was Granz guilty of stunting Parker's artistic development? Doris insisted not: 'Norman Granz did not conceive the idea. This was Charlie's dream and, perhaps, it bugged him later.'[30] The dream may have been less musical than socio-economic. After Europe, it must have been harder than ever for Parker to accept that in the land of his birth the colour of his skin made him an object of hatred and contempt. Strings and woodwind were standard trappings of the white musical establishment. So why should he not enjoy their benefits?

The first half of the twentieth century ended on a high note for Charlie Parker. On 15 December 1949 a new jazz palace, the grandest yet, opened on Broadway. An all-star line-up performed at the launch party. Parker was top of the bill. The new club was being named in his honour. They called it Birdland: the Jazz Corner of the World.

*

Norman Granz's next initiative was a recording session that reunited Parker with Dizzy Gillespie. To support them he booked Thelonious Monk, Curley Russell and the swing drummer Buddy Rich. The casting of Rich was perverse, but the occasion was momentous and the quality of the improvised solos was superb. Three new Parker compositions were recorded – all joyful melodies. The first, 'An Oscar for Treadwell', uses the 'I Got Rhythm' chords, shifted to the key of C. The other two, 'Mohawk' and 'Bloomdido', are both blues in B flat.

Despite the spelling, Parker insisted that 'Bloomdido' was dedicated to the long-suffering violinist Teddy Blume, who led the string orchestra and acted as Parker's personal manager when they travelled the country. 'This is my boy,' Parker would say, and pat Blume on the head like a dog. During what Blume described as 'the most tumultuous years a human being ever spent', he never ceased to goggle at Parker's gargantuan appetites:

> His life seemed to revolve around four things: music, junk [heroin], sex, and movies. He had sex three or four times a day with three or four different women. The girls chased after him from state to state. He always entertained them in my room, because it was dangerous for a white girl to be noticed going into a Negro man's room.[31]

On nights when, after all the entertaining, Parker still could not sleep, Blume used to play the violin for him. 'It soothed him. He loved the violin. I loved Charlie Parker. I'd forgive him anything.'[32]

Parker's favourite movie at that time – he saw it over and over again – was *The Third Man*, Graham Greene's story set in seedy post-war Vienna and backed with plangent zither music. The film's anti-hero, Harry Lime, was played by Orson Welles, who gave the doomed racketeer an enchanter's voice, a subversive philosophy and a devilish allure. No wonder Parker empathized.

*

In the summer of 1950, resting Blume and the Strings, Parker took an engagement at Birdland with trumpeter Fats Navarro (in the Gillespie class), plus a rhythm section led by Bud Powell. This fast company put Parker on his mettle, as we know from a recorded broadcast. Here he is, finding new ways to astonish, creating the illusion of wild abandon while remaining perfectly poised.

On 29 August 1950 the manager of Birdland, Oscar Goodstein, threw a party to celebrate Charlie Parker's thirtieth birthday – a good moment for a snapshot of his domestic affairs. Back in November 1948, while in Los Angeles with Jazz at the Philharmonic, he had slipped down to Tijuana for a wedding ceremony with Doris Sydnor, neglecting the awkward fact that he was still married to Geraldine. In the spring of 1950 he left Doris and set up home with another white woman, Chan Richardson, who had a little daughter called Kim. Their cosy ménage was far from Harlem, in the Ukrainian district of Manhattan's Lower East Side, where he relished the bourgeois lifestyle.

In November 1950 he flew to Sweden, played with adoring local musicians and consumed jumbo helpings of schnapps. From Sweden he flew to Paris, and was paid in advance for a concert. However, the carousing and the complimentary cognac made him so ill that he put himself on a plane home before the concert date, without saying goodbye. Back in New York he was diagnosed as suffering from an acute peptic ulcer and ordered into hospital for intensive care. Within a week he discharged himself and took a cab to Birdland, where Oscar Goodstein found him at the bar, downing whiskies.

*

In January 1951 Norman Granz financed Parker's reunion in a recording studio with Miles Davis and Max Roach. Completing the quintet on this special occasion were two youngsters who would become Parker regulars: Teddy Kotick on bass, and Bud Powell's disciple Walter Bishop on piano. Four top-class recordings were made, including a new Parker blues, 'Au Privave', whose terse phrases are bolted into a near-continuous 12-bar line. Parker's solo, skimming joyfully above Max Roach's buoyant drumming, is among his best on commercial record.

At the end of March, Parker was back at Birdland playing for a week with Dizzy Gillespie and Bud Powell (plus bassist Tommy Potter and drummer Roy Haynes). A fan hooked his recorder to his radio one night when this so-called 'Summit Meeting' was being broadcast. Introducing the players, compere 'Symphony Sid' Torin (who could not have foreseen the even more extraordinary gathering two years hence at Massey Hall) announced, 'It never in life again probably will happen where you can get three great gentlemen of modern music all together in one group.'

Gillespie's 'Blue 'n Boogie' is the chosen launch pad, and Parker is galvanized by the company and bursting with *joie de vivre*. He garnishes the 'Blue 'n Boogie' riffs with exuberant squeaks and squawks, and as usual he takes the first solo, a long, daring flight. The second number, 'Anthropology', is a rerun of the fast tune famously recorded by Parker in 1945 as 'Thriving on a Riff'. Now, it is played at outrageous speed with everyone sure-footed and Parker in his element.

Thelonious Monk's ''Round Midnight' is presented soberly, with Parker applying graceful curlicues to the lovely theme. And then to close the set 'A Night in Tunisia', with Parker and Gillespie resuming the dramatic roles they played at Carnegie Hall in September 1947.

*

On 17 July 1951 a daughter, Pree, was born to Parker and Chan, but what should have been a happy time was blighted by the State Liquor Authority, who revoked Parker's cabaret licence. Without it, he could not work in any nightclub in New York, and they were entitled to take it away because he had been convicted of a drug offence. The judge at his trial handed down a three-month suspended sentence, and could not resist adding a lecture: 'Mr Parker, if you ever have the urge to stick a needle in your arm again, take your horn out into the woods somewhere and blow.' As Chan observed bitterly in her autobiography, 'Even if Bird had followed that white man's advice, he would probably have been arrested.'[33]

The loss of the cabaret card was a dreadful blow. During this crisis Norman Granz remained supportive. In August he set up another recording session. Red Rodney was the trumpeter, and Granz booked the rhythm trio of John Lewis, Ray Brown and Kenny Clarke. From the exultant music you would never know that Parker was a man in deep trouble. The stand-out piece, his new composition 'Blues for Alice', preserves the spirit of the 12-bar sequence while opening up its harmonies.

His exile from the New York clubs continued through the autumn and winter, so there was a hollow ring to the December announcement by *Down Beat* magazine that its readers had voted him top alto saxophonist of 1951. However, no cabaret card was needed to appear in a New York TV studio, so he joined Gillespie (winner in the *Down Beat* trumpet section) on a programme on Channel 5, where they were presented with their plaques by the babbling compere Earl Wilson. Asked if he had anything to say, Parker answered, 'Well, Earl, they say music speaks louder than words, so we'd rather voice our opinion that way – if you don't mind.' Then, backed by a scratch rhythm section, he and Gillespie treated the TV audience to an abridged edition of Tadd Dameron's 'Hot House'. An invaluable telerecording preserves this show in both sound and image.

*

The year 1952 began with a flurry of recording sessions conceived by Norman Granz, who believed in presenting Parker to the public in various guises. At one session Parker played nothing but Afro-Latin numbers, leading a team that included, alongside Max Roach, a conga drummer and a specialist on the bongos. Granz marketed them as 'Charlie Parker and his South of the Border Orchestra'. Obligingly, the boys in the band let out fierce cries of *olé* during their rendering of 'La Paloma'.

On 10 August a son, Charles Baird, was born to Parker and Chan. At around the same time the authorities restored his cabaret licence, so he could work again in the New York clubs. Soon he was playing at Birdland, supported by a trio that included his passionate admirer Charles Mingus, who had migrated from the West Coast.

On 26 September Parker was a main attraction at a grand occasion in Harlem: a musical evening in the Rockland Palace Ballroom to raise funds for the campaign to free City Councillor Benjamin Davis. Davis, an African-American, was the last Communist Party member ever to hold elected office in the United States. The government accused him of sedition and threw him in jail; 14,000 Harlemites signed a petition calling for his release.

The organizers of the fundraising evening had booked Parker with both his quintet and the strings. On this special night the quintet welcomed the return of Max Roach. Two private tape recorders were running, capturing nearly two hours of Parker music. The peak moment is a quintet performance of 'Lester Leaps In', where the flames of Parker's long, searing solo are fanned by Roach's whirlwind drums.

*

When Parker was booked to play for a December week at the Hi Hat club in Boston, he took Charles Mingus with him.

The Sunday session at the Hi Hat on 14 December was broadcast over local radio, and as recently as 1996 a recording of that broadcast was recovered and published. Parker, in tremendous form, plays 'Ornithology', 'Don't Blame Me', 'Groovin' High', and two of his own: 'Cool Blues' and 'Cheryl'. Mingus provides muscular support and some virtuosic solos.

The last music made by Parker in 1952 (for Granz on 30 December) again involved Max Roach, this time with Hank Jones (piano) and Teddy Kotick (bass). It was, as they say, a 'blowing session', with scant formality and maximum reliance on Parker's genius for improvisation. The stand-out track, 'Cosmic Rays', is one of his classic 12-bar blues performances, the unique Parker mix of the sensual and the numinous.

*

Charlie Parker entered 1953 in wonderful artistic health but in poor shape physically. And his career was in the doldrums. To supplement his income he would sometimes teach saxophone at the Hartnett Music Studios on Broadway, and it was here that he was tracked down, on Sunday 25 January, by four eager youngsters from the New Jazz Society of Toronto. Their mission was to persuade him to perform, alongside other modern masters like Dizzy Gillespie and Max Roach, at their First Annual Festival of Creative Jazz. He liked the sound of the $200 guarantee plus a percentage of the profits, so they drew up a contract there and then – for just one concert, on 15 May in Toronto's Massey Hall.

On 30 January, putting at risk his exclusive and valuable contract with Norman Granz, he earned himself some extra money playing tenor saxophone at a Miles Davis recording session. The occasion caused Davis considerable unhappiness. According to him, Parker was drinking heavily ('a quart of vodka at the rehearsal') because, after the jailing for drugs of his young protégé Red Rodney, he was frightened of being captured in possession of heroin. Parker's behaviour in the studio made Miles seethe:

> He treated me like I was his son, or a member of *his* band. He said, 'All right, Lily Pons, to produce beauty we must suffer pain – from the oyster comes the pearl,' in that fake British accent. Then he fell asleep.[34]

At the beginning of February came another invitation from Canada, this time to play with local musicians on TV in Montreal. Parker accepted. The Canadians were astonished at their luck, and at what came to light when Parker opened his saxophone case: a white plastic alto! He assembled it and ran a couple of scales, and nobody had heard playing that *loud* before. According to the pianist Paul Bley, 'accompanying him was a shock because of the volume. He played about three times louder than I had ever heard anyone play.'[35] Billy Graham, the local drummer, remembered, 'It was like riding a fire engine around a corner at 90 miles an hour – you're just hanging on by the tips of your fingers.'[36]

Parker's loudness, by the way, was not a novel product of the plastic. It had always been there – embedded in the Parker philosophy. One of his pupils, Bob Newman, remembered how the lessons would go:

> Bird used to stress playing loud. He felt that a horn man should make his statements strong. 'Blow through your horn as if you were blowing out a candle.' He used a reed that was so stiff I could hardly get a peep out of it.[37]

On Sunday 22 February 1953, for a flat fee of $50, Parker went to Washington to play with a band of young enthusiasts calling themselves The Orchestra. They were proud of their tricky arrangements and wanted to talk them through with him, but he arrived too late for that. Taking the stage with no rehearsal, no written music, just his white plastic saxophone, he sailed with the big-band scores as if they had been designed expressly for him. The snatched recording of this casually produced art still has the power to astonish.

And what about the white plastic sax? A novelty, certainly, but also a legitimate instrument, important to our story. The one Parker played was given to him for promotional purposes, and he would use it whenever his regular horn was in the pawn shop.

The second week in March, Parker played at the Storyville club in Boston, where they laid on a good rhythm section. A recorded broadcast from here includes his deluxe solos on 'Moose the Mooche' and 'Ornithology'. Advertising in the March issue of *Metronome* magazine, the King Saxophone Company proudly quoted Parker's endorsement: 'I'm as happy as a Bird with my King Super 20'. Was the Boston engagement played on this classy King model, or on the white plastic oddity? From the recording we cannot tell. The only certainty is that we are listening to Charlie Parker. Which goes to illustrate a favourite Max Roach dictum:

that all the greatest performers in jazz distinguish themselves by their individual *sound*, regardless of the make or quality of their instrument.

During the first fortnight in May, Parker led a quartet at Birdland. On a recording of the 9 May broadcast we hear him soloing prolifically, and this time we are certain which saxophone he used, thanks to the MC who obliged with this plug: 'Hi Bird. It's a real pleasure having you back in Birdland once again. With your real unusual plastic axe here. It looks good.'

*

On Friday 15 May 1953 the members of the Definitive Quintet booked to play at Massey Hall assembled at La Guardia Airport for the flight to Toronto. All except Charlie Parker. Gillespie volunteered to stay behind and look for him . . . .

TWO

DIZZY ATMOSPHERE

'The other half of my heartbeat.'
Charlie Parker, describing Gillespie[1]

JOHN BIRKS GILLESPIE was born on 21 October 1917 in Cheraw, South Carolina, a racially segregated small town where a Negro boy who looked at a white girl stood a chance of being murdered.

John Birks was the last of nine children. To support them all, Papa Gillespie laid bricks during the week and led a dance band at the weekends. By the time John Birks was four he had discovered the parlour piano and would spend hours picking out popular songs of the day. At school he became famous for picking fights, probably inheriting his bellicosity from his papa, whom he describes in his autobiography as 'a real man, who roared when he talked'. Papa Gillespie beat his children without fail on Sunday mornings, on the assumption that during the week they must have done something to deserve it.

When John Birks was ten his father died and poverty struck. His mother took in laundry, but there was barely enough money for food and none at all for new clothes. John Birks grew more aggressive. Defying local custom, he refused to bow his head when gangs of white boys menaced him in the street.

When he was twelve years old his life was transformed. His school was given some musical instruments and appealed for volunteers to learn to play them for the end-of-term minstrel show. He was by far the youngest volunteer and had to take what was left in the box, which turned out to be a slide trombone. He gave his all to this physically demanding instrument but was hampered by the shortness of his arms. Then at Christmas the boy next door was given a trumpet, which he was happy to share. Within nine months Gillespie had mastered it.

Alice V. Wilson, the teacher who organized the school band, described him as 'a real show-off, but a good one'. When the band played for dances, young John Birks performed on a borrowed cornet, in a similar condition to Charlie Parker's first saxophone: 'It was all taped up: I was blowing through tape rather than through metal.' But he could make it work. He also earned a reputation as a dancer, and found he could make good money entertaining white folks up at the Country Club with a brazen dance called the snake hips.

Just as John Birks was beginning to believe what everyone told him – that he was the best young musician in Cheraw – he got his come-uppance. As with Charlie Parker's first humiliation, lack of theoretical know-how was to blame. The trouble was that Gillespie's mentor, Alice V. Wilson, played the piano entirely by ear and always in the key of B-flat. This limitation was exposed when an older boy called Sonny Matthews came home to Cheraw after playing trumpet up North. Gillespie describes in his autobiography what happened when he was invited to Sonny's house and Sonny suggested they should try a new song called 'Nagasaki':

> I didn't know the tune, but told him I would try it, relying on my ear. Sonny started playing in the key of C, but all I could do was fumble around. I couldn't find one note for 'Nagasaki'. I felt so crushed, I cried.

But not for long. Alerted to the existence of other keys besides B-flat, he mastered the technique of sight-reading and practised his scales.

What happened next was horrific but not unprecedented. The band's trombonist was kidnapped by white vigilantes who claimed he had been peeping into a white person's home. His body was not found. 'Our band never sounded the same again, but it made us want to improve ourselves so we could get the hell out of Cheraw.'

On Sundays the Gillespies joined the multitude of black families across America who escaped the ugliness of everyday life by attending church. Disappointingly for John Birks, his folks were Methodists – a prim denomination, unremarkable for its music. So he gravitated towards the more exciting Sanctified Church that stood in their neighbourhood. On Sunday nights he would sit at the back, entranced by the rhythms of the percussion instruments and by the counter-rhythms that were added when the congregation joined in, 'with foot stomping, hand clapping, and people catching the spirit and jumping up and down on the wooden floor, which resounded like a drum'.

The radio was another source of inspiration. The Gillespie family was too poor to own one, so John Birks used to prevail upon Mrs Harrington next door to tune in so he could listen to the nation's top bands, beamed from the hotels and ballrooms of New York.

*

The escape from Cheraw happened almost by chance, in 1933, when Gillespie was sixteen years old. The agent of fate was a local girl who had gone to study nursing at the Laurinburg Institute, a college for Negroes in North Carolina. When the Institute band lost its best trumpeter, she told the Principal she knew the perfect replacement. And on this informal basis Gillespie was awarded what amounted to a music scholarship. Officially his main subject was farming, but he put in long hours, day and night, practising the trumpet and exploring harmony at the piano.

Laurinburg was certainly more congenial than Cheraw, but he saw the college only as a temporary shelter. In 1935, when his mother moved the family up north to Philadelphia, he abandoned his agricultural studies and hurried to join them in their crowded apartment.

His brother-in-law took him to Henry's Pawnshop and bought him a trumpet for $13. Like Charlie Parker's first saxophone, it came without a case. He carried it in a paper bag to the job he found in a rowdy drinking club, where they paid him $8 a week. At that time in Philadelphia there was a union for so-called 'coloured musicians'. He joined, and this was a good decision because the union secretary, Frankie Fairfax, ran the best coloured band in town. Soon Gillespie was a member of the Fairfax trumpet section, sitting next to Charlie Shavers. Shavers was from New York, where his father ran a barbershop in the shade of the Savoy Ballroom. He won Gillespie's admiration mainly because he could play by heart all the solos recorded by the trumpet star Roy Eldridge. Soon Gillespie could do the same, but what impressed everybody most was the way he played the piano. He would arrive early for rehearsals so he could devote time to his keyboard experiments:

> I'd play chord changes, inverting them and substituting different notes, trying to see how different sounds led into others. I'd take them and play them on my horn, and used to surprise people with new combinations.

Partly to recognize the quirkiness of his methods, but mainly as an acknowledgement of his effervescence (he liked to spring to his feet in the trumpet section and do a dance), the boys in the Fairfax band nicknamed him 'Dizzy'.

*

In 1937, after two years with Fairfax, Dizzy Gillespie left Philadelphia for New York. At first he stayed in the tiny Harlem apartment of his brother James, on terms similar to those worked out two years later between Charlie Parker and Buster Smith. By day Dizzy occupied the bed while brother James was out at work. At night James slept while Dizzy did the rounds, sitting in at a dozen clubs, starting in Greenwich Village and finishing in Harlem. Sometimes he would turn up with his trumpet at the Savoy Ballroom and augment the strength of a band like Chick Webb's.

His impromptu performances at the Savoy brought him to the attention of bandleader Teddy Hill, previously the employer of Roy Eldridge and now looking for a new trumpeter in the Eldridge mould. Hill invited Gillespie to attend a band rehearsal that would count as his audition.

Gillespie took part without removing his overcoat or his gloves. He was a good sight-reader. He could play high, fast and hot. He knew the Eldridge licks. He got the job.

On 7 May 1937, when he was nineteen years old, Gillespie made his first recordings, playing forthright solos with the Teddy Hill Band on *King Porter Stomp* and *Blue Rhythm Fantasy*. His contribution was not credited, and most record buyers would have assumed that these solos were by Eldridge.

Later the same month the Hill Band sailed to Europe, with singers and a chorus line. Gillespie (the youngest musician) had a wonderful time with the girls, but went unnoticed by the European jazz buffs.

Back in New York, the local musicians' union told him that as a 'foreigner' (from Philadelphia) he could not work regularly with Teddy Hill until he had served three months 'quarantine'. To make ends meet and fill the time, he played gigs with the West Indian Cass Carr, whose speciality was performing 'My Buddy' on the musical saw. Carr was a favourite at the Communist dances in Brooklyn and the Bronx, where white–black relationships were actively encouraged. Gillespie relished the free-love ethos, and for a while carried a Communist Party membership card.

He also worked with the Edgar Hayes Band, with the Savoy Sultans and with the Afro-Latin Band of Alberto Socarras. On top of that he made what he always described as the best discovery of his life. She was Lorraine Willis, a strong-minded and comely dancer on the Theatre Owners Booking Association (TOBA) circuit, and he began courting her immediately.

When the three-month quarantine was up he rejoined Teddy Hill but kept working with Alberto Socarras and Edgar Hayes. Socarras (a schooled flute player from Cuba) ran a top-notch conga and rumba band. Gillespie played maracas as well as trumpet, and revelled in the Afro-Cuban experience. What appealed to him about the Edgar Hayes Band was the quality of the writing. One arrangement in particular stuck in his mind. It introduced him to the bewitching interval of the tritone, or flattened fifth, which he began immediately to incorporate into his solos. The most important creative stimulus of all, though, came from the drummer Kenny Clarke.

Clarke scorned to use his bass drum pedal for setting a tiresomely metronomic beat. Instead, he would keep the regular rhythm alive on the cymbals, using the bass drum to galvanize and dramatize. Teddy Hill called the technique 'klook-mop music' and objected strongly. Gillespie called it 'dropping bombs' and loved it.

*

The Hill band could find little work, and Gillespie's career was not prospering as he felt it should if he was to be worthy of Lorraine. The best-paid sidemen in the business were in the orchestra at the Cotton Club fronted by super showman Cab Calloway, so when Gillespie heard they were short of a solo trumpeter he put himself forward and was hired. He stayed from 1939 to 1941, and these were key years in his development.

First of all, he married Lorraine. Secondly, as a featured soloist in this most colourful of bands he was perfectly placed to develop his stage personality. Thirdly, the band made records, which spread his name. Although as a matter of fact the first recording to get him noticed was not for Calloway at all, but for another big personality, Lionel Hampton, who borrowed him for an all-star date. Using a cup mute, Gillespie played the opening solo on 'Hot Mallets'. His distinctive, stinging tone and the cascading quavers he unleashed were proudly described by Hampton as 'a crazy sump'n entirely new'.

In Gillespie's own assessment, the way he played when he joined Calloway was 'somewhere between Roy Eldridge and a style of my own. The unique thing about me was I was always with the piano, always a student of chord changes.' The solos he contributed to Calloway's records and his writing for the band pointed to exciting things to come. In particular, his Afro-Latin-tinged, minor-key 'Pickin' the Cabbage', recorded in March 1940, clearly anticipates such famous Gillespian exotica as 'A Night in Tunisia'.

When the Calloway band was not at the Cotton Club it was on tour. To avoid the Jim Crow treatment commonly endured by black musicians who ventured south, his outfit moved in style: either by private railroad car or chartered bus. One of their regular destinations was Kansas City, about which Gillespie noted two things in his autobiography. First, the theatre stuck in his mind because 'coloured people weren't allowed to come unless they sat in some out-of-the-way place: up in the balcony, called the "buzzards' roost". Secondly, he remembered his 1940 intro- duction to Charlie Parker. When they told him he had to hear the local hero of the alto saxophone, his first reaction was that in New York he was surrounded by the best, and he didn't need this. 'But the moment I heard Charlie Parker I said, "there is *my* colleague". However, two years passed before they were reunited.

*

Back at the Cotton Club in New York, between shows Gillespie and the band's bassist, Milt Hinton, would lug their instruments up the fire escape to the roof of the building. Hinton loved the spicy chords Gillespie was using to enrich his solos, and wanted the recipe. Gillespie, a natural teacher, was happy to pass on his discoveries. The bond between them was strengthened when Calloway denounced Gillespie for playing 'Chinese music'.

After his evening's work at the Cotton Club, Gillespie would rush to the spots in Harlem where adventurous spirits congregated. His was a familiar face, for example, at Minton's Playhouse on 118th Street – a haven for experiment long before Charlie Parker hit the New York scene.

Minton's had once been the dining room of the Cecil Hotel. By 1940 it was being managed as a music venue by ex-bandleader Teddy Hill, whose crafty policy was to hire only a rhythm section, and invite all comers to join in. The tactic succeeded partly because guest musicians were tempted with free food on Monday nights, and partly because of Hill's inspired choice of paid personnel. The drummer was Kenny Clarke, a Gillespie soulmate. At the keyboard was the enigmatic Thelonious Monk, who took the stride-piano style and made of it something entirely his own. By employing Clarke and Monk, Teddy Hill ensured that adven- turers like Gillespie would come to Minton's and play for free.

Gillespie always said he learned a great deal from Monk. No recordings have survived of them playing together at Minton's, but there *are* recordings, made by an amateur, of Gillespie jamming, either at Minton's or further uptown at Clark Monroe's, in May 1941.

Hoagy Carmichael's ballad 'Stardust' was recorded twice. On one version Gillespie is playing open trumpet, on the other he uses a mute. Both solos include modern touches, but the overall effect is hardly radical, it's simply beautiful. The third item preserved is a jam on the chords of 'Exactly Like You'. The recordist (a hip student called Jerry Newman) labelled it 'Kerouac', in honour of the beat-generation scribe who used to hang around Harlem digging the music.

On 'Kerouac' Gillespie toys with chromaticism and the whole-tone scale, placing defiant emphasis on just those notes that would have struck Cab Calloway as Chinese.

*

In September 1941 Gillespie and Calloway reached their bloody parting of the ways. The band was on stage in Hartford, Connecticut, and the trumpeters were sitting idle during a number that featured the rhythm section. Some spitballs (wads of chewed paper) landed at the feet of drummer Cozy Cole, and from their trajectory Calloway deduced, wrongly, that Gillespie must have thrown them. After the show, he cursed his rebel trumpeter and was shocked to be repaid in kind. Calloway was a big man; he grabbed Gillespie's collar. Gillespie was a fighter; he drew his knife and speared his boss in the thigh. The spurt of blood ruined Calloway's white suit, and cost Gillespie his job.

Despite the scandalous manner of his exit, he was soon working again: with Ella Fitzgerald, with Coleman Hawkins, and then with a septet led by the multi-instrumentalist Benny Carter, who had this to say about Gillespie's trumpet technique: 'The man who invented the trumpet knew there were certain things on the instrument that were impossible to do, but no one thought to inform Dizzy. So he just went ahead and did them.'

It was while he was with Carter that Gillespie wrote what is probably his most famous composition. Its original, dreary title was 'Interlude', but

this distinguished descendent of 'Pickin' the Cabbage' is now known to
the world as 'A Night in Tunisia'.

*

Gillespie was determined that he and Lorraine should live comfortably.
Whenever they were 'strapped for vittles', as he put it, he would accept a
commission to write an arrangement for a prosperous white bandleader.
He took pains over his writing, repeatedly testing his novel voicings at the
piano, and he charged high fees. The manager of Jimmy Dorsey's band
bought a package of arrangements at $100 each.

Gillespie left Benny Carter when he was offered irresistibly good
money to tour as the only black musician in the Charlie Barnet
Orchestra. After that tour, he went to play for Les Hite, a black bandleader whose operation was bankrolled by a wealthy white woman.
Gillespie impressed with his immaculate sight-reading, his dashing garb,
and the wicked little knife with a furry handle that lived in his pocket.
But he fell out with Hite because during a public performance in New
York he stopped playing and sat down midway through his solo, in
protest against the distracting racket coming from the drums.

Next he joined the band of Lucky Millinder. In July 1942 they made a
recording they called 'Little John Special', which included a significant
Gillespie contribution: a percussive 4-bar riff for the band to play, ending
in a pair of hiccuping octave leaps. This riff he later elaborated until it
became the full-blown party piece called 'Salt Peanuts'.

*

Above all else, 1942 was the year Gillespie linked up with Charlie Parker.

When Parker reached New York in January to play with Jay McShann
at the Savoy Ballroom, Gillespie headed the welcome. When Parker left
McShann and took a job at Clark Monroe's Uptown House, Gillespie
would go there and jam until breakfast time.

Towards the end of the year Gillespie joined the Earl Hines
Orchestra, and soon afterwards Hines was persuaded to bring Parker
on board. Gillespie was twenty-five. Parker was twenty-two. Earl Hines

was thirty-nine, a jazz legend whose piano playing had graced the classic recordings of Louis Armstrong.

Between shows, Hines observed, Gillespie and Parker would huddle together backstage, cooking up chord structures and rhythmic and melodic patterns. According to Gillespie:

> Charlie Parker and I inspired each other. I think I was a little more
> advanced, harmonically, than he was, but Charlie Parker heard rhythms
> and rhythmic patterns differently. And after we started playing together
> I began to play, rhythmically, more like him.

The bond between them was forged not simply from music. In an interview he gave more than fifty years later, Gillespie talked about touring the South with Hines, and vividly recalled what had to be endured when the band played for a white dance in Pine Bluff, Arkansas. During the intermission, while Gillespie was playing the piano, a redneck thumped down a nickel and called for his favourite tune. Gillespie ignored him. When the dance was over, the aggrieved racist lay in wait and attacked him from behind with a bottle: 'Bap! Hit me, and blood came all down my uniform.' Charlie Parker intervened: 'He came up and said to the guy that hit me, "You took advantage of my friend, you *cur*". He called him a cur. I'll never forget that. All this blood down me, but I thought it was funny even then!'[2]

Because of the recording ban imposed by the American Federation of Musicians in 1942, we have no evidence of how the Hines band sounded with Gillespie and Parker. Nor are there any records of the band playing Gillespie's compositions and arrangements, which is vexing because we know the repertoire included his orchestration of 'Interlude', for which Hines proposed the more attractive title 'A Night in Tunisia'.

What we do have is a private recording, made by Bob Redcross, of Gillespie jamming with Parker and Oscar Pettiford on the chords of 'Sweet Georgia Brown'. Gillespie's improvisation, full of virtuosic excitement, includes tricks with the whole-tone scale learned from Thelonious Monk.

*

Gillespie left Hines in September 1943, and he and bassist Oscar Pettiford formed a little band to fill an opportunity at the Onyx club on 52nd Street. This was the defining moment when modern music emerged from Harlem and penetrated white Manhattan.

Kenny Clarke had been drafted into the army, so the drummer was young Max Roach, whose playing Gillespie had admired at Monroe's Uptown House. Roach fitted perfectly, as Gillespie remembered in his autobiography:

> I said, 'Look, now you're in my band, never mind if Gabriel comes to ask you, don't you get off them damn drums! You sit right there.' At the Onyx all the drummers wanted to sit in. All the big guys. I said 'No'.

The ideal front-line partner for Gillespie, of course, would have been Charlie Parker, but he was out of town. And the ideal pianist, Bud Powell, was denied them because his mother thought Dizzy was crazy.

On opening night, 20 October, and for six weeks after that, the temporary saxophonist was no less a luminary than Lester Young. The pianist who filled the gap was Billy Taylor, who would run across from The Street from his regular job with Ben Webster. He was fascinated by Gillespie, who would sit down at the piano and show him not just the chords, but the exact voicings he required behind his rich and strange melodies. Taylor was astounded by the fast tempos ('ungodly', he called them) and in awe of the power of the bass and drums: 'Oscar Pettiford and Max Roach were two of the strongest rhythm players I'd ever played with.'[3]

By December Don Byas was the regular saxophonist and self-effacing George Wallington played the piano. Gillespie had convinced himself he could manage without Bud Powell, reasoning 'we didn't need a piano player to show us the way . . . We had Max and Oscar. We needed a piano player to stay outta the way.'

The importance of this quintet is hard to overstate. Every night at the Onyx Club new ideas would crop up. During the daytime the musicians would gather at the Gillespie apartment (2040 Seventh Avenue, in the heart of Harlem), analyze their discoveries, use the piano and write things down. Pettiford created a showcase for Max Roach, 'Max is Making Wax'. Gillespie worked up the riff in 'Little John Special' and added a hiccuping vocal refrain: 'Salt Peanuts'.

Another fine tenor saxophonist, Budd Johnson, took over from Don Byas in January 1944, and it was sometime during this month, while the quintet was broadcasting from the Onyx, that the diligent Bob Redcross made a disc-recording from his radio. This archive fragment was not widely published until 1995. Its technical quality is execrable – crunching surface noise almost obliterates the music – but its historical signifi-cance is massive. Lovers of classification have tagged it 'the first bebop record ever'.

Straining our ears, we hear first a busy tenor saxophone improvising in a minor key. Then Gillespie takes over, dramatic and brilliant, proudly addressing us in the new musical language, fluently supported by Roach. His solo is followed by a short one from the piano, then the trumpet is back, muted this time, leading the ensemble through the final bars of what we recognize with hindsight as 'A Night in Tunisia'. Beneath the snake-charming theme, the saxophone insists upon a drone-like counter-melody, and Roach and Pettiford create an Afro-Latin undertow. By way of coda, Gillespie dissolves the beat and delivers a suspenseful trumpet monologue.

At the Onyx new compositions emerged at such a rate that many were left without names. Gillespie used code to signal what the band would play next:

> I'd say, 'Dee-da-pa-da-n-de-bop', and we'd go into it. People, when
> they'd want to ask for one of those numbers, would ask for 'bebop'. And
> the press picked up on it and started calling it bebop. The first time the
> term bebop appeared in print was while we played at the Onyx Club.

There were those who objected that the label 'bebop', fixed to the new black music by white journalists, was condescending and offensive, but Gillespie was a pragmatist. He accepted that packaging and marketing were the American way. One of his most incendiary compositions from the Onyx era, leaping like wildfire through a thicket of staccato quavers, he called simply 'Bebop'.

Anxious to board the latest trend, the big names in the music business reconnoitred the Onyx. White bandleader Jimmy Dorsey offered Gillespie this thought: 'Boy, I'd love to have you in my band – if you weren't so dark.'

More civilized and fruitful was the approach from Coleman Hawkins. Now that the recording ban was over, the great tenor saxophonist was about to make a set of records, and wanted to sound up-to-date. The 10-piece band he booked included all the players at the Onyx, and he paid Gillespie the further compliment of asking him to write some arrangements.

The landmark recording session was spread over two days in February 1944. Of the six pieces recorded, the most striking was a new Gillespie composition, 'Woody 'n You' (titled in honour of Woody Herman), whose main theme generates its drama from a descending sequence of half-diminished chords.

In his autobiography Gillespie credits Thelonious Monk with alerting him to the virtues of the half-diminished, and describes how 'Woody 'n You' came into being while he was at the piano tinkering with a pleasing progression: 'The song came from the chords. Looking at the notes in my right hand, I discovered a melody and a countermelody. I didn't try to express anything particular, just what the chords inspired.'

Fifty years later 'Woody 'n You' is a classic, whose four-square phraseology is easier to grasp than the flowing asymmetries of Charlie Parker's compositions. Questioned about the different gifts Gillespie and Parker brought to the new music, several of their contemporaries offered insights. In Billy Eckstine's judgement, 'Bird was so full of spontaneity. It just – boom! – came out. But Diz knew methodically what it was. He pursued it.' According to Kenny Clarke:

> Bird was a genius . . . Dizzy is different: he's a saint. An extraordinary
> musician, in some ways more than a genius. Dizzy taught all the
> trumpet players, and a lot of the drummers, too. He gave much more of
> himself than Bird. Bird was like a prophet, who brings a message and
> disappears.[4]

*

During the spring of 1944, as well as setting the pace on 52nd Street, Gillespie was tending the budding big band of Billy Eckstine. In April they made some records, including an arrangement that Gillespie thought one of his best. 'Good Jelly Blues' benefits from ingenious orchestral writing, as well as an ear-catching introduction that we shall meet again, put to new use, at Massey Hall and elsewhere.

The first public appearance by the Eckstine Orchestra was in Baltimore in June, by which time Charlie Parker was leading the saxophones. Gillespie wrote arrangements to showcase himself and Parker as soloists, including big band versions of some Onyx favourites. Dancers were nonplussed. Musicians like Miles Davis were astounded.

What sold the band to the general public was the singing, especially the romantic vocals of Eckstine himself (the 'Sepia Sinatra'), but also the luxurious tones of Sarah Vaughan. To help Vaughan's career, Gillespie made an arrangement of his 'Interlude' ('A Night in Tunisia') for her, transforming the sizzling item played by his quintet at the Onyx into a wistful ballad, with the punchline 'Love was just an interlude'. A small company, Continental, financed a low-budget recording session, and the musicians gathered in a New York studio on New Year's Eve 1944. Not only was Gillespie composer and arranger of the vocal 'Interlude', he also played the piano and took the trumpet solo on this rare but telling record.

*

On 9 January 1945, having left Eckstine, Gillespie made his first commercial records as leader. His sextet included Don Byas and Oscar Pettiford, and the chosen pieces were from the Onyx Club repertoire. On 'Salt Peanuts' and 'Bebop' he played solos of tremendous flair and dash. To the ballad 'I Can't Get Started' he brought fresh beauty, elaborating the harmonies and creating a suspenseful coda. (This coda was later used by him, and afterwards by everybody else, as the introduction to Thelonious Monk's ''Round Midnight').

During the same month, once again 'strapped for vittles', he took a turn as a member of the Boyd Raeburn Orchestra. Raeburn already had

Gillespie's 'Interlude'/'A Night in Tunisia' in his library, and liked it so much that his band regularly performed both versions: the resigned vocal about fleeting love, and the feisty instrumental.

Raeburn's broadcast of the instrumental (recorded in 1944) is an exhilarating performance, featuring Gillespie's hero Roy Eldridge. But better still is the band's January 1945 commercial record, with the composer himself as solo trumpeter. This is as near as we can come to how 'A Night in Tunisia' must have been played by the Earl Hines Orchestra. The torrid theme builds its suspense in layers. First, a heavily-syncopated bass ostinato. Second, an insinuating saxophone riff. Third, a solo trombone, playing the quasi-oriental melody. Fourth, stabbing trumpets. After the theme comes a bold interlude in march-time, then the orchestra stops dead, leaving Gillespie to launch his solo with a two-bar break.

The Boyd Raeburn recording put 'A Night in Tunisia' on the map, but the glory days of this fine composition were still to come, not least because it became a favourite vehicle for Charlie Parker.

*

The chance for Gillespie and Parker to play together regularly in a small group came in February, when the Three Deuces (a narrow basement off 52nd Street) commissioned Gillespie to form a quintet. Gillespie chose Parker, Bud Powell, Curley Russell and Max Roach. Roach could not be there at the start, but his deputy Stan Levey suited Dizzy well because 'he was in the drawer behind Max and knew all the licks Max played'. When sickness ruled out Bud Powell, he was replaced by Al Haig, an attentive young man with a firm grasp of the style.

First night at the Three Deuces was preceded by an intense period of rehearsals, often in the Gillespie apartment. Much of the repertoire was original: written by Gillespie and designed for razor-sharp performance at high speed.

The seating capacity at the Three Deuces was not much more that 100, and when 'Dizzy Gillespie and his Band, featuring Charlie Parker' opened at the beginning of March 1945, the place was packed. Some of those present were baffled, some were thrilled, some enraged. Business was good enough to keep the quintet at the little club until July. None of its live performances were recorded, so the closest we come to how it sounded are the discs Gillespie made with Parker during that period for the Guild label.

As well as the breath-taking playing of the two of them, those records feature four Gillespie compositions of the highest quality. 'Groovin' High' (on the chords of 'Whispering') is elaborate fun. There's a teasing introduction; a theme that shuttles between simple questions and devious answers; a key change; and a melodramatic half-speed coda. 'Dizzy Atmosphere' is a riff on the 'I Got Rhythm' chords, with a chromatic middle eight. Its surprise (reserved until after the solos) is a delightful, fluting countermelody. 'Shaw 'Nuff' (named for agent Billy Shaw) opens with an alarm call in F minor, then switches to the major. Its theme (again on the 'I Got Rhythm' chords) contrasts a smooth A section with a spiky section B. 'Salt Peanuts' has grown by now into an extensive routine, with a teasing introduction and several bracing interludes. To round things off, the introduction is recycled as a coda, capped by a final, jovial shout from one and all: 'Salt Peanuts! Salt Peanuts!'

Gillespie and Parker also recorded Jerome Kern's 'All the Things You Are', complete with the introduction that has become, for jazz performers, an integral part of the piece. This bell-like summons, tolling the cadence D flat–C, is often attributed to Parker, but is in fact by Gillespie, adapted from the opening bars of his arrangement for the Eckstine band of 'Good Jelly Blues'.

Scores of musicians have testified to Gillespie's importance as teacher and enabler. According to the saxophonist Budd Johnson, 'all the guys who were trying to learn about this kind of music would go by Dizzy's, and sometimes he'd have as many as fifteen or twenty cats up there sitting around'. Max Roach was one of those cats, and so was young Miles Davis. In Miles's estimation, 'Bird might have been the spirit of the bebop movement, but Dizzy was its head and hands: the one who kept it all together.'[5]

Parker, too, came to the Gillespie home on Seventh Avenue, but only at times to suit his eccentric body-clock. Gillespie told Robert Reisner about a characteristic visit:

Three in the morning the doorbell rang. There was Bird, horn in hand, and he says, 'Let me in Diz, you must hear this.' I had been putting down Bird's solos on paper, which is something Bird never had the patience to do himself. 'Not now,' I said, 'Later, man, tomorrow.' 'No,' Bird cried, 'I won't remember it tomorrow.' From the other room my wife yelled, 'Throw him out,' and I obediently slammed the door in Bird's face. He then played the tune in the hallway. I grabbed a pencil and paper and took it down from the other side of the door.[6]

*

What snapped Gillespie's tolerance was Parker's aberrant behaviour at the Three Deuces: late appearances and sometimes non-appearances. Although the quintet had achieved wonders, Gillespie announced his intention to drop it and form his first big band. Helped by the arranger Walter Fuller, he orchestrated his best compositions and gathered New York's finest young talent, including Max Roach.

To make such an experiment more commercial, Gillespie's agent Billy Shaw slotted it into a singing and dancing package he called 'Hep-Sations of 1945'. The tour he fixed took the Hep-Sations into the Deep South, where they met the usual nasty problems, plus one Gillespie had not foreseen. Although Shaw had said this would be a concert tour, it turned out that all the bookings were for dances. Worse than that, the black audiences in the segregated Southern dance halls took against the new music. Gillespie still felt furious with them when he recalled that tour thirty years later:

> They said they couldn't dance to the music. *I* could dance to it. I could dance my ass off to it. But the unreconstructed blues lovers down South, who couldn't hear nothing else but the blues, didn't think so. They wouldn't even listen to us.

Not long after the tour Gillespie broke up the band. A lucky beneficiary of the sad demise was Charlie Parker, who was able to call upon his former partner for support during his first recording session as leader. Gillespie's contribution to this historic occasion, both as trumpeter and pianist, was crucial, but the Savoy record company was reluctant to acknowledge his generosity. On the original releases the only trumpeter credited is Miles Davis, and the piano player is mysteriously listed as one Hen Gates.

*

The next contract negotiated for Gillespie by Billy Shaw was with the Californian club owner Billy Berg. The deal was for an eight-week engagement at Berg's nightspot in Hollywood, starting on 10 December. What Shaw sold to Berg was the Dizzy Gillespie Sextet, including the vibraphonist Milt Jackson. What Berg was not told was that Parker's unreliability had become so acute that Gillespie was bringing Jackson so there would always be at least five musicians on the bandstand.

Gillespie described the coldness of Billy Berg's customers with his characteristic vigour: 'They thought we were just playing ugly on purpose. They were really *very* square. Man, they used to stare at us so tough!'[7] According to journalist Leonard Feather, it was not only the music that the audience found provoking. There were also prejudicial comments about the presence in this black-led band of the two white musicians, Al Haig and Stan Levey. A local radio station fuelled the antipathy, claiming that what was going on at Billy Berg's tended to pervert young minds. A local newspaper reported, 'Men from Mars land at Billy Berg's'.

Nevertheless, the sextet did see out the engagement, and left a handsome legacy of recordings on the West Coast. Mostly they involved Parker, but there was one session when the Gillespie Sextet with Lucky Thompson instead of Parker came to the studio and delivered a bumper crop. Two equally good versions of 'Dizzy Atmosphere' were issued (labelled *Dynamo A* and *Dynamo B*). An intense performance of ''Round Midnight' placed on record Gillespie's fitting (and universally adopted) introduction and coda to Monk's theme. Charlie Parker was represented in his absence by one of his finest compositions, 'Confirmation', on which Gillespie played an eloquent and passionate solo.

Also in Los Angeles, Gillespie made himself some pocket money as a sideman. Signing the register as John Burk, he beefed up the forces assembled for some big-band recordings by local showman Wilbert Baranco. The results are undistinguished, but worth mentioning because the bass player with Baranco and his Rhythm Bombardiers would go far. He was Charles Mingus.

*

On 8 February 1946 the sextet, minus Parker, took a plane to New York, where Gillespie was immediately snapped up to lend lustre to a series of records for RCA Victor called 'New 52nd Street Jazz'. The results, all classics of the small-group genre, included 'A Night in Tunisia', the first official recording of this composition to carry Gillespie's name as leader. A copy soon reached Charlie Parker in Los Angeles.

With a cavalier disregard for contracts, Gillespie also recorded for several small labels, using such pseudonyms as B. Bopstein and Izzy Goldberg. The clubs on New York's 52nd Street, meanwhile, were competing for his services. He chose the Spotlite. Its premises were large enough to accommodate a big band, and it was managed by Clark Monroe – previously famous for his Uptown House in Harlem. Gillespie opened with a sextet (using Sonny Stitt in place of Parker), while his dream orchestra was being recruited.

In May some records by the sextet were issued. One in particular, 'Oop Bop Sh'Bam', caught the popular fancy with its wacky refrain, although its prime feature artistically was Gillespie's dashing, shapely trumpet solo. Great trumpet playing is both an art and a physical feat. 'Putting that piece of iron on your chops,' Louis Armstrong said, 'is more than a notion.' Gillespie's autobiography reveals that a medical appointment during the engagement at the Spotlite Club marked a turning point in his playing. Troubled by a festering cut on his top lip that failed to respond to baking powder and scalding water, he visited Dr Irving Goldman, a top Manhattan surgeon:

> Dr Goldman stuck this reamer in my lip, then put this white stuff in there which burned a little bit. I went on playing, and very soon my lip was all healed up from the inside. I could hit Gs and As, sometimes B flat. Get up there and ride. All the trumpeters were trying to play my style.

Even those unmoved by the Gillespie trumpet playing must have felt their hair stand on end when the tight space at the Spotlite club was invaded by the full Dizzy Gillespie Orchestra: seventeen hand-picked musicians and their leader, playing arrangements that showed off their range, speed and power. According to Walter Fuller, the first night opened with a dramatic orchestration of 'Shaw 'Nuff', featuring Max Roach 'rolling and carrying on on those cymbals'. It closed with the overwhelming 'Things to Come' (a big-band magnification of Gillespie's pantherish 'Bebop').

The new venture needed nursing. Gillespie's first-choice pianist, Bud Powell, turned out to be catastrophically unreliable, so he was replaced by Thelonious Monk. When Monk, too, proved incapable of appearing on time, Gillespie turned for advice to his old friend Kenny Clarke (now back in civilian life). Clarke recommended a pianist he had met in the Army: the conscientious John Lewis, who also showed promise as a composer. And, since Max Roach was finding big band work not entirely congenial, Clarke himself took over the drums.

Private recorders roughly captured the full band at the Spotlite, and then in July it made its first official discs, including 'Things to Come'. The seismic force of this performance could hardly be contained by the recording techniques of fifty years ago, but what was trapped within the grooves still has the power to astound: from the incandescent introduction to the simmering coda. The same recording session produced the engagingly daft 'He Beeped When He Should Have Bopped', warbled by the band's now-forgotten vocalist Alice Roberts.

The New York media hailed Gillespie as 'Mr Bebop', and followers of fashion decked themselves in *bop* (goatee) beards, *bop* (French) berets, and *bop* (horn-rimmed) glasses. 'Real Gone Frames' for only $3.95 were advertised in *Ebony* magazine.

In November 1946 the Gillespie band, with Ella Fitzgerald as featured vocalist, began a long and successful American tour. When they returned to New York the Spotlite Club could hardly contain the swelling congregation. The more fitting Manhattan venues now were the Apollo Theatre and the Savoy Ballroom (where Charlie Parker, back at last from California, paid them a spectacular visit).

*

Impressed by the box office potential of Gillespie and his orchestra, the producer William D. Alexander financed *Jivin' in Bebop*, a full-length film built around them, which he sold as a 'Sensational Variety Musical, Studded with Star Names, Hummin' with Hit Tunes and also featuring the Hubba Hubba Girls'. These sultry beauties danced a scantily-clad interpretation of 'A Night in Tunisia', just one of the seventeen musical numbers brought to the screen. In the segregated America of those days, such a movie was not thought fit for picture palaces patronized by white folk, but *Jivin' in Bebop* did good business for Mr Alexander on the 'coloured' cinema circuit.

Another to ride the bebop boom was the jazz pundit Barry Ulanov. His wheeze, which he sold to the Mutual Radio Network in September 1947, was for a series of 'battles of the bands' – beboppers versus traditionalists. The mixed bunch he sent out to fight under the banner 'Barry Ulanov's All-Star Modern Jazz Musicians' included both Gillespie and Parker, so the bits of the broadcasts that have survived are not without historical interest: the first recorded examples of the two giants playing together after Parker's Californian absence.

Lumbered with unwieldy forces and the contrived, 'mouldy figs v moderns' atmosphere, Gillespie marshalled the Modern Jazz troops and did his best to play the game. For example, he took the New Orleans classic 'Tiger Rag' and presented it in a fashion designed to enrage the old fogies. As a shock entrance for the venerable beast, he recycled the introduction he had composed for 'Shaw 'Nuff'. And round the animal's sacred tail he wrapped the countermelody from 'Dizzy Atmosphere'.

*

On Monday 29 September 1947 the poster outside Carnegie Hall offered 'Dizzy Gillespie and his Orchestra with Ella Fitzgerald, plus extra attraction Yardbird Parker'. Pasted across it was the message 'Sold Out'.

That night a sumptuous feast of new music for big band was served, including 'Toccata for Trumpet and Orchestra' by John Lewis; 'Cubana

Be-Cubana Bop' by Gillespie and George Russell; Russell's fancy orchestration of Parker's 'Relaxin' at Camarillo'; and a writ-large edition of Gillespie's 'Salt Peanuts'.

The hair-raising Gillespie–Parker duel was supported by just the rhythm section, and notwithstanding all the other demands on his lip that night, Gillespie met Parker's fearsome challenge with a blazing response.

*

Searching for a percussion player to heighten the impact of his Carnegie Hall concert, Gillespie had found his man performing at a club in Spanish Harlem. Chano Pozo belonged to the Cuban *lucumi* faith, which drew on West African rituals. He spoke no English. He sang and he danced, and while he danced he beat the conga drum to inspire the other dancers. As soon as Gillespie heard him, he hired him: the first conga player in a jazz orchestra. The effect was dramatic, as Gillespie explained: 'Chano taught us all multi-rhythm: we learned from the master. The chants – the Nañigo, the Ararra, the Santo – each have their own rhythm. They're all African.'

Through Chano Pozo, Gillespie discovered the art of beating the conga drum with his hands – skin on skin. The title of the most famous Gillespie–Pozo collaboration, 'Manteca', means skin in colloquial Spanish. Chano Pozo's contribution was a set of interlocking patterns, modal and intensely rhythmic, known in Cuba as *montunas*. Gillespie produced a contrasting middle section, one of his typically rich harmonic sequences. The 1947 recording of 'Manteca' was a bestseller, and a prototype for that popular hybrid known as 'Afro-Cuban jazz'.

*

In January 1948, after a sickening Atlantic crossing in third-class berths, the Gillespie orchestra disembarked in Sweden and immediately gave the first concert of a crammed Scandinavian tour. For the next three weeks they played in packed town halls, sometimes giving three concerts in a day. The local enthusiasm was touching, but where was the money?

Fearing the worst about the promoter, Harold Lundquist, Gillespie took to sleeping in the corridor outside Lundquist's hotel room. But the crafty Swede managed to leave the band stranded without a cent.

News of their plight reached Paris and the ears of Charles Delauney, jazz connoisseur. Delauney treasured his rare copies of *Groovin' High* and *Dizzy Atmosphere*. Now here was the chance to be of service. A deputation set out to rescue Monsieur Gillespie and to assure him of a warm French welcome. Funds were raised. A hall was booked.

Gillespie had previously experienced a Parisian audience eleven years earlier, as an insignificant member of the Teddy Hill Orchestra. The crowd this time was different: younger, wilder, ready for anything, thrilled with what they got. A low fidelity recording, made on 28 February in the Salle Pleyel, allows us to share this atmosphere. Gillespie, on peak form, plays a commanding trumpet solo on every item. Sometimes he sings as well. And to bring down the curtain, 'Things to Come', faster than ever and with an extra-long Gillespie solo, fiery and majestic.

The plan to transport this cornucopia to England foundered on the opposition of the Ministry of Labour, who ruled that foreigners must not steal work from British musicians. The French took a different view: they induced Kenny Clarke to desert Gillespie and stay behind in Paris as an inspiration for local rhythm sections.

*

Back in New York the Gillespie band, with new drummer Teddy Stewart, gave a second concert at Carnegie Hall. Attendance was good but the press reaction was nasty. 'How Deaf Can You Get?', sneered *Time* magazine. Particularly offensive to Gillespie was the charge that his music was indebted to the self-proclaimed pioneer of progressive jazz – white bandleader Stan Kenton.

The consolation was the enthusiasm that greeted the band as it gave performances across America and the welcome it found in California. Here, after filling concert halls in Long Beach and San Bernardino, Gillespie returned in triumph to Billy Berg's in Hollywood. This was where his sextet with Charlie Parker had flopped. Now he was the darling of the film-star set. To reward Ava Gardner for her regular attendance, he presented her with a French beret.

Woolworth's in downtown Los Angeles placed a big order for 'Manteca' and had Gillespie come in and sign souvenir pictures of himself. The store also did a roaring trade in horn-rimmed sunglasses. And in a bizarre fashion twist, teenage girls took to painting goatee beards on their chins. During the band's concert at the Pasadena Civic Auditorium, the best of the Gillespie look-alikes were plucked from the audience and invited to sit on the stage. Chano Pozo entered the party spirit, beating his congas with a glass of water balanced on his head.

Gillespie relished the craziness. But then he acquiesced in a piece of lurid journalism that he came to regret: a six-page photo-spread in *Life* magazine, including a 'fun' picture of him dressed as a Muslim, bowing towards Mecca. The article purported to describe the genesis of bebop, but made no mention of Charlie Parker. As the band continued to tour, it was as if Gillespie's alter ego had never been. Until one night in September 1948, at the Pershing Ballroom in Chicago, when Parker swooped and helped himself to all the saxophone solos, rousing the audience of 3000 like a preacher exhorting his congregation.

*

According to Gillespie, the band of 1949 was the best he ever had, but this was the year when success slipped away. Keeping discipline was a strain. Costs of transport and accommodation swallowed the profits. Worst of all, public affection was switching to the raw product of marauding rhythm and blues groups. Gillespie signed a contract with Capitol records, who urged him to think box office. Results like 'You Stole My Wife, You Horse-Thief' made no money and made no one happy, least of all Gillespie's wife Lorraine. Identifying the band and its payroll as threats to connubial bliss, she presented her ultimatum: 'It's either me or the band.' The band was dismissed.

So Gillespie entered the spring of 1950 with no band, no recording contract and no definite plans. Sometimes he worked as a freelance

soloist, accepting whatever rhythm section he was given. He talked of
fronting a woodwind ensemble and touring as half of a double bill with
Charlie Parker and Strings, but this never happened. However, noting
that he was unattached, Norman Granz booked him to make a record
with Parker. The challenge of the reunion and the freshness of Parker's
compositions put Gillespie on his mettle. For example, on some takes of
'Relaxin' with Lee' (in D flat, on the chords of 'Stompin' at the Savoy'), he
elects to step up a semitone and improvise in the bracing key of D major.
The fizzing album became a classic, known and loved as *Bird and Diz*.

*

In 1951 Gillespie sunk his savings into the founding of a record company,
hoping that this way he could combine artistic freedom with material
prosperity. He would provide the musical talent. A fan of his, Dave Usher,
would take care of business. Usher worked in Detroit at his father's company, Usher Oil, so Detroit became the address of his joint venture with
Dizzy, which they registered as Dee Gee Records.

For the first Dee Gee recording session (in Detroit on 1 March 1951)
Gillespie picked some brilliant young musicians to play with him, including Milt Jackson (vibes and piano) and John Coltrane (alto and tenor).
And to celebrate his debut as what he called a 'musical industrialist', he
unveiled a new composition, 'Birks Works', a minor-key 12-bar blues
taking its title from his middle name. They also recorded the throbbing
'Tin Tin Deo', composed years earlier by Gillespie and Chano Pozo. In
1948 Chano Pozo had been killed in a fight in a Harlem bar, aged thirty-
three. Gillespie's statement of the lovely theme is intensely poignant. At
the other extreme they recorded 'We Love to Boogie', freighted with a
gutsy tenor solo by John Coltrane, and aimed deliberately but unsuc-
cessfully at the R&B hit parade.

The second session for Dee Gee took place six weeks later. The best
outcome this time was a tearaway 12-bar blues called 'The Champ',
another Gillespie composition to join the standard repertoire.

In August he was back in the Dee Gee studio again, still looking for a
hit. 'School Days' had a set of juvenile lyrics, bawled over a thudding back

beat by singing discovery Joe Carroll. 'Swing Low Sweet Cadillac' (with Gillespie himself taking the vocal lead) was an ironic updating of a beloved Negro spiritual. Both items became jazz festival favourites but neither triggered the nation's cash registers.

By July 1952, when the latest Gillespie quintet came to the studio, Dee Gee was faltering. 'Oo-Shoo-Be-Doo-Be' (sung jointly by Gillespie and Joe Carroll) was fair enough, but 'Pop's Confessin'' (mimicking Louis Armstrong) and 'Umbrella Man' (with minimal jazz content) were desperate strokes.

*

Gillespie's responsibilities as a 'musical industrialist' had never absorbed him completely. Throughout the Dee Gee period he kept busy as a freelance, always in demand for club and concert appearances. For seven nights at the end of March 1951 he played at Birdland with Charlie Parker and Bud Powell. And on one of those nights, when radio station WJZ was broadcasting from the bandstand, a home-listener plugged in his recorder.

Parker and Gillespie are both mightily motivated by this so-called 'Summit Meeting'. Indeed, Gillespie can hardly wait to get started. The first number is his composition 'Blue 'n Boogie'. While introducing it, the MC Symphony Sid starts to ramble down memory lane, but before he can get far, Gillespie's trumpet sounds the charge and the music sweeps Sid aside.

After 'Blue 'n Boogie' comes 'Anthropology', jointly composed by Gillespie and Parker, and played tonight at a ferocious 288 beats per minute.

Thelonious Monk's ''Round Midnight' benefits, as has become usual, from the handsome front and end extensions Gillespie built for it. And the closing number, 'A Night in Tunisia', comes with the by-now customary bonuses: Parker's famous alto break and Gillespie's rhapsodic trumpet coda.

*

In February 1952, in lieu of the financial security he craved, Gillespie received a plaque from *Down Beat* magazine 'for being one of the top trumpet players of all time'. At the same award ceremony the impecunious Charlie Parker was handed the trophy for 'best alto sax man of 1951'. New York's TV Channel 5 screened the double presentation and the consequent performance of 'Hot House'. The telerecording of this brief occasion is the only footage we have of Parker and Gillespie playing together.

Some of the Dee Gee records – particularly 'The Champ' – had been selling well in Europe. In their wake, Gillespie travelled to Paris in the spring of 1952 and enjoyed a lucrative spell giving concerts and making recordings as a star soloist with local musicians.

The most hyped event in New York's 1952 jazz calendar must have been the autumn concert at Carnegie Hall, billed by its organizers as 'The Greatest Musical Attraction This Side of Heaven'. The Ellington band was there, plus Billie Holiday, Stan Getz and Charlie Parker with his string orchestra. Squeezed into a small corner of this crammed November evening was a spot for Gillespie to play with Parker and the Parker rhythm section – minus the strings but plus the eager presence of the conga drummer Candido Camero. On the unbalanced recording that we have, Candido easily obliterates everything that matters about 'A Night in Tunisia'.

Early in 1953 Gillespie was back in Europe, this time at the head of his latest group, with singer Joe Carroll. Their concert at the Salle Pleyel in Paris on 9 February is ours to enjoy in a technically decent recording. Gillespie sounds in good heart, bounding about the stage with a conga drum slung across his shoulder, running through the favourites in the Dee Gee catalogue. What the audience did not know was that the Dee Gee company was now in mortal trouble. It had failed to meet its tax bill and the government had seized its assets.

*

Back in January, just before he left for Europe, Gillespie had been visited by those eager young Canadians who were assembling the Definitive

Quintet for their festival at Massey Hall. After their effusive reception by Charlie Parker, the youngsters were taken aback by the trumpeter's severely businesslike manner. However, a deal was struck. Gillespie would play the concert for $450.

On Friday 15 May, good as his word, he reported punctually at La Guardia airport for the flight to Toronto. And when Parker did not appear, it was Gillespie who went looking . . .

THREE

UN POCO LOCO

'He outbirded Bird and he outdizzied Dizzy.'
Al Haig on Bud Powell[1]

'A HUNDRED PEOPLE would crowd into one flat until the walls bulged. When we played the shouts, everyone danced.'[2] That's Willie 'The Lion' Smith, describing the parties thrown by the tenants of Harlem in the 1920s – called 'rent parties' or 'rent shouts' because guests paid to come in and the receipts covered the rent. The Lion was just one of the two-fisted pianists you could hire to provide the music. Rivals included James P. Johnson, Luckey Roberts, and Thomas 'Fats' Waller. These were the 'Harlem Ticklers', and the style they fashioned from ragtime and blues was labelled 'Harlem Stride'.

On 27 September 1924 Earl Rudolph 'Bud' Powell was born into this milieu. His father, William Powell, was one of Harlem's busiest ticklers, whose playing, we are told, 'really made the piano sing – he filled the room with sound'.[3] Bud's big brother Skeets studied violin and trumpet. At six Bud began to devour the European piano repertoire. When he was seven, according to his proud father, 'musicians would come and actually steal him, take him from place to place playing music, sometimes to two or three o'clock in the morning.'[4]

By temperament Bud was unsuited to the gregarious, rent-shout environment. According to his childhood friend Andy Browne, he felt uncomfortable at parties – and was always dragged to the piano and obliged to play. Another friend remembered Bud as a small fellow, '*always* protective of his hands'.[5]

Although he did well enough at High School, shining in the mathematics class, Bud left at fifteen to concentrate on his music. In another place, at another time, his gifts might have earned him the respect due to a concert recitalist, but this was America in 1939 and he was black. He found work in the burlesque houses over on Coney Island. His principal jazz model in those days was pianist Billy Kyle, whose melodic, 'trumpet-style' improvisations brightened the John Kirby Sextet.

By 1940 he was finding paid work in the Manhattan clubs, sometimes as a solo pianist and sometimes in tandem with drummer Max Roach, 'the kid from Brooklyn'. At the end of an evening's work, Bud, Max and other adventurous young spirits would descend on the after-hours joints in Harlem where fresh ideas were bubbling. In one of these, Bud met the composer, pianist and enigmatic genius Thelonious Monk, seven years his senior and a major player in the black music revolution. A profound friendship developed. Powell adopted Monk as a father figure; Monk was struck by the teenager's pianistic brilliance and uncanny ability to absorb the new musical language.

Monk and Powell took to visiting each other's homes and to going for walks through Harlem and the Bronx, pausing at the addresses where they knew they'd find a piano. Monk's regular job was with the rhythm section at Minton's, a favourite Harlem watering hole for the experimentalists. The drummer at Minton's, Kenny Clarke, remembered the night when Monk led Bud up on to the bandstand and invited him to play. Some customers complained, and the manager urged Thelonious to come back. Monk growled, 'Don't you hear what he's doing? If you don't listen to him, I won't play anymore.'[6] According to Clarke, 'Monk wrote for Bud just like a composer writes for a singer. When you hear Bud play Monk's music, then you really hear something.'[7]

Acceptance at Minton's meant you were a member of the avant-garde, up there with Charlie Parker and Dizzy Gillespie. Sometimes, during the day, Powell would join the assembly of youngsters, including Miles Davis and Max Roach, at the Gillespie apartment in Harlem, where the niceties of the new music were debated under Dizzy's benign tutelage. On other days, musicians leaving the after-hours jam sessions at around 9.00 in the morning would make their way to the Powell family apartment on St Nicholas Avenue. Bud's mother, Pearl, would cook them breakfast and they could carry on playing, with Bud at the piano.

*

In 1943, when Powell was eighteen, the bandleader Cootie Williams hailed him as a genius, hired him and assumed legal guardianship. According to Bud's father, it was while he was with Williams that the boy grew fond of alcohol and marijuana.

Before 1943 was out, Dizzy Gillespie tried to recruit him for the modernist group he was assembling to play at the Onyx Club on 52nd Street. His overture was rebuffed. According to most accounts, it was Cootie Williams who stood in the way – unwilling to part with the brilliant pianist for whom he was legally responsible. But in Max Roach's version it was Bud's mother who said no, because she feared Dizzy was crazy.

Either way, Powell missed taking part in the groundbreaking recordings Gillespie, Roach and the others at the Onyx made with Coleman Hawkins in February 1944. However, he recorded several times during that year with Cootie Williams, and although the context was conservative and Powell's solo space was tightly rationed, his contribution made other pianists sit up.

His first recordings (in January) were with the Cootie Williams Sextet – a band within the band, featuring the big personalities of Williams himself and Eddie 'Cleanhead' Vinson. Powell's versatility is dazzling. On the fast pieces 'Floogie Boo' and 'Honeysuckle Rose', the express delivery of the right-hand melody is of the school of Billy Kyle. On the ballads 'My Old Flame' and 'Sweet Lorraine', he shows how powerfully he has been affected by the example of Art Tatum, supreme master of rococo piano playing. While Cootie Williams's fruity trumpet declaims the tunes, Powell keeps fluttering by, leaving graceful trails of Tatumesque arpeggios.

The bouncy instrumental 'You Talk a Little Trash' demonstrates his skill at 'comping' (feeding harmonies to the front line in a discreetly propulsive manner). The novelty song 'Do Some War Work Baby' is notable for the dainty edging of arabesques he applies to Williams's gruff vocal. During 'Echoes of Harlem', beneath the trumpet growls, he spreads a dark, hypnotic mantra.

The full Cootie Williams Orchestra recorded eight sides during 1944, but found solo space for Powell on just one – a roisterous arrangement of 'Royal Garden Blues'. Here his deft right hand and discrete left are from the drawer marked Billy Kyle, but whereas Kyle at high speed radiates bonhomie, Powell crackles with an electric tension.

Without Powell's passionate campaigning, the Williams orchestra would never have recorded Thelonious Monk's intricate ''Round Midnight'. Ironically though, this is the disc where the piano is barely audible, buried by the engineer beneath the crashing of the ensemble.

*

Powell grumbled openly about Williams's artistic policy. Sometimes during an evening's performance he would refuse to play the number Williams announced, keeping his arms folded and shaking his head. But these were family quarrels, and there was no hint that the young rebel intended to quit. When the break came, in January 1945, it was involuntary and the circumstances were horrific. Cootie Williams has given his version of what happened:

> We went to play a job in Philadelphia and Bud was a little late. And high when he got there. So he didn't come back [to New York] with us that night when we finished. The next day the FBI called and told me they had him in jail. I gave them his mother's phone number. They'd beaten him so badly 'round the head that she had to go get him. His head was so damaged he ended in Bellevue; his sickness started right there.[8]

The FBI involvement is surprising, but the local police certainly played an active part. The location was Philadelphia's Broad Street railway station, where Powell tried to defend himself against arrest for disorderly conduct.

His mother came and paid the fine and took him to the family's country home at Willow Grove, a suburb of Philadelphia, and here she nursed him, helped by his teenage girlfriend, May Frances Barnes. But nothing relieved his extreme headaches, and after visits to Bellevue Hospital in Manhattan, he was consigned to the Pilgrim State Psychiatric Facility out on Long Island, where they kept him for many months.

Before the injury Powell was childlike and highly strung; afterwards he was pursued by demons. The blow to the head did not abort his creative brilliance – his full artistic flowering was still to come – but it condemned him to a life of mental torment.

His confinement during much of 1945 meant he missed several major episodes in the rapidly unfolding story of the new music. For example, when Dizzy Gillespie formed a group with Charlie Parker to play at the Three Deuces, the pianist he wanted was Powell. Since that could not be, the job went to another youngster, Al Haig, who was embarrassed by his sudden elevation and in awe of the hero he replaced.

In November, when Charlie Parker approached his first recording date as leader, he chose Powell to be his pianist. By now Powell had been released from hospital, but shortly before the session, he quit New York for the haven of Willow Grove. Dizzy Gillespie stepped into the breach and played the piano on that day.

*

In 1946 Powell was back on the scene, and his young trio – with bassist Curley Russell and Max Roach – was considered New York's sharpest. The records they made in January, as the bedrock of a quintet led by modern tenor man Dexter Gordon, show how Powell's playing had advanced since his Cootie Williams days.

During Gordon's solos, Curley Russell spells out the beat, while Roach and Powell create a kaleidoscope of secondary rhythmic patterns. When it's Powell's turn to solo, he attacks with tremendous power: more than a match for the beefy sound of Dexter Gordon's horn. Liberated from the Cootie Williams context and astutely backed by Roach, he can express himself freely, and although he refers glancingly to the styles of Earl Hines and Art Tatum, he now speaks a keyboard language of his own.

Worth a footnote here (because it was a permanent part of his performances) is the harsh whine of his voice, echoing the actions of his fingers.

*

In April Gillespie hired Powell to play in his big band at the Spotlite Club. 'Bud was the definitive pianist of the bebop era',[9] said Gillespie, who was nonetheless obliged to sack him because of his super-erratic attendance.

In June Powell recorded again, this time in support of the young wizard of the trombone J.J. Johnson, who could speak the language of Parker and Gillespie on his awkward instrument. The Savoy record company invited him to the studio with a little band, which they dubbed 'J.J. Johnson's Beboppers'. Four original pieces were recorded (three by Johnson and one by Max Roach), all of them bristling with flattened fifths and suchlike snazzy features. In this modish ambience Powell enjoyed himself enormously, launching two of the performances with rocketing introductions, and contributing powerful solos to all four.

The 'bebop' brand name was evidently a winner, because in August 1946 Savoy contracted another team of practitioners (including trumpeter Kenny Dorham, saxophonist Sonny Stitt and drummer Kenny Clarke) and labelled them 'The Be-Bop Boys'. Powell was their pianist, and two of the pieces they recorded were newly written by him. These fine compositions, Powell's first on record, are perfect examples of the creative use of the new musical language.

'Bebop in Pastel' is cast in the AABA song form, but with delightful twists and turns, and a dancing postlude.

'Fool's Fancy' is another brilliant, evasive melody, this time racing over enhanced 'I Got Rhythm' chords. And here again there's a twist: on its second appearance the melodic line enjoys a rhythmic metamorphosis.

*

In the summer of 1946 the French company Swing came to New York to track down and record *le Bebop*. They assembled 'Kenny Clarke and his 52nd Street Boys': a band led by the pioneering drummer, playing bebop anthems like '52nd Street Theme'. Powell was the pianist, and the front line included Fats Navarro, an eloquent and original trumpeter. The presence of Navarro seems to have inspired the combative Powell, whose solos take on an exceptional lustre. (He once told his disciple Walter Bishop, while demonstrating some aspect of his awesome technique, 'See this? Ain't no horn player in the world can outplay a piano player.')[10]

By now Powell's searing style had reached its maturity. At fast tempos his jabbing left hand acted like a spur, or angry drum, goading his right to create long strands of melody, often at double speed. His recorded solos up to this date disappoint only because of their brevity – he was always obliged to share the cramped solo space on 78rpm discs with the front line instruments, and usually he had to settle for a miserly portion.

On 10 January 1947 a small company called Three Deuces invited him to come to the studio with a trio, and he seized the chance to spread his wings. Supported by his favourite partners, Curley Russell and Max Roach, he recorded eight magnificent sides (only slightly blemished by some shaky engineering). These 21 minutes of concentrated piano music redefined African-American keyboard art.

Powell selected most of his themes from among the popular melodies of the day. Two of these – 'Everything Happens to Me' and 'I Should Care' – are languid love songs, and here, for the first time on record, he demonstrates his own, distinctive, post-Tatum ballad style. His expositions keep faith with the songs' melodic and emotional contours. What he brings is fresh harmonic colour, some of it from the palette of Thelonious Monk. Leaving Curley Russell and Max Roach to take care of the beat, he underscores the melodic line with thick, two-handed chords, delicately fastened using gossamer arpeggios.

To convey the lilting nostalgia of 'I'll Remember April', he drifts in and out of a gentle Afro-Latin rhythm. On 'Somebody Loves Me' (medium tempo) and 'Nice Work If You Can Get It' (brisk) he generates colossal swing as he dramatizes the familiar tunes in bold block chords, then spins them into fantastic melodic webs of his own.

The old war-horse 'Indiana' becomes his vehicle for a super-speed excursion. First the familiar tune flashes by at around 330 beats per minute. Then an unaccompanied piano break spearheads the improvisation: three torrid choruses, followed by a joust with Max Roach during which Powell switches from soaring melodic line to thunderously percussive octave tremolos. After the reprise, he signs off with a characteristic flourish – a jubilant two-handed scamper down the whole-tone scale, in homage to Claude Debussy and Thelonious Monk.

Just two of the eight pieces Powell recorded are by modern jazz composers. 'Bud's Bubble' (also known as 'Crazeology') is an 'I Got Rhythm' variant, assembled in Powell's honour by Benny Harris (he who compiled 'Ornithology' for Charlie 'Yardbird' Parker). Powell rockets through this one at close to his 'Indiana' speed. And that leaves Thelonious Monk's 'Off Minor'. This easy-paced but teasing tune is treated by Powell with tenderness and respect. His romantic reading offers a sumptuous alternative to the stark beauty of the version recorded by Monk himself.

*

In April 1947, after his extended stay in California, Charlie Parker was back in New York, where the Savoy company invited him to form a quintet and record. He chose Miles Davis as his front-line partner, plus the top rhythm team of Bud Powell, Tommy Potter and Max Roach. The group rehearsed *chez* Teddy Reig, recording director for Savoy, and at Max Roach's home in Brooklyn. Then, on Thursday 8 May 1947, they made an historic set of discs, the only studio recordings where Parker and Powell play together.

Four new pieces were recorded, some requiring several attempts before Parker was satisfied. Savoy eventually released all sixteen takes. The complete set reveals that Powell, though reduced once again to the role of sideman, was a creative force second to none.

On 'Donna Lee' and 'Chasing the Bird' he furnishes the solos of Parker and Davis with a springy chordal underlay, then does wonders with his measly half-chorus allocation. And to 'Cheryl' and 'Buzzy' (both 12-bar blues by Parker) he contributes modern piano solos of matchless power and beauty.

However, for the quintet's residency at the Three Deuces club on 52nd Street, Parker's chosen pianist was not Powell, but the more modestly gifted Duke Jordan. Miles Davis and Max Roach were disappointed, but their leader was adamant. He respected Powell's talent but was not prepared to accommodate his temperament in the working band. Parker was still feeling the benefit of his six months enforced convalescence in California's Camarillo State Hospital. He recognized Powell as another troubled being, close to the edge. He talked of taking the fragile pianist away with him to the countryside for a healthy holiday.

The rural idyll failed to materialize. Powell started drinking heavily, although alcohol, even in tiny quantities, had a ruinous effect. He developed a terror of being attacked in the street. He brooded on his colour and the hatred it attracted. He was seen in public trying to scrub the blackness from his skin. In November 1947 he suffered a mental collapse and was condemned to almost a year of confinement in the Creedmoor Psychiatric Facility in the New York borough of Queens.

Psychiatric treatment in the overcrowded state-funded institutions in post-war America could be brutal. Electroconvulsive therapy, which involved strapping patients down and repeatedly passing a hefty current through their temples, was a favourite way of dealing with so-called schizophrenia. Powell's belligerent outbursts made him an obvious candidate for this terrifying and punitive remedy. The most blatant effect of the electric shocks, noted by his dismayed visitors, was severe memory loss.

A friend of his youth, pianist Elmo Hope, went to Creedmoor and found that Bud, denied access to a piano, had tried to draw a keyboard on his cell wall. Hope managed to attract the sympathy of a young doctor, who arranged for Powell occasionally to play the hospital's wonky upright.

In October 1948 Powell was released. He went to live in the family's apartment on St Nicholas Avenue in Harlem, where he was tended by his mother and his girlfriend Frances Barnes. (His father, who had been so proud of him, had left home.) The other household member was Bud's kid brother Richie, who played the piano himself and was also proud to be related to such a marvellous artist. Passing the neighbourhood music store one day, and recognizing the sound of Bud with the Charlie Parker Quintet, he went in and announced, 'That's my brother on that record.' The boy looking after the shop, seventeen-year-old saxophonist Jackie McLean, refused to believe him. So Richie took Jackie and his saxophone to the Powell household.

In an interview with the author A.B. Spellman, Jackie McLean described that first visit:

> Two large French doors opened and: 'My brother tells me you don't believe I'm Bud Powell.' And so I said, 'I never saw Bud Powell. I only know Bud Powell by music.' With this, Bud went to the piano, and there was no question. It was Bud. He told me to take out my horn, and I was scared to death. He asked me what did I know, and I called a Charlie Parker blues, 'Buzzy', which I had been practising from the record. It was a gas.[11]

McLean became a regular visitor and an informal pupil. Bud, who had shown little interest in the pianistic potential of his younger brother, now dedicated himself to nursing the talent of Richie's friend. (Richie, meanwhile, switched to the drums and often started his day with a trip to Max Roach's home in Brooklyn, where he would wait for Max to wake up and then beg a lesson.)

Mrs Powell was delighted to see her problem son drawn out of his private world by the friendship with Jackie McLean. Although McLean was seven years Bud's junior, he was given the job of chaperone:

> If Bud had a gig, Mrs Powell would call me: 'Jackie, will you take Bud to play this job and wait for him and bring him home?' Or when I was there she would say, 'Jackie, you're taking Bud down to Monk's house. Remember now, he can't have any beer or go in any bars or anything.' Bud would be standing there, and her tone was 'and you better not!'[12]

Before setting out, Bud would fuss over his appearance. His favourite rig, for which he became famous around the city, was white shirt, black suit, black tie, black hat and black umbrella. McLean would help him dress, stand him in front of the mirror and say, 'Look Bud.' Powell would ask, in a high baby voice, 'Am I sharp?' To which McLean would reply, 'Yeah, man, you really are. Let's go.'[13]

Powell's regular gig was at the Royal Roost on Broadway, where he played a solo spot every Sunday afternoon. McLean used to take him there. On one occasion they spotted Charlie Parker at the bar. 'Look, there's Bird,' said Powell. 'I can introduce you to Bird.' Then he called out to Parker in a needling tone, 'Hey, Bird, you know who this is? He's an alto player too, and you should hear him. He plays real good and *he's only a kid.*'[14] Caught in the tense space between the two men he most admired, McLean hid his embarrassment by taking charge of Powell's coat and escorting him to the piano.

During the winter of 1948/9 Powell stayed busy on the New York scene. A private recording of a broadcast on 19 December captured him playing with a 10-piece band, at close to his thrilling best. According to a witness – the jazz writer Ira Gitler – during Powell's solos the front-line players turned round and gave him their full attention. Adding to the aura, Gitler noted, was Powell's vivid stage presence: 'right leg digging into the floor at an odd angle, pants leg up to almost the top of the shin, shoulders hunched, upper lip tight against his teeth, mouth emitting an accompanying guttural song'.[15] Once, after a particularly great solo, Powell walked off the stand, applauding himself as he went.

*

Early in 1949 Powell – now a hot property – was brought to the studio by record producer Norman Granz. Ray Brown was the bassist and Max Roach the drummer. The six inspired improvisations matched the ones Powell recorded with Roach and Curley Russell, and this time four of his starting points were original compositions.

The two standard tunes – 'All God's Chillun Got Rhythm' and 'Cherokee' – both move very fast. 'Cherokee' is particularly remarkable, just as devastating in its way as Charlie Parker's more famous reworking of this Ray Noble song. It begins with Powell beating out a ferocious rhythm low down on the keyboard, in parallel fourths, to suggest an American-Indian war dance. An unaccompanied piano break links the dance to a quicksilver presentation of the theme, all dissolving chords, one chord per beat, more than 300 beats per minute. Another piano break leads to the intense improvisation; the skittering recapitulation; and a final, furious burst of stomping.

The first of Powell's own compositions, the toccata-like 'Tempus Fugue-it', is similarly swift. At the other extreme, his ballad 'I'll Keep Loving You' is played rubato and loaded with sumptuous harmonies. 'Strictly Confidential' is something else again, a jaunty theme triggering a joyous impromptu.

The remaining item, 'Celia', is another beautifully constructed Powell ballad, whose gentle introduction and dainty melody are both adorned with little 'turns', trilling like birds under Powell's steely fingers. 'Celia' took its name from Powell's baby daughter, recently presented to him by Frances Barnes. Sadly, this new family member did not restore his peace of mind. Shortly after recording for Granz, he was sent again to Creedmoor and held there for nearly three months. This time the authorities, presumably meaning well, found him a place among the entertainers at the hospital's annual minstrel show.

*

In the summer of 1949 Powell was approached by Blue Note, the most enlightened of the jazz record companies. They invited him to assemble a quintet of his own choosing and come and record his own music in his own way.

His chosen trumpeter was Fats Navarro, one year Powell's senior and bursting with song. The choice of saxophonist was a surprise: not Jackie McLean, but McLean's eighteen-year-old friend Sonny Rollins (who had started on alto, but now played tenor). Tommy Potter played bass. Max Roach was unavailable, but Roy Haynes proved an effective deputy. The well-planned session took place on 8 August.

It began with 'Bouncing with Bud', a new name for the Powell composition previously labelled 'Bebop in Pastel'. Three takes were needed before Powell the leader was satisfied with the overall effect. Powell the pianist plays with equal brilliance on the first and last.

Next they tackled 'Wail', another fine Powell piece, known as 'Fool's Fancy' when he recorded it with the Be-Bop Boys back in 1946. This one moves very fast, and two takes were needed to get it right. Powell solos superbly on both of them.

The third composition Powell placed before his quintet was 'Dance of the Infidels', one of his rare contributions to the 12-bar blues form. The introduction is eerie, with saxophone and trumpet tiptoeing around the whole-tone scale. The theme itself is a tantalizing, chromatically-enhanced beauty. Charlie Parker adopted 'Dance of the Infidels', which he liked to perform prestissimo, but this premier recording by the Modernists remains definitive. Moving at a comfortable pace, it encourages us to drink in the composition's manifold delights. Powell properly claims the lion's share of the solo space and shows what a passionate blues player he can be.

The quintet's final recording is Thelonious Monk's high-speed '52nd Street Theme', whose essence is a short, rushing phrase, sounded thrice by the horns, with generous space between each sounding. Into these gaps Powell hurls his explosive responses. And then he crowns the flawless group performance with a glittering solo.

*

Powell next came to the studio on 11 December 1949. He had been hired, along with Curley Russell and Max Roach, to accompany the Prestige record company's new signing, Sonny Stitt. Stitt had recently switched from alto to tenor saxophone to escape the shadow of Charlie Parker. He enjoyed the spotlight, and found it amusing to goad his pianist by constantly addressing him as 'the great Bud Powell'. Anxious to assert himself, Powell yelled at Bob Weinstock, the portly president of Prestige, 'Hey, Fats, go out and get us some sandwiches.'[16]

The important and lasting consequence of Stitt's provocation was Powell's irresistibly aggressive playing. The studio piano is tinny, but he overwhelms it and obliges it to deliver his personal sound. The first tune, the zippy 'All God's Chillun Got Rhythm', sets the pattern for the whole session. Powell's unaccompanied introduction has the force of a gun going off, and he trumps Stitt's hard-blowing solo with an even more vigorous one of his own.

On Christmas Eve 1949 Powell, Russell and Roach were among the 'Stars of Jazz' who gave a concert at Carnegie Hall. The concert was broadcast and a recording of part of it has survived, including the trio number that launched the evening. The compere, 'Symphony' Sid Torin, correctly introduces them as 'one of the most exciting trios of our time', and they hurtle once more into 'All God's Chillun Got Rhythm'. Powell evidently relishes the conditions – concert grand piano, large hall, attentive audience, no time limit. He responds with an improvisation more playful, more risky and much longer than those he managed to fit on to commercial discs.

*

Powell entered 1950 at the peak of his musical powers, but not a well man. He would go for days without speaking to anyone, and on the bandstand his demeanour was disturbing. Between numbers, or when other musicians were soloing, he would confront the audience for minutes at a time with a fixed stare and a disconnected leer. There were rumours that he was shooting heroin.

On 26 January Powell, Russell and Roach returned to the studio for another session supporting Sonny Stitt. Four standard tunes were recorded, all of them brisk, and all serving to illustrate Powell's dictum that 'no horn player in the world can outplay a piano player'.

In February the Bud Powell Trio was booked to make more records for Norman Granz. Six standards were recorded, plus one Powell original, which he called 'So Sorry Please'. This is an altogether charming tune – a song without words, arising from the 'I Got Rhythm' chords. Powell's intensely pianistic performance redoubles its charms, dressing it in parallel fourths and tremulous ornaments. And when he comes to improvise upon it, his solo bubbles with optimism. Impossible to guess that this uplifting music was created by a soul in torment.

*

At this point the dynamic Oscar Goodstein made his entrance and took charge of Powell's life. According to his own account, Goodstein had been on the point of retiring to Miami when he visited Birdland and heard Powell for the first time. He put off his departure and went to hear Powell every night for a week. Then he cancelled Florida and appointed himself Powell's personal manager and minder. He took on the running of Birdland, too, on behalf of its gangster-owner Mo Levy.

Music was regularly broadcast from the club, and sometimes recorded from their radios by enthusiasts at home. Luckily for us, someone pressed the button on 30 June 1950 when Charlie Parker and Fats Navarro joined a trio led by Bud Powell.

The three principal players were as famous for the disorder of their lives as for the splendour of their art. Parker and Navarro were both in thrall to heroin, and Navarro was ravaged by tuberculosis. Powell's mental health was precarious, his relationship with Parker tense. He counted himself Navarro's friend but had always found the overweight, baby-voiced trumpeter an easy target for his jibes. On one notorious occasion when they were on stage together and Powell's tormenting became unbearable, Navarro raised his trumpet above his head and tried to bring it crashing down on Powell's hands. He missed his target and wrecked his instrument.

On this June night at Birdland the distress and the antagonisms are distilled into pure music. Some numbers are played fast. Others are played very fast indeed. Navarro sounds unhurried and sweetly reasonable. Galvanized by Parker, Powell sounds powerful and passionate.

*

Next day Powell was in the recording studio once again, this time with Norman Granz's choice of rhythm men: bassist Ray Brown and drummer Buddy Rich. It was an odd session. The two numbers they recorded – 'Hallelujah' and 'Tea for Two' – were driven by Powell at close to reckless speed. His 'Tea for Two' is particularly hair-raising. After a beguiling start, browsing lazily through Vincent Youmans's verse, he flings himself at the main theme and hauls it up and down through a series of keys. Art Tatum had treated 'Tea for Two' in much the same way when he recorded it in 1939, and Powell would certainly have known the Tatum record. His father liked to boast that by the time young Bud was ten, he could reproduce anything he heard of Tatum's. Now, at twenty-five, Powell could offer much more than a reproduction. The difference between the two masterly performances, Tatum's and Powell's, expresses the difference between the two men. Tatum's is a cool, controlled, technically stupendous feat of decoration. Powell's is a passionate, ultra-dramatic, high-risk act of recomposition.

It was around this time that Powell and Tatum had their falling out, a clash of the titans that has been variously reported. What follows is a composite of the commonest accounts.

The place was Birdland, where Tatum was playing and Powell was in the audience. As was his custom, Tatum included in his programme a selection of tit-bits from the classics. During the interval, Powell put it to the great man that his rendering of a Chopin Prelude had been less than entirely accurate. Displeased by such impertinence, Tatum replied that Powell was no more than a right-handed piano player, whereas he, Tatum, had a whole rhythm section in his left hand. To the horror of those present, Powell took out a pocketknife, slashed his right hand, and crudely bandaged it up. Then he went to the piano and played 'Sometimes I'm Happy' at full pelt, using only his left.

*

When Powell made his next set of recordings for Norman Granz in February 1951, he elected to play entirely on his own, without the benefit of bass or drums. Part of his purpose may have been to prove to the world that he, too, could call upon 'a whole rhythm section in his left hand'. Like Tatum and the other old-timers, Powell has a left hand that can span a tenth with massive ease. On 'A Nightingale Sang in Berkeley Square' and 'The Last Time I Saw Paris', he gives short demonstrations of how to stride, but mostly he plays just as he would if bass and drums were present: punctuating and promoting the melodic flow with subtly timed left-hand jabs. The colossal forward momentum is generated by what is implied, and the daring procedure rests on his infallible metronomic sense.

His prestissimo improvisation on Cole Porter's 'Just One of Those Things' tests his capacities almost to destruction. He can finger all the notes, but can he produce new ideas, non-stop, at this monstrous speed? Sometimes, fleetingly, he falters. The listener is on the edge of his seat. Ira Gitler described the experience as like watching 'a man walking on a tightrope over a chasm of poetic beauty and madness'.[17]

This fabulous set of recordings is made doubly special by the quality of the new Powell compositions, five perfectly formed creations.

'Parisian Thoroughfare' (written five years before Powell's first visit to the French capital, and probably inspired by George Gershwin's *An American in Paris*) is an intensely evocative piece. The A section – the main highway – bustles with diatonic quaver triplets, while section B twists and turns through the devious side-streets.

'Oblivion' (Powell's titles frequently describe states of mind) rides on a blissfully simple harmonic pattern, reminiscent of Dizzy Gillespie's 'Woody 'n You'.

'Dusk in Sandi' (some say Powell meant this to be 'Dusky 'n Sandy', for a beautiful woman fitting the description) is a dreamy ballad. He plays it molto rubato, romantically blurring its contours.

'The Fruit' has long, flowing lines that he articulates superbly. His improvisation upon it is a model of buoyancy and invention, although there's a curious lapse of concentration (eight bars are missing from his second chorus).

'Hallucinations' is a catchy quickstep with a stop-go beginning. By the time of this recording the tune was already in circulation, thanks to a modified version recorded by Miles Davis as 'Budo'. However, to appreciate fully the intricate character of 'Hallucinations', you have to hear Powell play it the way he wrote it.

*

On 31 March 1951 a home-recorder captured the so-called 'Summit Meeting' from Birdland, when Charlie Parker and Dizzy Gillespie joined Bud Powell, Tommy Potter and Roy Haynes.

Powell is below his best, but his contribution is superlative by any standard except his own. Recognizing his eminence, Parker and Gillespie grant him equal solo space. During his long improvisation on 'Blue 'n Boogie' he sometimes sounds disconnected, and his double-time passages (usually a match for Parker's) are less crisp and coherent than we have come to expect. 'Anthropology' is a happier story. Tonight it's taken at a killing pace, and Powell holds his own proudly and easily. Powell and Gillespie had both championed Thelonious Monk's ''Round Midnight', and here they are playing it together. Parker, Gillespie and Powell share the exposition of Monk's lovely tune, with Powell taking the last eight bars and presenting them with reverence and passion.

To close the broadcast they play 'A Night in Tunisia', with Gillespie and Parker in their familiar roles. When it comes to Powell's solo, he gets off to an agonizingly slow start. Dissatisfied with his first chorus, he embarks on a second, where his ideas start to flow, but time is up and the others cut him short.

*

By the time of that Birdland big night, Alfred Lion of Blue Note records had become Powell's frequent companion. Worried by the pianist's often-agitated behaviour, he discovered that the best medicine was to take him to the cinema to see a Western. The trusty horses, the rocky mountains and the backlit desert dust were all balm to Powell's anxious spirit.

Whenever Powell gave a performance in New York, Lion would be there. One night he went up to Minton's and joined the audience waiting for Powell to appear. Suddenly someone rushed on to the stage, opened the piano lid and started making frantic hand movements above the keys, without producing a sound. Unaware that this was the great Bud Powell, some people laughed. Others complained to the bouncer, who picked him up by the neck and threw him out the front door. Appalled by the madness and the violence, Lion hurried into the street, but of Powell there was no sign:

> There was a car parked near the club entrance. He wasn't in it. I saw an old man with a shopping bag standing on the opposite side of the street. I asked him if he had seen someone run out of the club. He pointed to the car. I looked inside again and no Bud. The old man pointed down. Sure enough, Bud had crept under the car like an injured cat, and was lying there.[18]

Lion talked Powell into coming out and took him home.

A second Blue Note recording session was arranged, for 1 May 1951, with Powell's favourite accompanists, Curley Russell and Max Roach. Keen to keep track of Powell the night before the session, Lion invited him to his house out in New Jersey, gave him dinner and put him to bed. Next morning during breakfast Lion's black cat jumped on to the table. 'And Bud went crazy. He took a big knife from the table and tried to kill the cat. We had to get the cat out of the way.'[19]

The drive from New Jersey to the Manhattan recording studio took them through Harlem. Here Powell ordered Lion to stop the car. He had to see his doctor, he said. They went down to a basement and entered a waiting room crammed with patients. Realizing that if they joined the queue they would miss the recording session, Lion managed to persuade Powell that they should leave.

At the studio Curley Russell and Max Roach were waiting. Powell asked for the key to the men's room and disappeared. After ten minutes Max Roach went to look, and discovered Powell had left the building. Lion spent the next hour and a half trying to convince Russell, Roach and himself that the star would return. Then 'all of a sudden in rushed Bud. Before you knew it, he was sitting at the piano saying, "Okay, okay, we're ready. Let's go." Boom, we made the first take of UN POCO LOCO.'[20]

Although it may have felt that way at the time to Alfred Lion, the piece that Powell called 'Un Poco Loco' is clearly not an unpremeditated outburst. Many elements figure in its careful construction. The percussive introduction establishes the Afro-Latin rhythm and harps on the harsh chord that will dominate the first subject. There is a pugnacious codetta and a vamp-'til-ready lead from the first subject to the second, a sparse line in the right hand, against a pummelling, Afro-Latin ground bass. This minimal theme is repeated like a mantra, and out of it grows Powell's solo, a right-handed scalar exploration above the stubborn left-hand ostinato. The three takes of 'Un Poco Loco' issued by Blue Note map the journey towards the definitive performance.

Take 1 ends prematurely because Powell's solo refuses to take wing. It seems he blamed the failure on Max Roach, who had been laying down a familiar Afro-Latin rhythm. For Take 2 Roach offers a fresh, more challenging polyrhythmic pattern – precisely the stimulus Powell needs. His solo comes to life and the take is a good one, but it is decided to try once more, with Roach doing the same again. On Take 3 Powell's extended solo achieves architectural perfection. He starts with short, staccato phrases, hardly more than a bar in length, and builds until he is producing long, florid traceries. Then he rests his right hand for four bars (continuing the ostinato in his left) before putting the process into reverse, playing lines that grow shorter until they shrink to nothing.

After the intensity of 'Un Poco Loco', Powell records 'Over the Rainbow' as a piano solo, staying unusually close to the decorative manner of Art Tatum, and sounding utterly at peace with himself.

Next he chooses to play Dizzy Gillespie's 'A Night in Tunisia', and recalls Roach and Russell to apply the polyrhythms. Powell is of course familiar with Charlie Parker's famous alto break. Inspired rather than intimidated by that formidable precedent, he invents an unaccompanied break of his own – four dazzling double-time bars – and follows it with a solo of unremitting intensity.

Resting Roach and Russell again, Powell offers a solo interpretation of the ballad 'It Could Happen to You'. Like 'Over the Rainbow', this is a carefree reading, rejoicing in its pianism, and harking back to those childhood days when Bud amazed his father with his Tatum simulations.

Four numbers are in the bag and there is time to spare. Powell calls Russell and Roach to join him on a bonus recording: a trio version of his 'Parisian Thoroughfare'. When it starts, it seems this performance is going to trump the piano solo version he recorded back in February.

Soaring above Curley Russell's oak-like bass and Max Roach's supple brush-work, Powell achieves a feathery lightness. But by the fifth chorus his concentration is waning and his articulation has become ragged. Vexed, he starts the sixth chorus with a sarcastic quotation from 'London Bridge is Falling Down', then stops playing. Russell and Roach plough gamely on. The last thing we hear before abrupt silence is Powell, sounding peeved, ordering the recording engineer, 'Hey, cut it man.'

*

By June 1951 Powell was close to mental collapse, and this was the moment the New York Police Department chose to arrest him for a marijuana offence. He was taken to the Tombs prison, where he became agitated and kept shouting that there was a plot to kill him. His lack of humility did not endear him to the custodians at the Tombs, who doused him with buckets of ammoniated water.

He was shipped to the Psychiatric Unit at Bellevue Hospital and hauled before a panel of assessors. When they questioned him about his occupation, he told them he was a composer. Deducing from this answer that here was a black man suffering from 'delusions of grandeur and a detachment from reality', they consigned him to Pilgrim State for the application of more electric shocks.

After eleven months, he was passed to the more progressive regime at Creedmoor. Here he was visited by the English pianist Marian McPartland, one of his most ardent fans, now living and working in New York. When she arrived in the day room at Creedmoor where the inmates could meet their visitors, Powell was waiting for her. There was a piano in the room, which he played for her while the other inmates and their guests carried on talking. Then he fixed her with a terrible look and asked, 'Marian, do people still remember me?'[21]

On 11 December 1952, eighteen months after his arrest, Powell was let out of Creedmoor on an overnight pass, arranged by Oscar Goodstein, so he could come and play at Birdland with Curley Russell and Max Roach. During this testing time Roach was supportive in every way, and the experiment was judged a success. But now Powell's mother, Pearl, felt unable to cope, so papers were drawn up making Goodstein Bud's legal guardian.

On 5 February 1953, when Powell was discharged from Creedmoor, Goodstein installed him in an apartment conveniently close to Birdland, and kept him under lock and key. Those, like Alfred Lion, interested in acquiring Powell's services, or even in seeing him, had to negotiate with the Goodstein office.

Shortly after Goodstein took the guardianship, Powell went through a wedding ceremony with a white woman, Audrey Hill. He and Audrey never lived together, and it has been generally assumed that the sudden and mysterious match was engineered by Goodstein to consolidate his control. There was even a rumour that Goodstein supplied Powell with hard drugs to entice him to play. Whatever the truth of these allegations, he was certainly loyal to Powell's genius, which he promoted with vigour. Almost from the moment Powell came out of Creedmoor he was steadily employed.

His first job was at the Royal Roost in New York City, leading a trio with bassist Oscar Pettiford and drummer Roy Haynes. Several broadcasts from the Roost during February and March were recorded, so we know how he sounded and can make comparisons with his earlier, classic recordings.

'Tea for Two' recalls the version he made back in 1950. The same routine is observed, but the spirit is very different. The man at the piano in 1950 was a fire-eater. The same artist in 1953 has suffered much. He settles for a gentler tempo, and instead of hurling the Vincent Youmans tune through those chromatic shifts, he raises and lowers it gingerly. When he comes to improvise he shows that his timing is still true and his keyboard command more or less unscathed, but he has become more reliant on appoggiaturas and their blurring effect.

'It Could Happen To You', which he had previously recorded for Blue Note, shortly before his incarceration, comes as a shock. The earlier account was carefree. The new one is heavy-hearted, seeming to brood upon the title of the song. 'What happened to me could happen to you,' Powell seems to warn, 'and you'd better pray it does not.'

*

The Bud Powell Trio stayed busy in New York until the end of March, by which time Oscar Pettiford had been replaced on bass by rising star Charles Mingus.

Deeming that Powell was now fit to travel, Goodstein took a booking from the Club Kavakos in Washington, DC, where the trio played on the afternoon of Sunday 5 April. The proceedings were privately recorded by a local enthusiast and issued thirty years later as a commercial disc.

The concert programme includes familiar repertoire like 'Somebody Loves Me' and 'Nice Work If You Can Get It', and these retreads of his earlier recorded masterpieces make sad listening. The themes are slightly fumbled, as if he is fighting to remember; and during the improvisations the long, eloquent sentences of Powell in his prime have been replaced by stubby phrases that seem to be gasping for air.

Missing from the concert (and from all his performances since his release) are any compositions, new or old, by Powell himself. Instead, he concentrates his damaged faculties on the works of others: a mock-baroque treatment of Jerome Kern's 'Sure Thing'; a canter through the chordal complexities of George Shearing's 'Conception'; two versions of the same composer's 'Lullaby of Birdland'; and long improvisations upon two by Dizzy Gillespie – 'Woody 'n You' and 'Salt Peanuts'.

The last time he had played with Gillespie was at Birdland two years earlier: the so-called 'Summit Meeting' also attended by Charlie Parker. Now, unknown to him, a grand reunion was brewing. Oscar Goodstein had been taking calls from Canada apropos of an extraordinary concert in Toronto. The organizers' first choice of pianist had been Lennie Tristano, but now they were after Powell, and to secure his services they were obliged to do business with his guardian. The $500 fee was the highest for any of the five musicians, although of course none of the money would find its way directly to Powell himself.

On Friday 15 May, Canadian concert day, Goodstein presented himself at La Guardia airport with Powell in tow. He was coming to Massey Hall to make sure his charge stayed on the straight and narrow . . .

FOUR

WEIRD NIGHTMARE

'*A little of everything, wholly nothing, of no race, country, flag or friend.*'
Charles Mingus, describing himself[1]

CHARLES MINGUS, JR. was born on 22 April 1922 on an Army base in Arizona. His lineage was not straightforward. His father, blue-eyed Staff Sergeant Charles Mingus, Senr., was the consequence of a liaison between a black farm-hand and a well-to-do white lady, rumoured to be a cousin of President Lincoln. The sergeant's wife, Harriet, was also of mixed descent: half black and half Chinese. Soon after the birth of Charles, Jr., Harriet became ill. Her husband took early retirement and they moved to join Harriet's folks in Los Angeles. Here Harriet died of heart disease on 7 September.

When baby Charles was one year old his father remarried and moved his family to 1621 East 108th Street. This bungalow in the Watts suburb of Los Angeles would be the home address of Charles Mingus, Jr. for the next twenty years.

Charles's stepmother Mamie, half black and half American Indian, seems to have been relegated by her husband to the role of domestic servant. Charles Mingus, Senr., like Dizzy Gillespie's father, was an aggressive man who ruled his household using strap and fist. And he espoused middle-class values, including a belief in the improving qualities of European classical music. At his command, young Charles's older sisters, Grace and Vivian, took lessons on violin and piano. Charles pleaded for and was granted a mail-order trombone. And when no teacher could be found, he explored the lengthy instrument for himself.

Like his father, Charles, Jr. had light skin, and at home he was encouraged to believe that this paleness signalled his superiority over his darker neighbours. So he was shocked when a white schoolteacher advised him scornfully that he was no better than a 'yellow nigger'. Charged with peering up girls' dresses, he was told he'd be transferred to an institution for problem pupils. His father challenged the decision and Charles was allowed to stay – a podgy, amber, bow-legged outcast in his own community and a favourite target for playground bullies. To add to his misery there were ructions at home, because father was neglecting Mamie in favour of his lighter-complexioned mistress – 'that high-yellow woman', as Mamie called her bitterly.

Where young Charles felt snug was in the world of music, and that good feeling swelled into love when he tinkered with his father's radio and chanced upon the Duke Ellington Orchestra playing their theme tune, 'East St Louis Toodle-oo'.

Seeking to improve his trombone playing, he approached an older boy, Britt Woodman, who came from a musical family and excelled on the instrument. The friendship lasted all his life and yielded several immediate benefits. First of all, Britt praised Charles's keen ear and coaxed him through the rudiments of music theory. Secondly, he introduced him to the local Holiness church, where the congregation rocked with a reckless abandon foreign to the Methodist services attended each Sunday by the Mingus family. Like Dizzy Gillespie before him, young Charles was deeply impressed by the fervent, polyrhythmic hullabaloo. Thirdly, Britt Woodman took him to a live show featuring the Duke Ellington Orchestra. Said Mingus, 'I never heard no music like that in church. I screamed.'[2] Finally, Woodman put it to Mingus that the trombone was not his destined instrument, and persuaded him to transfer to the cello.

Charles the cellist joined his sisters to form a trio that gave concerts at the Methodist Chapel. When he was old enough to move to Jordan High School, he signed up for the school's symphony orchestra, but he could not read music well enough to satisfy the management, so he was out. After the 'yellow nigger' incident and others similar, he had come to expect little from institutional education, preferring self-improvement through home study. Mingus the autodidact borrowed library books on yoga, reincarnation and the oriental religions. He lurked in the high school music department and in the music stores, gleaning what he could about the European tradition. He came to love the Bach cello suites and the melancholy side of Debussy and Ravel; and he developed a particular fondness for Richard Strauss's tone poem *Death and Transfiguration*.

He needed practical help, someone who could pull his yearnings into focus. That person turned out to be his fellow pupil Buddy Collette, a clarinet player in the high school orchestra and also in its jazz band. Collette proposed to Mingus that what the jazz band required was not the wispy sound of his cello, but the propulsive thud of a double bass. And this argument was backed by a friend of Mingus's father, who pointed out that a black man with a bass could find employment, 'because he can play *our* music'.[3] A bass was acquired, and Collette's next good turn was to introduce Mingus to Red Callender, a veteran bassist of twenty-two, who had played with Louis Armstrong. Mingus learned a lot.

Outside the world of music, the consuming question remained: what kind of non-white man was he going to be in America's loaded society? In his autobiography he describes a transcendent moment from his schooldays when the anguish seemed resolved, at least temporarily. It happened while he was making love to an ebony-skinned and regally beautiful girl, who cried out to him, 'You're black as I am, Mingus!'[4]

*

Keen to master the craft of writing music down, he began seriously to study the piano, and took lessons in theory and orchestration from Lloyd

Reese, a respected teacher in the black community. And in 1939 (if we accept his own dating) he composed 'The Chill of Death', a mixed-media piece in which a poem he had written about the after-life was to be declaimed against an orchestral background.

Although their subject matter is ostensibly similar, Richard Strauss's *Death and Transfiguration* and Charles Mingus's 'The Chill of Death' are poles apart. Strauss intended his orchestral tone poem to express the flight of a hero's soul into the unknown, where it finds, 'gloriously achieved in eternity, those ideals that could not be fulfilled here below'. 'The Chill of Death' lacks this grand optimism. In rhyming couplets Mingus tells how, while seeking the pathway to Heaven, he is tricked into taking the road to Hell. His music, more Hollywood film-score than jazz, ebbs and flows in obedience to the dictates of the solemn text. A recording of this extravaganza was finally made in 1971. Its style owes something to the popular recordings of Orson Welles reciting poetry, his sultry voice cloaked in fitting mood music. Welles was one of Mingus's earliest heroes, but the essence of 'The Chill of Death' – its fixation with our passage beyond this life – can be linked to another source.

During the summer of 1939, before he graduated from high school, Mingus played gigs in a band that travelled as far north as San Francisco. Here he met a man who would influence him profoundly: the painter Farwell Taylor. Taylor was thirty-four – twice Mingus's age – and a leading figure in San Francisco's bohemian counter-culture. Mingus was drawn not just to this white man's art (Taylor painted murals around the Bay Area) but to his freewheeling life-style and his radical opinions. 'Everyone is a child of God,' was a favourite Taylor maxim. He and his wife Faye invited Mingus to stay in their home, and encouraged him to develop a sense of himself as an artist. 'You're the greatest. Remember that,'[5] Taylor would tell him. He introduced young Charles to Vedanta Hinduism, which teaches that the divine spark lives within us all and that death is a consummation to be wished for.

*

Back in Los Angeles, Mingus left school, resisted pressure from his father to take a job in the Post Office, and entered the lists as a freelance musician. Gigs as a bassist in the Watts district paid poorly, so at first he bolstered his income with work as a colourful extra at the Hollywood film studios. (He and Buddy Collette helped to populate the exotic background during the shooting of *The Road to Zanzibar*.)

When America entered World War II, many established musicians were drafted, improving the work prospects of those left behind. Mingus (who failed his medical on the grounds of diabetes) was one who stayed. The consequence, in August 1942, was a job at the Trouville club as junior member in a band made up mainly of New Orleans veterans. Here he came to the attention of Louis Armstrong, who was in Hollywood to appear in the all-black musical *Cabin in the Sky*. Once filming was over, Armstrong assembled a band to go on tour and chose young Mingus to be his bass player.

Although he felt privileged to be working with a genius, Mingus could not bear the antics Armstrong performed to amuse his white audiences. After he had been in the band for a couple of months, they told him they would be touring the South, where a humble attitude was essential. So he quit, went back to Los Angeles and took lessons from Herman Rheinschagen, a white bassist formerly with the New York Philharmonic. Rheinschagen demanded perfection. Mingus responded by slaving over his technique, while grumbling that perfection was a subjective thing.

By 1943 he was playing regular club dates with a sextet led by the drummer Lee Young (brother of Lester). This group never recorded, but we have the word of band member Art Pepper that Mingus already had a style that was completely his own.

In January 1944 he married his girlfriend Canilla Jeanne Gross. The match pleased his father – Jeanne's middle-class family was respected in the black community – but by September, when their son was born, Charles and Jeanne were living apart. For a time Mingus's habitat was the Venetian Room at Long Beach, where he played in a trio called Strings and Keys and conducted an affair with the club owner's wife. According to the description of their frolics in his autobiography, she was a white woman from the South who wore skin-tight dresses and nothing underneath.

Mingus was a bulky man – weight 200 pounds – whose lust for life and passion for bass playing were making him locally famous. The disc jockey Jimmy Lyons first came across him in an after-hours club, playing 'Body and Soul' for forty-five minutes perched on top of a table.

In the summer of 1945 he made his first records as leader: two 78s featuring forgettable vocalists. He recorded again in January 1946, and this time the memorable results included 'Weird Nightmare' (words, tune and arrangement all by C. Mingus). Like 'The Chill of Death', 'Weird Nightmare' is strong on atmosphere but its construction is more conventional: a minor-key ballad in AABA song form, apostrophizing a bad dream.

For his next set of recordings he listed the personnel as 'Baron Mingus and his Octet'. The output of this royal assembly included 'Weird Nightmare' rendered as a piano showpiece; but the most significant consequence of the session was 'This Subdues My Passion', a new Mingus orchestral piece with distinctly Ellingtonian overtones.

*

Curiously, it took a band of Californian white boys to convert the reluctant Mingus to the music of Charlie Parker. Deputizing one night for the band's regular bass player, Mingus was impressed by the unanimous enthusiasm for everything Bird did. The leader of the band, saxophonist Dean Benedetti, had dissected the records Parker made with Gillespie, transcribing the solos and learning to play them by heart. When Parker arrived in California in December, Benedetti rushed to study at his feet. Mingus at first stayed aloof, but the fanaticism of Benedetti and the others made him think again.

By the spring of 1946, when Parker was the resident attraction at the Finale club, Mingus had joined the devotees. Miles Davis wrote about those days in his autobiography:

Charlie Mingus loved Bird, man, almost like I have never seen nobody love. Maybe Max Roach loved Bird that much. But Mingus, he used to come to see and hear Bird almost every night. He couldn't get enough of Bird.[6]

After Parker collapsed and was committed to Camarillo State Hospital, Davis decided to leave Los Angeles and join the Billy Eckstine Orchestra. When he told Mingus of his plans, the reaction was characteristically emotional:

He thought I was abandoning Bird, who was still up in Camarillo. He asked me how I could go back to New York without Bird. He said, 'Miles, Bird is your musical papa. You're an asshole, Miles Davis. That man *made* you.'[7]

*

Putting the Venetian Room and its carnal pleasures behind him, Mingus joined a co-operative called the Stars of Swing, an idealistic venture that defied the pressures of commerce. These were happy days. His wife had come back, he had started practising the cello again, and he was making extra money ghostwriting bits of film scores for Dimitri Tiomkin.

In September 1946 his second son was born, but what should have been a happy event snuffed out his marriage. His wife took the nativity as her signal to go back to mother, and this time the separation was permanent. Failure as a husband and a father left Mingus depressed. He fled to San Francisco, lodged once more with his friend Farwell Taylor, failed to find paid work as a musician, and took a Christmas job with the Post Office.

Early in 1947, urged by Taylor to pursue his artistic calling, he was back in Los Angeles, prising sufficient funds from Columbia Records to make a recording of 'The Chill of Death'. But Columbia, having paid for the large and unusual orchestra, declared the result unsaleable and declined to issue it. The consolation was that Charlie Parker – now released from Camarillo – came to the studio while 'The Chill of Death' was being recorded, and gave it his blessing. According to Mingus, Parker made no comment on his bass playing but warmly acknowledged his gifts as a composer.

*

Parker left Los Angeles in the spring of 1947. Mingus busied himself in his home town until the autumn, when he was invited to join the Lionel Hampton orchestra as featured bass soloist. His wife was divorcing him, so he was not unhappy to go on tour.

The band's music policy was hardly adventurous, and the leader's stage antics could be embarrassing, but there were compensations. The scores Mingus wrote added spice to the band's regular fare, and several were recorded, including his arrangement of his own composition, 'Mingus Fingers'. Inspired by 'One Bass Hit' (recorded a year earlier by the Dizzy Gillespie Orchestra with bassist Ray Brown), 'Mingus Fingers' pits a string-bass virtuoso against the power of a big band. It was a popular success, issued by Decca, a major label. But Hampton infuriated Mingus by assigning the music to his own publishing firm and helping himself to a co-composer credit. In the autumn of 1948 Mingus left the band, taking all his arrangements with him.

By Christmas he was leading a quartet at a club in Oakland, the black suburb across the bay from San Francisco. They made a record with fashionable bebop touches and called it 'Lyon's Roar'. Their hope (unfounded) was that regular airplay by disc jockey Jimmy Lyons might make it a hit.

More important than the quartet (and even less lucrative) was the San Francisco big band that Mingus formed and rehearsed. Early in 1949 this band recorded two fine examples of his writing: a quasi-symphonic arrangement of 'He's Gone'; and a new composition, 'The Story of Love', featuring the shifting rhythms and polyphonic excitement for which he would become famous.

*

Although San Francisco was a fertile field for Mingus creatively, he could barely scratch a living, so he went back to Los Angeles. Here jobs were equally scarce. When no major label could be persuaded to take an interest, he recorded for the music store Dolphin's of Hollywood. On 'Boppin' n' Boston' his scat singing bears an uncanny resemblance to Dizzy Gillespie's, but few copies were sold. By the spring of 1950 Mingus had turned his back on the music business and was working full time as a mailman.

Enter Red Norvo, vibraphonist and bandleader – the same Red Norvo who had booked Parker and Gillespie to record with him in 1945. Now, Norvo's trio (vibes, guitar and bass) was working in Los Angeles and suddenly found itself without a bass player. Local connoisseurs advised him to add Mingus to his hitherto all-white ensemble, and directed him to the post office where the disillusioned bassist could be found. Mingus stayed with Norvo for more than a year, first in his home town and then on tour.

The chamber jazz of the Red Norvo Trio managed to be both popular and revolutionary. Not the least of its virtues was the transparency of the ensemble texture, in which all three instruments played an equal part. Norvo was no doubt grateful for the exhilarating swing that Mingus generated, and for the bassist's melodic gift, allied to an awesome technical command. Surprisingly, though, he made no use of Mingus's skills as composer and arranger.

Mingus's private frustration did not impinge upon the appeal of the trio's performances, and when they came to San Francisco early in 1951 they were jazz celebrities. On 2 April, amidst the euphoria, Mingus remarried. His bride was a redheaded jazz fan named Celia Gemanis, who adored the music of Charlie Parker. Mingus had met her during an earlier visit to San Francisco with Lionel Hampton, and then persistently wooed her by phone and letter. Farwell Taylor choreographed the wedding party.

Next time the Norvo Trio went on tour, Celia went with them. In his autobiography Mingus describes the grim farce they were obliged to play out when they reached the Southern States: two white men, one black man and one white girl, riding in two cars:

> Before you get to town, out on the empty highway, your girl changes
> cars and pretends to be the wife of one of the white men so you can
> check into hotels. You trade rooms that night, and again in the morning,
> so she can walk out with her 'husband'.[8]

By the summer of 1951 the horrors of racism were apparently behind them and the Norvo Trio was a fixture at New York's swanky Embers club. Mingus had re-established contact with Charlie Parker, and his bass playing was causing a stir in the big city. These were happy times – until September, when what should have been a further fillip to his career turned into a deep humiliation.

Television station WCBS booked Norvo and his men to appear, five afternoons a week, on one of the first-ever series to be transmitted in colour. But when the trio reported to the TV studios for rehearsals and revealed themselves to be a racially mixed group, they met fierce resistance. Ranged against them were the combined prejudices of the programme's sponsors and the musicians' union, who insisted Mingus could not take part. After two days of deadlock, Norvo caved in and replaced him with a white bass player. Then, hoping to soothe Mingus's feelings, he assured him he could keep his job with the trio at the Embers. Not unnaturally, this olive branch was spurned.

*

In spite of the rebuff, Mingus chose to put down roots in New York City. There was no further obstruction from the union, but freelancing as a twenty-nine-year-old newcomer to the East Coast was not easy. Celia's steady income as a secretary paid their bills.

Mingus's first gig in New York, a week after the break with Norvo, was with a sextet led by Miles Davis at Birdland. Then he turned up in the studio when Miles was recording an album for Prestige. Still carrying his bass on his back, he stood at the piano demonstrating tunes. No composition of his was chosen, but Miles allowed him to play bass (uncredited) on one track.

His next paid work was with the trio of pianist Billy Taylor. They played at the Storyville club in Boston, and here Mingus met Nat Hentoff, the writer and broadcaster who would become his champion. During this Boston visit, Mingus appeared on Hentoff's radio programme, arguing for the benefit to jazz of European techniques like the fugue.

Mingus sued Red Norvo for dismissing him without notice, won $500 in compensation and used the money bravely to start his own record company. He called the company Debut, and intended it as an outlet for music by himself and his neglected contemporaries. Celia partnered him in the venture, investing $600 provided by her mother and taking charge of all the paper work. A later partner and investor would be Max Roach, with whom Mingus had formed a mutual admiration society.

As Roach remembers it, Miles Davis made the introduction. According to Mingus, he was hooked the first time he heard a Max Roach drum solo, and could identify the melody from the solo's construction. When the two men talked, they discovered they shared strong views on the abusive nature of American society and a passion for the music of Charlie Parker. It's hard to pinpoint the date, but it seems that during the spring of 1952, when Parker was playing at Birdland, they got their first chance to serve him as a bass-and-drums team. Looking back on those exciting times, Mingus had this to say about Parker:

> He put something else in there . . . more than just the blues or the pain black people have been through. He brought hope . . . I felt a whole change in my *soul* when I joined up and accepted that I liked Charlie Parker.[9]

He was deeply affected by one of Parker's phone calls:

> He called me and said, 'How does this sound?' and he was playing – ad-libbing – to the Lullaby section of Stravinsky's *Firebird Suite*! . . . I'd like to write a suite of three or four hours and have a solo that is like Charlie Parker, playing ad lib.[10]

No such project was realized, and the first recordings made by Debut, in April 1952, featured the wintry alto saxophone of Lee Konitz, a follower of the blind pianist and pedagogue Lennie Tristano. Mingus and Roach were both Tristano enthusiasts, and Celia took piano and composition lessons from him. 'Extrasensory Perception', the piece Mingus wrote for Konitz to play, tells its story in the dispassionate Tristano manner, with a cello bowing a countermelody.

Striving to make Debut more commercial, Mingus and Roach also recorded the hip crooner Jackie Paris singing a clutch of love songs Mingus had composed, including the epic lament 'Paris in Blue'.

In December Mingus was flattered to be invited to join Charlie Parker for a week at the Hi Hat club in Boston. A recently unearthed recording of a broadcast from that week reveals the swing, virtuosity, precision and empathy that made him Parker's choice.

While they were still in Boston, an amateur soundman captured them playing together at a jam session. Mingus takes a three-chorus solo on 'I'll Remember April', and his huge presence transcends the fuzziness and flatness of the recording. Having gripped our attention with extravagant cross-rhythms and flamboyant note-flurries, he throws in a set of sly quotations, including an ironically triumphant snatch of 'All God's Chillun Got Rhythm'.

Profits from the sales of Debut records were modest and opportunities to play the music he liked were scarce, so during Christmas of 1952 Mingus again found work at the Post Office. He later insisted he would have been happy to stay as a mailman, 'but this security was taken from me by Charlie Parker, who called me up, reminded me of my aesthetic responsibilities, and made me give up my chance at a pension'.[11] In a more elaborate version of the story, told on television, Mingus claimed he protested to Parker that the Post Office job was too valuable to give up, but Parker swept this argument aside, promising, 'I'll pay you $400. I want you in my band.' However, by the time pay night came, Parker's drug habit had created the usual cash-flow crisis, so Mingus offered him a compromise:

> I said, 'Look Bird, don't pay me no salary. Just pay me the money you've been borrowing from time to time.' And he closed his eyes. And then his eyes opened and you saw all white. And he said [with Wellesian resonance], 'Mingus, do you remember that time in California I loaned you $2000? That cancels the whole debt.' And you know, when he said that, I almost thought it happened![12]

Once the job with Parker had run its short course, Mingus was thrown back on New York's crowded freelance market.

*

In January 1953 the post of bass player with Duke Ellington's orchestra fell vacant, and Mingus was invited to fill it. This situation should have been the fulfilment of a boyhood dream, but it turned out nasty, brutish and short. In his autobiography Mingus concedes that the disaster was self-inflicted. According to his brightly coloured account, violence erupted during the preliminaries for a stage show at the Apollo Theatre. Ellington's Puerto Rican trombonist Juan Tizol (composer of 'Caravan' and 'Perdido') had written a new arrangement for the band featuring a solo for bowed bass. Before curtain up, Mingus was practising his part, playing it an octave higher than written in order to avoid a muddy sound. Tizol accused him of being unable to read music. Mingus interpreted this as a racist attack, and insults were still flying when the band struck up the Ellington signature tune, 'Take the A-Train'. The curtain rose, revealing to the audience that Tizol was threatening Mingus with a knife. Mingus rushed from the platform and returned swinging a fire axe. Tizol dodged what would have been the fatal blow. Mingus sublimated his rage by reducing the trombonist's chair to matchwood.

After the show, the Duke invited Mingus to his dressing room and treated him to lavish helpings of Ellingtonian charm. 'Why didn't you and Juan inform me about the adagio you planned, so that we could score it?' he wondered. 'I must say, I never saw a large man so agile.' More outrageous flattery led at last to the point: 'Juan's an old problem, I can cope with that, but you seem to have a whole bag of new tricks. I must ask you to be kind enough to give me your notice, Mingus.'[13] Somehow made to feel that he was being honoured, Mingus shook hands with the great man and tendered his resignation.

*

At the end of March 1953 Mingus landed (and this time held on to) another valued assignment: bassist in the latest edition of the Bud Powell Trio. This meant regular nightclub work in New York and, on 5 April, a concert at the Club Kavakos in Washington, which was privately recorded. The quality of the amateur recording is poor and, as so often in these circumstances, the double bass suffers most. But through the acoustic murk one can sense Mingus's resilient contribution, transcending time keeping, finely tuned to the impulses of Powell's left hand.

Five days after the Washington concert, Mingus was at a studio in New York, lending moral support (but not participating) while his friend and business partner Max Roach made his first American recordings as a bandleader. For Debut of course.

*

How Mingus came to be recruited to play at Massey Hall in Toronto on 15 May is not entirely clear. In a version of events given by himself, he was the one who put the Ultimate Quintet together. However, on 25 January, when the young Canadians were in New York signing Parker, Gillespie and Max Roach, Mingus was a full-time member of Duke Ellington's orchestra, hardly anticipating that he would shortly be sacked. And when news of the Toronto concert broke in the Canadian press on 6 February, the stars named were Parker, Gillespie and Roach. There was no mention of a bass player.

In all probability, the bassist the Canadians first sought was Oscar Pettiford, who had been at the cutting edge with Parker, Gillespie and Roach long before Mingus joined the New York scene. But when Pettiford declined the booking, Roach advised the Canadians to go for Mingus. Supporting this scenario is an item about the Quintet in the Toronto *Telegram* of 14 March 1953, announcing that Mingus was 'just signed up this week'.

Mingus's fee was $150 – the same as Roach's – and he had no complaints. He and Roach saw the forthcoming event as something far more important than just another gig for the transient enjoyment of some lucky Canadians. It would be an historic occasion, crying out to be preserved – on their Debut label.

They liaised with Dick Wattam, president of Toronto's Jazz Society and principal organizer of the concert. By day Wattam worked as a clerk for General Electric. He assured Mingus and Roach that for the evening of the Massey Hall concert his employers would lend him a brand new Ampex tape recorder. For their part, the two musicians undertook to bring some reels of the latest, high-quality Scotch recording tape, only available in the USA. Parker, Gillespie and Powell almost certainly knew nothing of these arrangements. Parker's exclusive recording contract with Norman Granz was a bridge that Mingus and Roach would cross when they came to it.

On Friday 15 May, when the musicians (except Parker and Gillespie) took the pre-arranged flight to Toronto, Mingus required two extra seats on the aeroplane: one for his double bass, and one for his wife Celia, his unsung partner in Debut Records . . .[14]

FIVE

MAXIMUM

'*I wanted it to sound just perfect, so only Max could play with us.*'
Dizzy Gillespie[1]

MAXWELL LEMUEL ROACH was born on 10 January 1924 in Dismal Swamp, a vast, soggy expanse that blurs the border between Virginia and North Carolina and fades into the Atlantic Ocean.

Before the Civil War, this uncharted and treacherous waste was a hideout for runaway slaves, pirates and renegade Indians. After the war, pockets of the territory were turned into farmland by newly emancipated Negroes, some of them called Roach. (The Irish surname is a legacy from the plantation owners.)

Max's great-grandfather, Mr Ivy Roach, founded the local Baptist Church and preached vigorous sermons. Max's father, Alphonso – light-skinned, quietly spoken and of a slight build – married the dark and handsome Cressy Saunders. Like the Roaches, the Saunders were numerous in Dismal Swamp, and in their case the line had been enriched by intermarriage with Native Americans.

Cressy was the daughter of the local midwife, so when her son Max was born he was delivered exclusively into the hands of his immediate family – the perfect start, he says, to a secure and loving home life (and a joyful contrast, we might add, to the fractured beginnings of Parker, Gillespie, Powell and Mingus).

The family was close, but these were hard years for farming in general and for the black farmers in particular. The boll weevil was destroying crops, the big corporations were fixing prices, and on market days the produce offered by the blacks was auctioned last.

In 1928 Max's parents abandoned the agricultural struggle and travelled north to look for work in New York.

*

The Bedford-Stuyvesant district of Brooklyn (known locally as Bed-Stuy) is a miniature Harlem. Less than a year after the Roaches came to live here, the Great Depression took hold. Job opportunities were few and black applicants stood at the end of the line. Max's father found some work washing cars and taught himself the trade of automobile mechanic. Max's mother scrubbed floors. Their earnings were tiny and irregular, so they had to join the grim game of home-hopping played by many big-city black families. Max explains:

> We were always moving. If you had one month's rent, you could move into an apartment. And then, when you couldn't pay your rent, you could stay there for two months, maybe three at the most, before the landlord could get a notice to have you legally evicted. And then he would put your furniture literally on the street. So you may come home from school and all of your family's furniture is on the sidewalk.

After three bumpy years came the best move yet – to a fifth floor walk-up apartment on Gates Avenue. The landlord had dumped the previous tenants' stuff on to the street, all except the heavy upright piano. The tenants themselves could not afford to have it moved, so there it stayed. Not only that, the apartment was big enough to accommodate an extra family member, so Aunt Clarkie Henton joined them from Dismal Swamp. Back home she had been the church pianist. Now she set about teaching Max and his brother keyboard and sight-reading skills, taking as her texts the gems of black gospel music:

'Sometimes I Feel Like a Motherless Child'; 'Joshua'; 'Standing in the Need of Prayer'.

Displeasing to Aunt Clarkie but thrilling for Max was the discovery that their instrument included machinery for playing piano rolls, and that the previous tenants had left some blatantly secular rolls behind, including performances by stride-piano master James P. Johnson. Max and his brother would set these rolls playing in slow motion, 'so we could see what notes the chords were. And we'd put our fingers over the notes. Then we'd play the roll faster and see how it all connected up.'

In Brooklyn, as previously in Dismal Swamp, Max's mother was an active member of the local Baptist Church and a soloist in its choir. Her boys sang in the children's choir, and then, when Max was eight, they were recruited into the drum and bugle band. 'That's how I began to play drums,' Max remembers. 'I picked up my first pair of drum sticks in Concord Baptist Church on Adelphi Street.'

In December 1936, shortly before his thirteenth birthday, Max graduated from elementary school. To mark Christmas, the birthday and his graduation, his parents said he could choose a very special present. He said he wanted a drum set:

> So my dad took me over to the Bowery, that's Lower Manhattan, where they had all the music shops. It was snowing like hell that Christmas Eve. And he bought me a bass drum; two Chinese tom-toms: one sock cymbal; a foot cymbal; and a snare drum. That was my first set of drums. And on Christmas day I woke up the neighbourhood.

*

Music did not figure officially in the curriculum at Max's high school, although there was a spare-time school symphony orchestra in which he sometimes played timpani or xylophone. His main musical educator was the late-night radio. He and his friends would stay up listening to the broadcasts by the top bands of the day. The one led by drummer Chick Webb was a hot favourite, and Max was captivated by the drumming of Jo Jones with the Count Basie Orchestra.

By now the Roach family was living in a small rented house on Green Avenue. In the house opposite lived the Dubonski family who ran the local tailor's shop. Young Perry Dubonski was another aspiring drummer:

> We used to have across-the-street drum battles. His room was in the front, too. We would have a ball. Open up the windows and just go crazy. I was the Chick Webb, he was the Jo Jones. Can you imagine that? And when the neighbours would come and say, 'Mrs Roach, please, your son is driving us all crazy!' she would run them away from the house, and say, 'At least he's not in the street, maybe like your son.'

All the nation's best bands used to come and play in the big theatres in Brooklyn: the Apollo on Fulton Street, for example, or the Paramount on Flatbush Avenue. Within these people's palaces young Max Roach and hundreds of other Brooklyn schoolboys first set eyes on their radio heroes:

> On Saturdays, after we did our household chores, we were allowed to take our lunch and go into these theatres and stay until the last show. They would have four or five shows a day, with a motion picture in between. So Saturday, I would say, was like our lecture day.

Before he was sixteen, Max had become an authority on his chosen subject. As well as Chick Webb ('the first major drum soloist') and Jo Jones ('the first I heard who played broken rhythm'), he had observed Gene Krupa ('one of the finest brush players'), Cozy Cole ('the technical man, the military style'), Sid Catlett ('fast hands, but when he played a solo he played the character of the piece') and many more. He was also developing a drum sound of his own. His friend Cecil Payne, who played saxophone in the same rehearsal bands, claimed he could tell if Roach was the drummer just by listening from outside the building.

By 1939 Max's father had a steady job in a garage, so the family took an agreeable apartment on Monroe Street and installed a piano. The basement of the building was divided into storage units, one for each tenant. Max appropriated his family's allocation for his drum kit, 'and I would bang all day'.

In the teenage rehearsal bands you earned no money. To join the world of professional music-making, you had to offer your services at one of the dozens of corner bars. On the corner nearest to the Roach apartment stood the Dew Drop Inn, and here, against his parents' wishes, Max applied. The management engaged his services on Friday and Saturday nights to support a pianist playing popular songs of the day.

Increasingly serious about his craft, he invested his earnings in private lessons on the drums and the piano. Before he was seventeen, Max was looking beyond Brooklyn – casting his eyes across the East River towards Manhattan.

Within Manhattan was Harlem, whose population of more than 350,000 made it the largest urban black community in the world. Two Harlem institutions attracted young Max immediately: the Apollo Theatre on 125th Street, arena for the finest concerts; and, further north, the Savoy Ballroom, 'Home of the Happy Feet'. Here at the Savoy, Max first experienced Chick Webb close-up:

> He sat in front of his band, so you could come up to the bandstand and be right at his bass drum. His bass drum would go all through your body. And he was fast. A power-house of a percussionist. When he was on the stage, it was *Chick* on that stage.[2]

Also at the Savoy, Max met Mildred Wilkinson – a teenager crazy about dancing. It turned out that Mildred, too, came from Brooklyn – she lived on Madison Street, just round the corner from the Roach home. Seven years later Max and Mildred would marry.

*

Although the Apollo and the Savoy welcomed all comers, it was not easy (legally it was impossible) for a sixteen-year-old to enter Manhattan's nightclubs. Max used to draw a moustache on his top lip using his mother's eyebrow pencil, and gruffly insist he was nineteen. Sometimes it worked, sometimes not. The best guarantee of admission was a reputation as a capable musician. Once the regular drummers found they could trust him to deputize while they took a break, club owners all over Manhattan started to use him:

> You worked in all-white clubs in downtown Manhattan (we called it 'white town') from nine to three, and then went uptown to the after-hours spots in Harlem (which we called 'black town') from four to eight. That's when I met Bud Powell and we became friends. These after-hours spots were elaborate places with maître d's and nice tables, and they had shows. And they would give young guys like Bud Powell and myself a chance. They used just to have a pianist and a drummer. And they'd have singers and fire-eating dancers, so you had to read music: Khachaturian's *Sabre Dance* and things like that. They paid maybe a dollar or two dollars a night. In some cases you just got sandwiches, and maybe some beer. But it was *playing* time for us, and it meant a lot. After the show, somebody would maybe bring in a bass, and then the horns would come in. They closed at eight in the morning, and that would give you time to scurry to school.

Max Roach and Bud Powell were almost exact contemporaries, but Bud was more familiar with Manhattan. He introduced Max to Minton's Playhouse on Harlem's 118th Street, where a new musical language was evolving. Powell's idol Thelonious Monk was the resident pianist. Sometimes Monk would invite Bud to come up and play. And once in a while the regular drummer, Kenny Clarke, would let Max take over.

The crucial night at Minton's, for Max, was the one on which his playing caught the attention of the entrepreneur Clark Monroe. Known locally as 'the Dark Gable', the dashing Monroe (whose brother Jimmy was married to Billie Holiday) kept several irons in the show business fire. Monroe's Uptown House, the after-hours spot he ran up on 133rd Street, was one of the most popular in Harlem. A superior band accompanied the floorshow, and the jam session that followed the set entertainment was the best in town. By 6.00 a.m. Monroe's would be full of top players, including those, like Dizzy Gillespie, looking for action after Minton's closed for the night.

Monroe appointed Max as his regular drummer. This meant not just the after-hours stint each night at the Uptown House, but also an earlier engagement, from 9.00 p.m. to 3.00 a.m., downtown at Georgie Jay's 78th

Street Taproom. Monroe had the contract to supply the entertainment here. He told jokes, sang and danced a bit, introduced the turns and went through the motions of conducting the band (whose effective leader was the Harlem cornettist and violinist Victor Coulson). Between the acts there would be a jam session, all-comers welcome. One night Coulson warned his players that tomorrow he would be introducing a stranger, who just happened to be the world's greatest musician. But Max and the others had been jamming with such legends as Lester Young, so when the unassuming new boy arrived they were unwilling to be impressed, as Max remembers:

> Sure enough, Victor brought down Charlie Parker. And during the jam session part, between shows, when he came to play with us, he played *Cherokee*. And he turned to the rhythm section and he asked us for stop time. You know: Bap! duddle uddle uddle uddle uddle ah. And it was *fast*. Well, we ran through it, but I don't think any of us realized what was happening at that moment.

'That moment' must have been in or soon after January 1942, when Parker reached New York with the Jay McShann band.

In the summer, when McShann took his band on tour again, Parker stayed behind. He found himself a steady job, playing for his supper and a share of the tips, as a member of the house band at Monroe's Uptown House, which meant that Max was now working with him every night. It also meant that the jam sessions at Monroe's became essential dates for all the thrusting jazz musicians in New York City. Dizzy Gillespie for one was always there. But young Max remained unfazed. When Kenny Clarke dropped into Monroe's one night, he witnessed an astonishing demonstration by the kid from Brooklyn:

> Max was playing and whistling at the same time, and he seemed not to care very much about what Parker was doing. He was using brushes, and when I asked him why he wasn't using sticks he replied, 'Because I haven't learned that yet'. He was already playing whatever he felt like, because he was so gifted, with a fantastic left hand.[3]

This was Max's last year in High School, and it was crowned by a summons to play with the Duke Ellington Orchestra. Clark Monroe was the go-between. Ellington had contacted him urgently because his regular drummer, Sonny Greer, had gone sick and all the usual deputies had been called into the Army. Did Monroe know of a reliable drummer who could read music? One was needed right away at the New York Paramount, where the band was part of an extravagant stage show. Monroe sent Max, who takes over the story:

> I was overwhelmed by the pageantry. Duke Ellington's band was set up like a pyramid, with the drummer at the apex. And Sonny Greer had everything in the world in his drum kit. He had all the mallet instruments: xylophone, vibraphone, chime, bells and timpani. And I searched for drum music – there wasn't a sheet of music anywhere! I was scared to death. So now Mr Ellington comes on stage, and he must have seen the panic in my face. He smiled and said, 'All you have to do is keep one eye on me, and one eye on the act.' And he was a great conductor, because he gave me everything just before it happened out there on the stage. And that lasted about two days, and I became a local hero.

In December 1942 Max graduated with honours from Boys' High in Brooklyn and committed himself fully to music.

*

Standing in the eerie silence that followed the Harlem riot of 1943, the writer James Baldwin noted the spectacular trails of discarded loot along the avenues of broken glass. All the commercial premises had been ransacked on the assumption that they were owned by whites. The immediate cause of the mayhem was the shooting of a Negro soldier by a white policeman. The underlying reason was the anger among the African-American population about the segregation and abuse of black conscripts in the US Armed Forces.

Although he was to become a dedicated Civil Rights warrior, back in 1943 Max Roach lived almost entirely for his music, and was caught unawares by the Harlem eruption. After leaving school he had continued in the employment of Clark Monroe, and by the summer he was also working at another Harlem club, Murrain's on 7th Avenue, where he earned not just tips but a guaranteed wage. To celebrate, he was buying new drums on the instalment plan. As soon as news of the Harlem rumpus reached him in Brooklyn, he dashed to catch the subway uptown, anxious to reach Murrain's and protect the expensive kit he had just installed. But the police had blockaded the Harlem subway stations. When at last he reached Murrain's, the drums were gone. The payments for them, however, had to be kept up.

As well as costing Roach dear, the riot ruptured the pattern of New York's musical life. In the pre-war years the Harlem jam sessions had attracted big names from mainstream show business, like Benny Goodman and Peggy Lee, who brought with them crowds of well-heeled white customers. But the troubles drove the carriage trade away, so the black music makers were obliged to move downtown – where work was waiting for them in the clubs proliferating along 52nd Street.

Roach's first regular job on 'The Street' was at Kelly's Stables, where he took over from Kenny Clarke (drafted into the army) as drummer for the venerable Coleman Hawkins. Then in October 1943 he was approached by Dizzy Gillespie, who was forming an experimental small group – one that would bring to 52nd Street the bold modernism previously found at Monroe's and Minton's. They were about to open at the Onyx Club, and Gillespie was adamant that Roach should be the drummer.

It was during this breakthrough for modern music that Roach came to fully appreciate Gillespie's genius: not just his instrumental brilliance and his originality as a composer, but also his inspirational qualities as leader and teacher. Most remarkable, from Roach's point of view, was Gillespie's ability to explain and demonstrate, in detail, what he required his drummer to do. Whenever he is asked to compile a list of those who have influenced the way he plays the drums, he always puts Dizzy near the top.

*

In February 1944, invited to make a set of recordings, Coleman Hawkins assembled a band of the most exciting new talent on 52nd Street. Dizzy Gillespie helped the maestro pick these young players, so of course Max Roach, who was just twenty, was chosen as the drummer.

On five of the six numbers he is confined to providing an apt accompaniment. The sixth, 'Bu-Dee-Daht', is his chance to impress. He enhances the theme statement with his frothing hi-hat in the Jo Jones manner, and plays a crisp, militaristic solo that could have come from Cozy Cole.

The conservative nature of Roach's contribution to these discs shows a proper sensitivity to the character of Hawkins' playing. To hear Roach the revolutionary from this same period, we must turn to the pirate recording of the Gillespie group at the Onyx club playing 'A Night in Tunisia'. Here, while Gillespie creates his startling solo, Roach provides exactly the required stimulus, breaking up the 4/4 time with provocative rhythmic patterns.

*

Early in March 1944, after a quarrel, Gillespie and Oscar Pettiford ended their partnership. Pettiford stayed at the Onyx with the rump of the quintet. Gillespie moved to the Yacht Club with a splinter group that included Roach. But Max did not stay for long. Although he loved playing with Dizzy, when the chance came to help a friend by joining a big band and touring America, he took it.

The friend was George Russell, a budding composer who had been playing drums with the touring band of Benny Carter. Like many out-of-town musicians passing through New York, Russell headed for the Roach apartment in Brooklyn, renowned for its homely comforts. Russell suffered from tuberculosis. When it turned out that he was too poorly to continue with the tour, he took long-term shelter under Max's mother's wing while Max hit the road as Benny Carter's drummer.

He stayed with Carter for a year. This was his first regular experience with a professional big band, his first exposure to the USA beyond New York City and Dismal Swamp, and the most congenial of apprenticeships. His courtly boss felt no revolutionary zeal. His style of playing was elegant and refined, and so was the sound of his band. According to a notice in the June 1944 issue of *Metronome* magazine, 'The big kick in this band is supplied by drummer Max Roach. He is fast, with a steadiness and a rhythmic inspiration found only in the very great.'

In the spring of 1945 when the band was in California, Roach received a telegram from Dizzy Gillespie announcing that he and Parker were forming a quintet to play at the Three Deuces club on 52nd Street. They wanted Max back in New York in a hurry.

*

In New York in the summer of 1945 Roach was not only the first-choice drummer of the elite Parker–Gillespie Quintet, he was also (because alternatives like Kenny Clarke were in the army) the undisputed king of the modern drummers on 52nd Street. And it went to his head. Fifty years later he still likes to tell the story of how Charlie Parker rescued him from the sin of pride. (To fully appreciate this story bear in mind that the Japanese prime minister during World War II, General Tojo, was always pictured wearing horn-rimmed spectacles.)

> I'd come to the rehearsals a little late. And I remember coming to one rehearsal, at the Three Deuces, and Charlie Parker was sitting behind my drums. He had a nickname for everybody, and since we're in the war, and I wore these thick horn-rimmed glasses, I was Tojo. And he said, 'Hey, Tojo, can you do this?' And he did a quarter note on the bass drum; a Charleston beat on the foot cymbal; a shuffle rhythm on the snare drum with his left hand; and the jazz beat, chick-chi-chang, chick-chi-chang, with his right hand on the ride cymbal. All at the same time, comfortably, with the saxophone across his lap! Then he got up, and I walked over to the drums and attempted to do it. And I knew I had to practise it, so he put me back to where I should have been all the time.

It would be wrong to deduce from this parable that Parker was wedded to punctuality. Unlike Gillespie, he refused to acknowledge the tedious claims of time. He was rarely present for the start of the quintet's evening performances. Roach remembers one occasion when Parker came in long after the rest of the band had started playing, and went straight to the bathroom at the side of the stage. When he failed to reappear, Gillespie left the rhythm section playing and went to check. He came back furious, shouting to Roach that Parker was in there fixing himself with all the heroin paraphernalia. Unfortunately, Gillespie was standing next to an open microphone, so his tirade was relayed to everyone in the club, including Parker. 'And,' says Roach, 'you heard spoons dropping and needles, and Bird came rushing out of the bathroom. He said, "Diz, man, why would you do something like that to me?"'[4]

Sometimes when the night's work at the Three Deuces was done, Parker would take the subway to Brooklyn with Max, arriving at the Roach apartment as Max's parents were leaving for work. Then the day could be spent snoozing, relaxing and consuming illegal substances in a safe and cosy environment. And when Max's mother got back home after a day of scrubbing floors, this God-fearing lady was always greeted with smoothness and charm:

> He'd be down on the floor, *ripped*, and yet he'd be the first to hear the key in the door. He'd grab the Bible and sit in the big chair, and open up the Bible and look as though he was in it. And when my mother came into the room he'd smile at her and say, 'Hey, mom.' She loved Charlie Parker. And after he'd gone she would say, 'Now you've got to be like that boy, Max. That's a *good* boy.'

Dizzy Gillespie had formed a different view. So vexed was he by Parker's self-destructive behaviour that he dissolved the quintet and concentrated on forming his first big band. This 18-piece outfit started rehearsals at Nola's Studios in New York City during the first week of July 1945. Max Roach was among its members. Charlie Parker was not.

For eight weeks in the summer the Dizzy Gillespie Orchestra toured the Southern States of America and had to cope with the inevitable racism. Roach's description of the standard indignities is matter-of-fact:

> We had a problem if we had to find food in an area where they did not serve blacks. Other than that, we were self-contained: we stayed in black homes, and everything we came into contact with was black. Except occasionally we might be harassed by the state police. They'd come on the bus and do what they call 'having some fun': give us a few nasty epithets and ask us would we give them a concert, or 'Can you dance?'

More agreeable for him to recall is the loving care bestowed on him by Dizzy Gillespie. By the time of the tour, Max (probably not helped by those afternoons at home with Charlie Parker) was addicted to heroin. During their travels through the South, he says, 'Dizzy nursed me like a baby.' He feels grateful to this day that his leader, with all his other responsibilities, still found the time 'to make me feel that I meant something'.

After the Southern tour the orchestra soon broke up, releasing Max Roach back on to 52nd Street. Here Charlie Parker was at the Spotlite club, fronting a new group that included Miles Davis on trumpet and Stan Levey on drums. Roach took over from Levey, and was the only drummer Parker considered when he selected the musicians to play with him on his first recording date as leader.

Parker's November 1945 session for Savoy produced six magnificent examples of the new music, including one breathtaking masterpiece, 'Koko', where Max Roach's contribution was vital.

'Koko' is framed by a fiendishly difficult introduction and coda of Charlie Parker's devising. Miles Davis had been booked to play the trumpet part but he refused. This material was way beyond him, he said: 'the damnedest introduction I ever heard in my life'.[5] But it held no terrors for Gillespie and Roach, who had been playing it with Parker at the Three Deuces earlier in the year. Written at Roach's request, it involves just the trio of saxophone, muted trumpet and drums, with Max's brushes pattering and slithering over the drum heads, intensifying the fiercely intimate climate. Then trumpet and saxophone play an unaccompanied four-bar break, which is Roach's chance to make the switch from brushes to sticks. This done, he detonates a precise explosion, to give Parker's improvisation a cracking launch, then provides supple support for one of the greatest solos in the history of recorded jazz.

He follows Parker with an exciting solo of his own, one entirely in keeping with the character of this extraordinary piece and steering us surely towards its coda. The coda is a mirror of the introduction, again played by the trio of trumpet, saxophone and drums; but here Max has no opportunity to revert to the brushes. Instead he achieves a hushed fury by concentrating his sticks upon the cymbals.

*

Within weeks of creating 'Koko' the quartet responsible had scattered. Parker and Gillespie were in California. Roach and Curley Russell had joined the resurgent Bud Powell to form one of the top trios in New York City.

When Gillespie came back to New York and formed a big band, Roach and Powell were both recruited but neither stayed long. Demand for their services continued to be heavy. In June 1946 they were part of a recording team led by the trombonist J.J. Johnson. One of the numbers they recorded was a catchy Roach original, playing merry games with on- and off-the-beat rhythmic figures. He called it 'Coppin' the Bop'.

*

Although he was the supreme modern drummer, Roach felt incomplete. So he enrolled at the Manhattan School of Music in East Harlem ('the poor kids' Juilliard', he calls it) and paid his tuition fees from his earnings on 52nd Street. He had planned to take percussion as his major subject, but his first date with the percussion tutor convinced him that the gulf between European and jazz technique made progress impossible:

> The first thing Mr Allbright asked me to hit was the snare drum. And before I could strike the drum he walked over and adjusted the sticks in my hands. And he said, 'Now each stick should come up and hit this button on your shirt, son.' And I knew that if I got into this I couldn't work on 52nd Street, because by the time I raised my hands up like he said, then a whole chorus would have gone by! So I went to the Registrar's Office and changed my major to composition.

On 10 January 1947 (Max's twenty-third birthday) the trio of Bud Powell, Curley Russell and Roach, long supreme on The Street, assembled in a recording studio. The consequent discs – eight 78rpm sides – brought new lustre to the piano trio genre. What catches the ear, of course, is the stupendous originality of Powell, and at first we hardly notice the immaculate brushwork of Roach, so closely does he shadow every pianistic nuance. As with his contribution to Parker's historic 'Koko' session, everything he does is designed to enhance the total effect.

*

In the spring of 1947 Charlie Parker returned to New York from his Californian exile and immediately recruited Roach for his new quintet. For the group's first recording session Bud Powell and bassist Tommy Potter completed the powerful rhythm section. To the delight of Max's mother, who adored the spiritual quality she found in Parker's blues playing, rehearsals for this important date were held at the Roach home in Brooklyn.

Although Parker had trouble with his reed during the recording session, there is a daring and footloose swing to his playing on these New York sides that is never quite there on the Californian discs. The added stimulants here, of course, are Powell and Roach. Out on the West Coast there had been no equivalents.

In spite of the success of these recordings, and the campaigning by Davis and Roach, Parker declined to employ Powell as the pianist for the residency at the Three Deuces club. He settled instead for Duke Jordan, a lesser talent but free of personality disorders. According to Miles Davis, it was Roach who nightly bore the brunt of Jordan's shortcomings:

> Max would scream at Duke not to try to follow Bird, because Duke wouldn't have been able to keep up. When Bird went off on one of his incredible solos, the rhythm section had to stay where they were. Eventually Bird would come back to where the rhythm section was, right on time.[6]

*

Twice during September 1947 Roach and Parker were summoned away from the quintet to broadcast as members of a group of modernists assembled by critic Barry Ulanov for a so-called 'battle of the bands: mouldy figs versus moderns'. Dizzy Gillespie, too, was among those chosen, so the surviving airchecks are valuable documents: rare examples of the great drummer supporting the two peerless horn men. However, because of the fatuous format the whole occasion amounted to less than the sum of its extraordinary parts.

The reverse could be said about the New York recordings made by the Parker Quintet for Ross Russell's Dial label during the winter of 1947. Here, within the confines of the three-minute 78rpm discs, Duke Jordan's slight but charming musical personality, Miles Davis's smouldering diffidence and Tommy Potter's steadiness combine with Max Roach's speed and elegance to form a fitting jewel box for Parker's genius.

Roach's role as a soloist here is a minor one. On those numbers where he is granted any space, it is usually no more than eight bars. Unfailingly, he fits a cunning story into these little nooks. On 'Bird Feathers' his allocation is increased to one 12-bar chorus, and he turns in a solo that is abstemious yet quietly sensational. But these moments are not his most valuable contribution to the recordings. What matters more is his priceless gift for what might be called on-the-wing orchestration: the empathic provision of background colours that shift and dance, catching exactly the character of every new Parker composition.

*

On 1 January 1948 the second ban on recordings by the mighty American Federation of Musicians came into effect.

In September, when this ban had been in force for nine months, the buccaneering Savoy record company organized two secret sessions for the quintet, risking the union's terrible wrath. Under these desperate circumstances some of the twentieth century's greatest music, including 'Parker's Mood', was recorded. Max Roach likes to draw attention to this paradox. And since this book hinges on one immortal night of extempore brilliance, it's right that we should hear his testimony on behalf of art under pressure:

> Some of the records were done 'under the table', because you were fined and thrown out of the union if you did record. It was always a hustle and a rush. Much of the music written by Charlie Parker was written in taxi cabs on the way to the studio. He would write just one part – the trumpet part. He would transpose his own part off the trumpet part.

And he would tell the harmonic progression to the pianist and the bassist. Then he would look at me and say, 'Max, you know what to do'. It was get in, get out immediately, because the union was always lurking around the corner. And it's amazing to me, when I remember how it was done, how today it is considered so profound.

*

Although the music was sweetly concordant, cracks were opening in the 1948 Parker Quintet – particularly between the leader and Miles Davis, who objected violently when his boss tried to keep all the band's earnings for himself. He urged Roach to support his rebellion, and was infuriated by the drummer's stubborn reverence for genius.

But even Roach's tolerance had its limit, and Parker breached it on the bandstand at the Royal Roost on Christmas Eve, when he left his musicians looking foolish while he entertained the audience with party tricks. That night Miles Davis left the band for good, and Roach insisted that he, too, must take a break.

During his short absence he made a telling contribution to a set of recordings by the Miles Davis Nonet: delicate arrangements that would become famous collectively as 'The Birth of the Cool'.

He also married his long-time sweetheart, Mildred Wilkinson. The wedding ceremony took place in Brooklyn on 14 January 1949, and when the couple emerged from the church, Charlie Parker was waiting with a surprise for them, as Max recalled: 'There was Bird with this beautiful smile on his face, and a great big black Cadillac with a chauffeur to take us to the wedding party. And he called out, "You're gonna ride in *this* kid!"'

In the spring of 1949 Roach was back in the familiar drum chair, and on 7 May the latest edition of the Parker Quintet, with trumpeter Kenny Dorham and pianist Al Haig, flew to Paris for the 1949 International Jazz Festival. Here Roach and the other sidemen found themselves caught up in a whirl of European enthusiasm, not just as satellites of Charlie Parker, but as stars in their own right. Spotting that the four of them, unlike Parker himself, were not contracted to any record label, the

Vogue company invited them to make some recordings under Roach's leadership. To complete the line up, Roach borrowed tenor saxophonist James Moody (ex-Gillespie big band) who was here at the Festival with a group led by Tadd Dameron and Miles Davis.

The Max Roach Quintet came to Vogue's Paris studios on Sunday 15 May and recorded four original compositions. The best (written by Roach and Dorham in tandem) is 'Prince Albert' – a wriggly melody drawn from the chords of Jerome Kern's 'All the Things You Are', and fitted with Dizzy Gillespie's standard introduction.

The composition credited solely to Max Roach, punningly called 'Maximum', moves exceedingly fast – around 320 beats per minute. In spite of the title, the theme is minimal: two punchy phrases, with spaces between for killer bursts of drumming. Trumpet, tenor and piano take most of the solo space, but Roach's is the dominant musical personality, driving the others forward, supercharging the group performance.

'Maximum' was ahead of its time. The ruthless emphasis on momentum would be a key feature of the so-called 'hard bop' movement of the mid- and late fifties, and Roach would become the movement's emblem. But his next move in 1949 was the return flight to the United States for more toil in the shade of Charlie Parker's restless persona.

*

The commitment to Parker was not an exclusive one. Within days of returning to New York, Roach accepted an invitation from Norman Granz to come and record with Bud Powell. These May 1949 recordings (with bassist Ray Brown alongside Roach) were Powell's first for Granz, and comparable in quality to the masterpieces he made for Three Deuces with the support of Roach and Curley Russell. Again Roach confines himself to brushes, and plays silkily even at the highest speeds; and once more the results ('Tempus Fugue-it', 'Cherokee' and the rest) are major additions to the piano trio oeuvre.

In the autumn of 1949, having satisfied his conscience by recruiting the estimable Roy Haynes as his replacement, Roach left Charlie Parker's employ. His first steady job leading a group of his own was at a club near his home in Brooklyn called Soldier Meyers. At the same time, despite his jazz pre-eminence, he became a student again, resuming his lessons in composition at the Manhattan School of Music.

Years would pass before he made his first American records as a leader, but there was non-stop demand for his stamp on the recordings of others. He was there in October when a new record company, Prestige, put together a session fronted by J.J. Johnson and Sonny Stitt. And he was there again in December, together with Curley Russell and Bud Powell, to back Sonny Stitt's first solo album on tenor saxophone. Immune to the sparks that flew between Stitt and Powell, he clinched this well-recorded occasion with his authoritative stick-on-cymbal sound.

On Christmas Eve, Powell, Russell and Roach were central to an All-Star concert at Carnegie Hall. Although we can feel Roach's power lifting Powell to extraordinary heights, it's hard to hear the drumming details through the low-fi recording, which wraps his kit in an acoustic fog.

In February 1950 Roach, Russell and Powell were invited by Norman Granz to make more records as the Bud Powell Trio. This, the last Powell–Roach session for more than a year, gave us six performances of standard tunes, plus a glistening account of a Powell original, 'So Sorry Please'. Here the discreet patter of Roach's brushes serves to enhance the sheen, until the middle eight of the closing chorus, where Powell invites him forward and he writes his neat signature with a wristy flourish.

*

During the summer of 1950, keen to correct the Eurocentric bias of his studies at the Manhattan School, Roach invested his savings in a trip to Haiti.

Here he searched for Tiroro – the drummer who had thrilled him a decade earlier at the 1939 World's Fair in New York City:

> When I finally found him, he was giving a lesson, with a partition
> between him and the student. And the reason he gave me was that
> everybody's hands are different, and the student has to learn to create
> the sound with his own particular anatomy. Tiroro did amazing things
> on the drum with his hands: skin on skin.

Roach invited Tiroro to visit him in his small hotel, and was shocked when the owner refused to let the master drummer in:

> And then I realized there was a caste system, because Tiroro couldn't read or write. He was good enough for Haiti to send him to the World's Fair, but here there was a caste system separating black from black. This was a revelation to me – coming from the United States, where I lived under the same system, but separating black from white.

*

In January 1951, still a student at the Manhattan School, Roach said yes to a reunion recording session with Charlie Parker, produced by Norman Granz. Miles Davis also agreed to play his old part. Completing the rhythm section were new boys Teddy Kotick on bass and Walter Bishop, Jr. (a Bud Powell devotee) on piano. Fine music was made, with Roach outstanding on 'Au Privave', where his 12-bar solo pins down precisely the larky spirit of Parker's theme.

In May, Roach was crucially involved with the creation of another masterpiece by Bud Powell. Powell was teetering towards a mental break-down and the recording session almost failed to happen. Roach and Curley Russell had been waiting for an hour and a half when Powell rushed in and attacked a new composition of his, entitled 'Un Poco Loco'.

For Take 1 Roach lays down a classic Afro-Latin rhythm: entirely serviceable, but for Powell uninspiring. The take is aborted. For Take 2 Roach produces a drastically different polyrhythm: three distinct but inter-locking patterns, played on cowbell, tom-tom and hi-hat. Powell is galvanized, 'Un Poco Loco' is transformed, and Roach's capacity to respond to the moment is perfectly illustrated.

The story of 'Un Poco Loco' has a tailpiece (told to me by Max in 1984), which shows what a thankless task nursing a genius can be. On a Manhattan street a few days after the recording, Roach was ambushed by Powell, who leapt out and demanded, 'Man, why did you ruin my record?'

*

By the spring of 1952 Charles Mingus had settled in New York and he and Roach had formed a soul brotherhood. The material outcome of their close tie was the self-help record company Debut, without which the Massey Hall concert by the Quintet of the Year would never have reached a global audience.

A binding ingredient in the friendship between Mingus and Roach was their shared passion for the music of Charlie Parker. In September, after a three-year gap, Roach was brought together with Parker again, not by Norman Granz this time but by the Harlem community. To raise funds for the campaign to free the communist Benjamin Davis, a grand musical event was staged at the Rockland Palace Ballroom, where you could hear Roach with Parker and his quintet, with and without the Parker Strings.

Enthusiasts tape-recorded Parker's music, but their machines were not running when the guest of honour, Benjamin Davis's friend Paul Robeson, gave his solo performance. Roach described to me how Robeson took command of the stage that night:

> The government had put a gag on him. And he said, 'You know I'm not
> supposed to talk to you folks tonight'. Then he sang workers' and
> freedom songs in every language you can imagine: Chinese, French,
> Russian. When he sang an old spiritual called 'Water Boy', Charlie Parker
> walked on the stage with a pitcher of water and a glass! *These* are the
> things you remember.

The year 1952 ended with Roach making more recordings with Charlie Parker for Norman Granz. The pianist was Hank Jones, the bassist Teddy Kotick, and this time Parker was the only front-line soloist. In the extra space the rhythm men could shine, and Roach's shapely solos show how he earned the title 'supremely melodic drummer'. On the two blues tracks 'Laird Baird' and 'Cosmic Rays' his playing achieves the quality of ardent song.

*

On 25 January 1953, when the four enthusiasts from the New Jazz Society of Toronto tracked Max Roach down and made an offer for his services, they were impressed by his coolness and charm. He politely checked their credentials and then said yes, he would be happy to join Parker and the others for the Massey Hall concert on 15 May. When they asked him about Bud Powell, he directed them to Powell's protector Oscar Goodstein. And when they sought his advice on whom they should book to play bass, he had no hesitation in recommending his soul mate and business partner Charles Mingus.

In the early spring, while Roach and Mingus were plotting to tape the Toronto concert, Roach was doubly busy. He had moved from the family home in Brooklyn to a basement apartment on East 30th Street in Manhattan, which he shared with his girlfriend Margo Ferraci. He was also gearing up for his first recordings in America as leader of his own group. The Max Roach Quartet, with Roach's young discovery Hank Mobley playing the tenor saxophone, rehearsed a mixture of standard tunes and originals. To boot, four arrangements were written for a specially formed septet. On the eve of the 10 April session for Debut records, conscious of his responsibilities, Roach retired to bed early. But at around 4.00 in the morning he was awakened by a hammering and ringing at the door of the East 30th Street apartment. It was Charlie Parker, looking for a pal to talk to:

> So I said, 'Not tonight, please Bird. I'm recording tomorrow.' And he sat
> down at the table and took a piece of manuscript paper and wrote a piece
> for me, like you'd write a letter. And the title he gave it was 'Chi Chi'.

'Chi Chi' – a typically eloquent 12-bar blues – replaced one of the tunes planned for the quartet. It is taken at a comfortable walking pace, with Mobley declaiming the soulful line while Roach points up its rhythmic intricacies.

Roach's own composition for his quartet, 'Cou-Manchi-Cou', is a 12-bar theme in a minor key, performed in the group's characteristically rugged, hard-driving fashion.

For his septet Roach wrote 'Sfax', another 12-bar theme in C minor – this one composed of snappy ensemble phrases walled in by percussion. Like the brilliant 'Maximum', recorded in Paris four years earlier, 'Sfax' is frankly a drummer's vehicle.

Another presageful track on the Debut LP has Roach playing entirely alone in a beautifully shaped soliloquy called 'Drum Conversation'.

*

On Friday 15 May three representatives of the Debut record company – Mr and Mrs Mingus and Max Roach – boarded the plane at La Guardia for the journey to Toronto. Their bulky luggage included a double bass, a drum kit and a stack of good-quality recording tape.

———

SIX

JAZZ AT MASSEY HALL

'The thing that's most important is that
Mingus and I had this little record company.'
Max Roach

IN 1892 HART A. MASSEY, prosperous Canadian manufacturer of agricultural implements, bought land bordering Shuter Street and Victoria Street in Toronto and commissioned the construction of an auditorium to rival Carnegie Hall in New York and the Royal Albert Hall in London. This was to be his gift to the city on the shore of Lake Ontario.

In 1894 the 3,500-seat Massey Music Hall opened with a performance of Handel's *Messiah*. In 1897 the Toronto Philharmonic Society filled the huge stage with a celebration of Queen Victoria's Diamond Jubilee. In 1901 a concert was laid on to honour the visit of the Duke and Duchess of York (the future King George V and Queen Mary). The royal couple arrived late during an aria sung by the operatic diva Emma Calvi, who was then left stranded when the orchestra hastily switched to the National Anthem.

During the 1920s the Toronto Symphony Orchestra made Massey Hall its home. In 1934 George Gershwin appeared as soloist in his *Rhapsody in Blue*.

During the 1940s, following the example set by Carnegie Hall, Massey Hall opened its doors to big name jazz events. Louis Armstrong, Duke

Ellington and Count Basie became regular visitors, and Norman Granz brought his Jazz at the Philharmonic package for an annual bash. However, the task of assembling five of the crucial creators of a new musical language on one platform was undertaken not by a canny impresario, but by an inexperienced and impecunious group of young idealists calling themselves the New Jazz Society of Toronto. To comply with musicians' union regulations, their 1953 Festival of Creative Jazz had to include a local big band as well as their dream Quintet, so recouping their costs meant selling a lot of tickets.

When, back in January, the concert had been scheduled for Friday 15 May, the date was free of rival attractions. But since then the fight for the heavyweight boxing championship of the world, between Rocky Marciano and Jersey Joe Walcott, had been postponed from April and reset by malignant fate for concert night. This hugely resonant bout of fisticuffs between a white and a black American would be shown live on TV throughout the USA and Canada.

Towards the end of April advance ticket sales for the concert were still far below the safety level. The New Jazz Society met to consider their position. They had inserted an escape clause into the musicians' contracts, allowing withdrawal by either side, without penalty, up to 1 May. Should they exercise this option? Believing, probably correctly, that never again would they bag such a haul of lions, they decided the show would go ahead.

*

The supporting band, drawn mainly from musicians on the payroll of the Canadian Broadcasting Corporation, was dubbed the CBC All-Stars. Its leader for the night would be trumpeter Graham Topping, who, incidentally, had chosen Dizzy Gillespie as his idol and model.

On the afternoon of the concert, Topping was rehearsing his men on the Massey Hall stage. They became aware that their American heroes had landed when Max Roach started to move among them, setting up his unshowy equipment. Once the pieces were assembled, he thrilled the CBC All-Stars by playing along with them. 'We were dragging,' remembered trumpeter Erich Traugott, 'and Max wanted to get us off our asses.'[1]

Other scattered sightings of the stars were reported. In the lobby of the Park Plaza hotel, Jazz Society members Alan Scharf and Boyd Raeburn were approached by Bud Powell, who must have given Oscar Goodstein the slip. Scharf remembers that Powell begged them for cash:

> We dug into our pockets and found like 60 cents. Bud disappeared into the bar. Immediately afterwards a harried Mingus rushed in. 'Have you seen Bud? Did you give him any money? How much exactly?' Then Mingus, too, rushed into the bar.[2]

Scharf met Powell several more times during the course of the day, and was disturbed by the consistent peculiarity of his appearance: eyes rolled back with only the whites showing. At a gathering of musicians and fans in Max Roach's hotel room, somebody happened to ask who composed 'Lullaby of Birdland'. Powell snapped out of his trance just long enough to answer 'George Shearing', and then his eyes rolled upwards again. As far as Scharf could tell, the great pianist was neither drunk nor drugged.

Having escorted Parker to Toronto airport and then having lost him, Gillespie headed for Massey Hall and warned the Jazz Society that they might have a problem. Of Parker there was no sign until 8.30, when he presented himself at the Massey Hall stage door, as per contract, and asked to see Dick Wattam, the New Jazz Society president. Wattam remembers that Parker was 'in a beautiful mood, sober as a judge'. All he asked for was a drink. Wattam took him across the street to the Silver Rail. Here Parker downed a triple scotch almost in one gulp and said, 'Dick, I'm ready.'[3]

*

In 1953 the ties binding the Dominion of Canada to the mother country were much tighter than now. Queen Elizabeth II had recently succeeded to the English throne. Her Coronation Service would take place in Westminster Abbey on 2 June – less than three weeks after the concert – and that day had been declared a Canadian national holiday. It's likely that a portrait of the popular young monarch hung in the Massey Hall foyer.

As Graham Topping and his band took their places on the stage, the management reminded them they had a patriotic duty to perform. The law of the land required 'God Save the King' (or 'Queen', as the case may be) to be played on all such public occasions, and during the rendition the audience was bound to stand respectfully to attention.

Topping and his All-Stars had come unprepared for this obligation. To meet it, volunteers stood in a corner of the stage and busked the anthem in shaky unison. 'It was very embarrassing, a horrible way to start, and it unnerved us all,' remembered baritone saxophonist Norman Symonds.[4]

Recovering from this grisly beginning, the band moved smoothly through its book of jazz arrangements and was loyally applauded by the meagre audience. Although Charles Mingus claimed in a 1975 interview that the concert was a sell-out, reliable evidence points the other way. Reviewers at the time described the hall as about half full, and a photograph of the stalls taken during the show by Alan Scharf shows the majority of seats to be empty. Perhaps there was more take-up for the cheaper accommodation in the balcony. One customer up there was Brian Dale, a passionate Parker fan who had chosen to leave his home in London, England and emigrate to Canada after reading stories about the planned Quintet concert in the British jazz press. We know about Brian because nearly fifty years later he published a log of his experiences. We shall return to him after the performance.

*

Under the terms of the contracts, each member of the Quintet was to be paid, on top of his fee, a percentage of the net profit. From a glance at the house they would have known that this meant a percentage of nothing, which may explain the sound of angry voices heard coming from the dressing room where they assembled while Topping's team was playing.

By the time the Canadian musicians left the stage and came to pay homage to the stars, a hush had descended. Gillespie was gnawing on a T-bone steak, and some local girls were in attendance. There had been no

Quintet rehearsal, and as yet no consideration of what they might play. As Max Roach remembers it, the running order dictated itself once the players were on the stage.

However, there *was* an element of calculation and forward planning. A borrowed state-of-the-art Ampex machine had been installed in the Massey Hall sound booth, loaded with professional tape and connected to the hall's public address system. According to Alan Scharf, the New Jazz Society paid $100 to an engineer from the Canadian Broadcasting Corporation to take care of the recording.[5]

As the Quintet members took up their platform positions, Gillespie was heard to exclaim, 'Oh, *baby*,' presumably referring to the fun to come in this lofty acoustic cavern, where a proportion of the music generated reaches the audience directly and the rest ascends to the barrel-vaulted ceiling then bounces back. To get their bearings Gillespie and Parker set aside the modernistic showpieces in their repertoire and opened with 'Perdido'. Composed for the Ellington band by Mingus's old enemy Juan Tizol, this catchy number harps on a simple three-note phrase. Tonight the theme statement ends with an extempore flurry from Gillespie – a chivalrous gesture ushering Parker forward to take the first solo.

Action shots taken by local photographers Harold Robinson and Alan Scharf prove that Parker was playing the white plastic alto, but as always his intensely personal tone transcends the material means. He plays three shapely choruses, utterly relaxed and beautiful, with no hint of the competitive edge that marked his tussle with Gillespie at Carnegie Hall back in 1947. Indeed, his first chorus ends with an ingenious melodic twist, causing Gillespie to chortle. Midway through his second he turns preacher, giving out a wailing message to which Gillespie responds with a shout. During his final chorus the poetic intensity is mounting, but here Gillespie evidently decides to titillate the audience with some extra-musical antics. The response is led by a lady with a dirty laugh. Parker proudly ignores the vulgarity. For those with ears to hear he executes a double-time passage of crystalline brilliance before bowing out with a plangent, infectious phrase that Gillespie's trumpet takes up immediately. Applause.

Having toyed with Parker's valedictory flourish, Gillespie caps it with a quote from 'Laura', David Raksin's lush film theme, famously recorded by Parker with Strings. While the audience is guffawing, Gillespie hits his stride, swinging intensely and asserting his huge musical personality. To start the second chorus the trumpet rips savagely upwards to a strangulated, sustained half-valve trill. When at last it explodes free, the effect is like champagne bursting from a bottle. The third chorus gets down to rhythm-and-blues basics, endorsed by Roach with a socking back beat. At the end of the chorus Gillespie quotes from his bluesy composition 'Birks Works', recorded for his Dee Gee label two years earlier. This citation rings no bells with the folk in Toronto. Undaunted, Gillespie sails into a fourth chorus – one more than Parker – and proceeds smoothly and soberly until the last eight bars. Here he delivers a grandstand finish, shaking and worrying a single medium-high note, aiming at those accustomed to the circus excitements of Jazz at the Philharmonic. Their prolonged applause smothers the start of Powell's piano solo.

When the Quintet made its entrance, Powell had been escorted to his place on the stage by Oscar Goodstein, giving rise to the persistent legend that the pianist was drunk and incapable that night, a legend that ignores the quality of his music. The closely-positioned piano microphone allows us to appreciate the vigour and precision of his attentive comping during the solos by Parker and Gillespie. And when his turn comes, his solo on 'Perdido' is a match for theirs: sweetly lyrical, swinging and technically commanding.

In the background during Powell's solo the voices of Gillespie and Parker can be heard, presumably planning how the piece shall end. The out-chorus they decide upon comes as a surprise. Instead of 'Wahoo' (the chromatic variant on the 'Perdido' dear to the beboppers), they strike up the swing-style counter-melody that was recorded by the Ellington band. (The Cootie Williams Orchestra used this same riff, by the way, in 1945, when Parker was briefly a member.) Roach's resplendent drums occupy the middle eight, then Tizol's tune at last emerges, with Gillespie soaring high above Parker to supply a good old-fashioned barnstorming ending.

Having warmed the hall with nostalgic delight, the Quintet turns to a key item in its modernist repertoire. Charlie Parker makes the announcement:

> At this time we would like to play a n-tune that was composed by my worthy constituent Mr Dizzy Gillespie in the year of 1942. We sincerely hope that you do enjoy – 'Salt Peanuts'.

Parker may have said more, but these are the only words preserved on the awkwardly edited tape. The little speech has been seized upon by those promoting the notion that Parker and Gillespie were at daggers drawn. According to their theory, 'my worthy constituent' is an obscure term of abuse, hurled by Parker because he was angered by Gillespie's distracting stage antics. But you need not listen to his announcement very hard to realize that something more light-hearted is going on. Finding himself in a wonderland where the distant Queen of England requires to be saluted, Parker has reached for his notorious British accent. He retracts the word 'number' before it is out of his mouth, replacing it with the more genteel 'tune'. And his juxtaposition of the highfalutin 'worthy constituent' and the earthy 'salt peanuts' comes with a smile and satirical intent.

The date he assigns to the composition is impressively accurate: 1942 was when Gillespie hatched the essence of the piece and gave it a first outing as part of the Lucky Millinder recording of 'Little John Special'. The Earl Hines orchestra used to play a version of it, and then the small group edition was honed by the Gillespie Quintet at the Onyx club. By the time Parker and Gillespie recorded it together, in May 1945, 'Salt Peanuts' had found its final form: racy and virtuosic. In December it went to California with them. After they split up, Gillespie arranged it for his big band and Parker played it with his various quintets – singing the hiccuping punch lines himself.

Max Roach is a 'Salt Peanuts' veteran. He played it with Gillespie at the Onyx and with Parker at the Royal Roost and in Paris. Tonight's drum introduction is yet another variant upon the dozens he has served up to give the piece a kick-start. After hushing the hall with a cymbal flurry, he foretells the octave leaps of the coming tune by alternating between his bass drum and his snare.

The opening salvoes scorch past: 8-bar introduction, toying with the 'leaping' motif; 32-bar theme, played by Gillespie and Parker in unison; then the showpiece chorus of instrumental calls and sung responses. Here the first eight bars follow established routine, with steady exhortations from Parker's soulful alto, met by Gillespie's squeaky pairs of replies, 'Salt Peanuts! Salt Peanuts!' But at the end of the second eight Gillespie swaps his regular answer for a protracted labial explosion: 'Salt – Peeeeanuts!!' While the audience screams, Parker improvises a whirling dervish of a middle eight and Powell spins a skein of counter-melody. During the last eight bars Gillespie finds room for a very quick joke, a preposterously redundant announcement – 'The name of this song' – squeezed in before his final set of repetitious namings.

When Parker starts his solo with sly references to the hiccuping catch-phrase, Gillespie feels bound to respond, and there follows a passage of sensational interaction. While Parker's alto makes the running, Gillespie bellows 'Salt Peanuts!' over and over with increasing savagery as he retreats into the vast hollows of the Massey Hall stage. Then he lies low until the end of Parker's meaty first chorus, whereupon he lets out a final carnivorous roar.

Parker continues for two more choruses, utterly composed and fiercely intense. To signal that the end is nigh, he pre-echoes a fragment from the ensemble passage always used in 'Salt Peanuts' to launch the trumpet solo. Gillespie picks up his cue, and the two of them skim through the traditional 8-bar link.

Gillespie's three-chorus solo is one of his best ever, an awesome demonstration of power, speed, swing and drama. To give advance warning that it is coming to a close, he quotes from the cascading ensemble passage that always ushers in the 'Salt Peanuts' piano solo. Parker joins him at the microphone for this tricky bridge, and then Powell takes off.

The solo that follows is as good as any heard all night, and withstands comparison with Powell's very best work. Gone is the desperation of the 'Salt Peanuts' he played with his trio in Washington just six weeks ago. Instead, his long, graceful phrases flow as freely as a mountain stream.

Max Roach's playing behind the solos of Parker, Gillespie and Powell has been a miracle of empathy. Now the spotlight is on him for four choruses, during which he applies his fastidious perfectionism to some traditional showmanship. His bass drum pounds steadily, four to the bar, his hi-hat ticks the off-beats, while his sticks expose the sharply different tone colours of snare drum and tom-toms in this grand acoustic. At the solo's midpoint the onslaught on the drums is magically hushed by a single cymbal splash. Then the violence is redoubled, egged on by Gillespie with a wild yell that sounds like 'Chaaarge!'

The drum solo leads to a reprise by the ensemble of the 'Salt Peanuts' opening, which doubles as its coda, and is capped by a lusty final unison shout of 'Salt Peanuts! Salt Peanuts!' When all is accomplished, Gillespie's quiet laughter seems to say, 'What about *that* for no rehearsal!'

Next the Quintet plays Jerome Kern's romantic and harmonically rich ballad 'All the Things You Are', a satisfying choice for the historically minded, because Gillespie and Parker recorded it together in 1945 – the same year they delivered their 'Salt Peanuts'. Back then they introduced the Kern song with a catchy device of Gillespie's – a solemn carillon which proved so effective that jazzmen have been applying it to 'All the Things' ever since. Unsurprisingly, it sets the ball rolling here at Massey Hall. A pity, though, that the first five of its eight bars are missing from the recording.

The first sixteen bars of the theme are declaimed by Gillespie's open trumpet. Parker takes over for the middle eight, and here Roach sets up an Afro-Latin rhythm behind him – as he did on the Parker Quintet's exemplary 1947 recording. (Parker loved 'All the Things You Are', which he referred to fondly as 'Yatag', an acronym formed from the words with which the middle eight begins. 'You are the angel glow . . .')

Gillespie returns to play the last section of the theme, and then Parker takes the first solo, as we have come to expect. Entirely unexpected – astonishing even – is the background activity of Bud Powell.

Jerome Kern's exceptionally elaborate composition rarely looks in on its home key of A flat. By the end of the middle eight it has roamed as far as E. The way back turns on the enharmonic modulation G sharp–A flat, using an augmented triad suggesting the whole-tone scale. Tonight at Massey Hall, Powell chooses to pay tribute to Kern's harmonic treasure house and to enrich it with chordal substitutions of his own. During the opening theme statement and on through the solos of Parker and Gillespie, he eschews the mundane duties of jazz accompanist and creates instead a misty, impressionistic backdrop, often woven from as many as four chords per bar. Kern's harmonic contour is never disregarded, and Powell is clearly listening intently to the soloists because his musical offering constantly shimmers in the light of theirs. There is no precedent in his own work for this bold and challenging style of accompaniment, but it is similar in spirit to the provocative comping of his mentor Thelonious Monk.

For years scholars have been vexed by Powell's behaviour during 'All the Things You Are'. Two theories have been put forward to explain it. According to the first, Powell was furious because the horn men chatted during his solos on 'Perdido' and 'Salt Peanuts', thus he took revenge by sabotaging their next excursions. The snag with this theory is that Parker and Gillespie thrive on Powell's rich chordal feed.

The alternative could be called the sinister conspiracy theory. It argues that the pianist on the Kern ballad is not Bud Powell, but someone else. And it goes further, claiming that 'All the Things You Are' was recorded not at Massey Hall but back in New York, where Canadian applause and atmosphere were deceitfully added. This contention gained ground in the months and years following the concert, and was published as fact on the sleeve of the UK edition of the *Quintet of the Year* LP, which names Billy Taylor as the pianist and warns record-buyers to listen out for his inferior contribution. We shall see how this story started when we come to the post-production work done on the tapes. It is sufficient for now to confirm that it is untrue.

Parker and Gillespie both play solos lasting for two choruses. Parker, relaxed and witty, incorporates a deranged quotation from 'The Kerry Dance'. Gillespie places a mute in the bell of his trumpet and shows how to infuse quietness with heat.

When it's Powell's turn to solo, he ditches radicalism and reverts to his familiar best – spinning long melodic lines with his right hand and adding punctuation with his left. After just one chorus he withdraws to the role of accompanist for Mingus.

While Mingus extemporizes, Parker and Gillespie stealthily join in, breathing background figures that by the end of the chorus have merged with the chiming phrase which doubles as introduction and coda. Beyond that, Gillespie embarks on a grand cadenza, but Parker cuts across him, belting out Thelonious Monk's hectic '52nd Street Theme'. In the clubs on the eponymous street this theme was the signal for an intermission. Gillespie, Powell and Roach get the message and join Parker's sprint through the exhilarating set-closer.

*

After barely twenty-five minutes of music, the Quintet has left the stage – conveniently for the boxing fans among the Massey Hall crowd. If they hurry across the street to the Silver Rail, which has a TV set, they will catch the 10.00 p.m. start of the title fight between Rocky Marciano and Jersey Joe Walcott. Pity the poor stragglers, though, because it's all over in just 2 minutes and 25 seconds. Result: victory by a knockout for Marciano.

Gillespie – a vigorous supporter of Jersey Joe – takes the African-American boxer's downfall personally. And his mood does not improve when Mingus calls a dressing-room conference to announce his dissatisfaction with the way the concert is going. A proven leader, Gillespie has naturally assumed charge this evening. What's the problem?

As Max Roach remembers it, Mingus's grievance was that the other four musicians had been slipping into practised routines, established over years of working together in the clubs of New York. As a newcomer from the West Coast, he felt disadvantaged.

On top of that, he may have felt meanly provided with solo space (just one chorus so far). But his chief worry (unsuspected by Gillespie) would have concerned the tape-recording and the judgement of posterity.

*

When the music finally resumes, after a break of forty-five minutes, it does so dramatically. Instead of five performers returning to the Massey Hall stage, only Max Roach appears. He seats himself carefully and raises his sticks in a ritual gesture, and it dawns on the hushed audience that a drum exhibition is about to be served. 'Go, Max!' calls a thrilled voice from up in the gods.

The solo that follows is comparable in its design to the 'Drum Conversation' Roach recorded for Debut one month ago. Both begin and end pianissimo, and they follow similar contours, linking peaks of tension to quiet moments of release. But the live performance, as you would expect, is more expansive and more flamboyant, with broader gestures to suit the huge, excited ambience. It lasts four minutes, and when it tiptoes to a conclusion the audience response is rapturous.

A further burst of applause greets Mingus's return to the stage, and a huge cheer goes up when Oscar Goodstein again leads Powell to the piano. We are about to enjoy a set by the Bud Powell Trio, with its current bass-player and the most illustrious of its past drummers.

The introduction and the first chunk of 'Cherokee' are missing (probably because of unreadiness in the sound booth), and the piano sound is remote – far more distant than the bass or drums – presumably because the piano microphone has yet to be reactivated after Max Roach's solo.

In spite of the poor technical quality, it is worth comparing this night's performance with the masterpiece recording of 'Cherokee' made by Powell back in 1949. The tempo is similarly breakneck, Roach's brushes again provide supple support, and the way of presenting the tune has not changed – one chord for every beat, 300 beats to the minute. The difference is in the emotional quality of the improvised choruses. In 1949 the tone was attacking, furious, passionate; now it is withdrawn, quietly scintillating from sorrowful depths.

After the recapitulation, Powell attempts the keyboard 'war dance' he invented years ago to frame this tune, but the percussive acrobatics sound alien to his present mood.

The remainder of the trio's programme is drawn from material Powell had been performing regularly since his February discharge from Creedmoor. 'I've Got You Under My Skin' (often broadcast from the Royal Roost) is a faithful, near-literal presentation of Cole Porter's lengthy melody above an Afro-Latin beat. 'Embraceable You' is recited in dense block chords of extreme solemnity, with post-Creedmoor Powell at his darkest and most introspective, conveying a special desolation. Mingus later claimed that kids in the audience were crying during this performance, and so was he.

After such despondence, Vincent Youmans's 'Hallelujah!' feels like the silver lining: always bright and sometimes lovely over six improvised choruses. The contrapuntal arrangement of Jerome Kern's 'Sure Thing' springs from Powell's and Mingus's shared love of the European tradition. Like 'I've Got You Under My Skin', it's a fixed presentation, but this time paying homage to the world of the baroque, with Mingus's agile bass-line often doubling Powell's busy left hand.

Since his release from Creedmoor into Oscar Goodstein's care, Powell had been using 'Lullaby of Birdland' as his sign-off music. On this recording the whole of the opening theme statement is missing and we are plunged deep into his flowing improvisation. Perhaps the Massey Hall sound booth was confounded because Powell played the Shearing as an encore.

*

Parker and Gillespie have been absent for more than an hour, and lurid gossip is spreading about how they have been spending their time.

Their extramural activities have certainly not dulled their musical appetites, because the pair restart their performance with gusto, ramming into an up-tempo bebop variant on the 'I Got Rhythm' chord pattern. On the original Debut LP and all the re-issues, this variant is entitled 'Wee', with the composer credit going to Denzil Best. Sometimes there is a footnote to say the number is also known as 'Allen's Alley' and credited to Allen Eager. Buried until 1990, when the archive of recordings by Dean Benedetti came to light, was the fact that in March 1947 Charlie Parker was playing this tune nightly at the Hi-De-Ho club in Los Angeles. He called it 'Big Noise', and it was presumed to be a Parker original.

If 'Big Noise' is indeed by Parker, then it is the only one of his compositions played at Massey Hall. Perhaps it was chosen because it is less complex and elusive than most of his writing, and so more appropriate to the ad-lib nature of the occasion. In any case, his high-speed improvisation upon it (or rather upon its 'I Got Rhythm' chordal foundation) is overwhelmingly eloquent.

Having endorsed Parker's magnificent outburst with approving shouts, Gillespie can't quite produce a solo of his own to match it. For all its animation and fierce swing, his improvisation here is less substantial than his other work this evening. Bud Powell, still on song after the set with his trio, relishes the blistering pace and plays a solo that never falters. Max Roach adds three imperious choruses, all throaty tom-toms and sibilant snare, before Parker and Gillespie bring this theme of doubtful provenance to an emphatic close.

Primitive tape-editing kills the lively applause and strips Gillespie's announcement to its bare essence: 'Thank you. And now we'd like to play "Hot House".'

Gillespie and Parker first recorded 'Hot House' together back in May 1945 (at the same session that produced 'Salt Peanuts'). Since then, Tadd Dameron's quirky and beautiful line, slithering over the chords of Cole Porter's 'What Is This Thing Called Love?', has enjoyed favoured status in both their repertoires. Their most recent joint performance of it, just over a year ago, was a cramped affair for an awards ceremony on TV in New York City.

Although Roach's introduction sets an easy pace, the unison statement of the theme by the horns is less than perfect. Gillespie is much closer to the microphone than Parker, so the little blemishes in his articulation are cruelly exposed. Had he known he was being recorded he would have applied more polish.

Parker's remoteness from the microphone gives the start of his improvisation a curious and misleading air of detachment. Like Gillespie, he is unaware that a tape is running, and feels no need to follow the rules of recording. Enjoying the freedom of 'live' performance, he moves about the stage at will, easily capable of filling this huge auditorium without electronic assistance. Towards the end of his second chorus, oblivious to the startling effect this will have on the recorded sound, he bears down on the microphone and almost touches it for a moment with the bell of his sax. The third chorus is delivered from optimum range. Behind these random distractions lies a solo packed with musical incident. Labyrinthine double-time passages are offset with soulful simplicities. A snatch of the 'Habañera' from Bizet's *Carmen* lends an air of insouciance.

Gillespie's three choruses come close to architectural perfection. Beginning as a prolonged, tantalizing echo of Tadd Dameron's twisty line, his solo evolves into a soaring edifice, all space and light, where the kingly trumpet roams at will. At one peak moment it hails the spirit of Charlie Parker: quoting Parker's extract from *Carmen* and then repeating it an octave higher.

Bud Powell's relaxed and confident solo – sometimes proudly resplendent, sometimes gently lyrical – matches the grace of what has gone before. When he closes, the horns begin the 'Hot House' recapitulation. Halfway through they step aside to allow Mingus a solo, which fills the rest of the chorus, the whole of the next, and the start of a third. But this time, at the mid-point, Parker and Gillespie insinuate a curly, Dameronesque figure, before taking charge and declaiming the theme's final eight bars.

For the benefit of any French-Canadians in the audience, Gillespie brings a bilingual touch to his announcement of the concert's climax: 'And now we would like to play "Ce Soir en Tunis" – "A Night in Tunisia".'

'A Night in Tunisia' (formerly known as 'Interlude') has been a running theme of this book: one of Gillespie's finest compositions; the first 'bebop' record; platform for some of Parker's most inspired improvisations; and beneficiary of a classic interpretation by Bud

Powell with Max Roach. Tonight's combined effort is among the most exciting performances in the history of African-American music.

During the long, involved exposition the serpentine bass line is casually doubled by Parker's low-register alto, as well as embellished by Roach's metallic filigree. When Gillespie's muted trumpet enters with the quasi-oriental main theme, Parker adds the usual countermelody plus some fancy ornamental braid. The middle eight shifts to 4/4 time and has a straightforward melody based on familiar harmonies. Here Parker takes the lead. He plays the melody as composed for four bars, then cuts loose and fills the other four with a fantastic double-time invention.

Appended to the theme is a thrusting interlude that finds relief at last in Parker's climactic four-bar break. The first edition of this alto break (recorded in a Los Angeles studio in 1946) astounded the jazz world with its unremitting brilliance: sixty semiquavers in five seconds. Here in reverberant Massey Hall the outburst is just as exciting, but the pace of the note-flow is more varied and relaxed, leaving the acoustic to do some of the work. And the solo that follows sustains the laid-back mood, sometimes lingering to savour the effect of a phrase in the lively air. This is a sweet and carefree invention, sometimes in double-time, sometimes in measured and soulful accents that make Gillespie shout for joy.

Gillespie's own solo displays all the virtues: searing tone, maximum swing and a grand sweep of dramatic ideas. Indeed, the architecture of its three choruses is immaculate – from the ingenious opening which toys with Parker's closing phrase, to the final subdued cadence that graciously cedes the stage to Bud Powell.

Buoyed up as ever by Mingus and Roach, Powell plays another of his effervescent improvisations, sometimes flirting with the main 'Tunisia' melody, sometimes exploding in new directions. Towards the end of the third piano chorus Max Roach (who has served as trusty helmsman all night long) unfurls the drum roll that cues Parker and Gillespie to proclaim the closing strains of 'Tunisia'. These merge into Gillespie's valedictory trumpet cadenza, supported loyally by his colleagues until the very end, when Powell breaks ranks and throws in two enigmatic chords. Ecstatic applause completes the recording.

*

And still the concert was not over. The band of local musicians reassembled and played three more numbers.

Meanwhile, backstage another row had broken out, with Mingus complaining to Gillespie that he had been starved of bass solos.

In spite of the friction, Parker, Gillespie, Mingus and Roach (but not Bud Powell) came back on stage and joined the Canadian band for a jam session finale. The extraordinary get together was captured in photographs, but not, unfortunately, on tape. What did they play? No one remembers for sure. Some think it was a blues.

Twenty minutes after the last notes had died away, Parker was spotted standing in the empty auditorium. He was sweat-stained but relaxed, smoking a cigarette. He agreed to have his photo taken by Alan Scharf, and asked if there was anywhere else in Toronto where he might sit in and play that night. The answer evidently was no, and shortly thereafter he was called to a meeting in the Massey Hall basement where the New Jazz Society president Dick Wattam had a grave announcement to make. Quite simply, the box office receipts, after the deduction of expenses, were insufficient to pay the Quintet members the cash they were owed. Parker protested that his responsibilities to his wife and children made payment vital.

Hoping to calm the situation, Wattam made it generally known for the first time that the concert had been recorded. He urged the musicians not to worry about money, because the tapes must be worth thousands. Parker again objected, pointing out that he had signed an exclusive recording contract with Norman Granz. The reaction of Gillespie, whose own record company had just collapsed, can be imagined.

Wattam's offer to pay everyone by doubtful cheque was universally unpopular, although Roach does not blame him for the financial fallout; he remembers Wattam as a sincere music lover who did his best.

*

Ere long the tapes were under Mingus's arm. A friendly enquiry about them from New Jazz Society member Roger Feather provoked the aggressive response, 'They're *mine*, white boy.'[6] And now he wanted to hear them. At around 3.00 a.m. Dick Wattam guided him on the short walk to the local radio station, where they found facilities for a playback. What they heard was condemned by Mingus as an outrage. After all he had done to make sure the concert was properly recorded, he was now listening to tapes where his bass was barely audible! Wattam took him seriously when he shouted that the whole lot must be destroyed. One thing was certain: Mingus's grip on the tapes had become absolute. And he rejected Wattam's cheque, saying he would only accept cash, and if it was not forthcoming he would sell his double-bass. This would mean the New Jazz Society would forfeit the bond they had been required by law to lodge with Canadian customs. Society member Boyd Raeburn (no relation to the American bandleader) paid Mingus from personal funds.

*

British jazz fan Brian Dale was a single-minded young man. To fund his sea passage from England to the New World he had sold his large collection of rare records, all except his precious set of bootleg acetates of Charlie Parker's broadcasts from the Royal Roost. These he had brought with him, and when he managed to speak to Parker before the concert, he told the great man about them. Would Parker like to see them? Yes, he would, and he invited Dale to bring them to his hotel on the morning after the performance.

I interviewed Brian Dale in September 2000. This is what he told me about his noon meeting with Charlie Parker at the Royal York Hotel, Toronto, on Saturday 16 May 1953. Entering Parker's room nervously, with the acetates under his arm, he found his hero sitting up in bed drinking Scotch, with a jazz-loving local girl called Cookie at his side. Savouring Dale's accent, Parker listened as the young Englishman described the reverence in which his music was held in London and the Holy Grail-status the bootleg recordings had achieved. When Dale asked him to autograph them he said he would be happy to oblige, but gave the impression that he was distinctly *un*happy that this illicit material (for which he had been paid nothing) was in circulation around the world. At this moment Dave Usher entered the room. Usher – Dizzy Gillespie's partner in the doomed Dee Gee record company – had travelled up to Toronto to enjoy the Massey Hall concert. Parker suggested that Dale should loan Usher the acetates for the purpose of quality evaluation. How could he refuse? He never saw the records again.

He was then invited to accompany Parker and Cookie on a final piece of Toronto business. Parker was holding a cheque from Dick Wattam he was sure would bounce, and he was keen to find someone to cash it before he left the city. First they tried the candidates in the hotel lobby: the florist, the airline office, the front desk. No joy. Then they worked their way up Yonge Street, dropping into all the bars (Dale found himself buying a double shot of whisky for Parker in each one). But nobody would touch the cheque. At Cookie's suggestion they ended up at a record store called Premier Radio, owned by a Parker devotee who had sold tickets for the concert. This friendly retailer agreed to cash the dubious item, provided Parker would autograph all the many Parker records the store contained. Parker signed the lot, got his money and said goodbye to Brian Dale. The store owner subsequently framed the cheque and hung it over his counter.

*

On 25 May, ten days after Massey Hall, Parker, Mingus and Roach found themselves together in a New York recording studio. The occasion was an experimental session in which Parker's alto was complemented with woodwinds and voices. Mingus and Roach had been booked to provide underpinning. In charge was Norman Granz, who lost patience when the unusual elements failed to blend and shut down the session prematurely. The less than convivial atmosphere did not deter Parker, Mingus and Roach from making Granz a proposition. They talked up the Massey Hall concert and offered to sell him the recording for $100,000. Granz asked if he might borrow the tapes and study them properly. Mingus, whose suspicions were easily aroused, said no.

*

In the autumn of 1953 the Debut record company began releasing its Massey Hall treasures. First to appear was a 10-inch LP containing 'Perdido', 'Salt Peanuts' and 'All the Things You Are'. According to the sleeve, the saxophone player was Charlie Chan. This transparent disguise (a play on Parker's wife's name and that of the B-movie character) could have fooled no one – least of all Norman Granz, whose exclusive contract with Parker was being circumvented. But Granz elected to turn a blind eye.

Jazz at Massey Hall, Volume 2, another 10-inch LP, contained the set played by the Bud Powell Trio, with one omission and one addition. Missing was 'I've Got You Under My Skin'. In its place we find 'Bass-ically Speaking', a long, healthily recorded bass solo by Mingus with a pallid accompaniment.

Although no such admission comes with the record, 'Bass-ically Speaking' (a D minor sequence similar to 'Weird Nightmare') was recorded in a studio in New York. The pianist was not Bud Powell but Billy Taylor, and applause was added to create a make-believe Massey Hall. Once news of this subterfuge leaked out, rumours started. One of these claimed (imaginatively but mistakenly) that the Quintet's performance of 'All the Things You Are' was another New York studio confection, and blamed Billy Taylor for the eccentric piano accompaniment.

The missing 'I've Got You Under My Skin' turned up on a Debut compilation LP called *Autobiography in Jazz*, where it was joined by Max Roach's Massey Hall drum solo.

Jazz at Massey Hall, Volume 3 (again a 10-inch LP) was released early in 1954. It contained the remaining items performed by the Quintet: 'Wee' (or 'Big Noise'), 'Hot House' and 'A Night in Tunisia'. Here again we are not given a straightforward concert record, although the interference is less drastic than the 'Bass-ically Speaking' substitution. What we have is an early example of the technique of overdubbing. Still vexed by the feeble reproduction of his playing at Massey Hall, Mingus added a second bass line to all three tracks. The only passage he allowed to stand unassisted was his solo on 'Hot House'.

He must have been pleased with the results, because by the time the contents of *Volume 1* were reissued, they had been likewise bass-reinforced.

And this time, on 'All the Things You Are', he went a step further. He added a new solo to the one he had played at the concert, thereby creating an eerie duet between his booming New York present and his faint, almost vanished Canadian past.

This reissue (which came out in June 1956) brought all the Quintet material together on one 12-inch LP. When Celia Mingus was preparing the packaging, she wrote to Norman Granz begging permission to drop the pretence and use Charlie Parker's real name. The reply came from Granz's lawyers: an absolute no. So the flimsy fiction of an alto saxophonist called Charlie Chan had to be maintained.

*

The complete set of Mingus overdubs has been the source of the worldwide stream of re-issues (including *Quintet of the Year* in the UK, which was where I came in).

The Bud Powell Trio recordings have been repackaged several times. For one edition 'Bass-ically Speaking' was dropped and 'I've Got You Under My Skin' was restored. For another the Trio tracks were bundled together with the Quintet material under the defensible heading *The Greatest Jazz Concert Ever*.

In 1990 Fantasy Records (who had long since taken over the Debut catalogue) produced *Charles Mingus: the Complete Debut Recordings*. Research for this exhaustive 12-CD box set uncovered material that had lain in the vault for the best part of forty years. Most interestingly for us, they found the original, undoctored Massey Hall recordings and included them alongside the versions revised by Mingus. We can hear that during the copying process, when the second bass part was added, the sound quality of the other instruments was somewhat diminished. We are also offered, patched together from tape bits and pieces, the first twenty-four bars of 'Perdido', hitherto presumed lost.

One of a series of small advertisements placed in the Toronto newspapers. 'There were no posters. Marketing was something we knew nothing about,' says Alan Scharf. (Courtesy of Ron Fritts)

Jazz Festival

DIZZY GILLESPIE • CHARLIE PARKER
BUD POWELL • MAX ROACH
• CHARLES MINGUS

Plus

CBC All-Stars • 17-Piece Orch. led by Graham Topping

MASSEY HALL—TOMORROW—8.30 P.M.

Tickets NOW at all agencies and Premier Radio

A meeting of the concert planning team. New Jazz Society president Dick Wattam is in the armchair. On his left is Roger Feather. (Photo by Alan Scharf)

LEFT: Before the event, Max Roach entertains on Charles Mingus's bass. 'You can't work with Oscar Pettiford and not pic[k] up a little something,' he says.

(Courtesy of Tony Williams, Spotlite Record[s])

RIGHT: Bud Powell.

(Courtesy of Tony Williams, Spotlite Records)

LEFT: Roach and Powell listen to the local band rehearsing.

(Courtesy of Tony Williams, Spotlite Record[s])

The Quintet takes charge of the stage. (Alan Scharf)

LEFT: The front rows at the start of the evening. The four suited black men sitting together in row 8 may be members of the Lionel Hampton Orchestra (in town to play at the Colonial Tavern, just around the corner). (Alan Scharf)

Max Roach alone opens the second half of the concert. (Alan Scharf)

A set by the Bud Powell Trio. (Alan Scharf)

Dizzy Gillespie and Charlie Parker rejoin the action.

(Alan Scharf)

The Quintet (minus Powell) joins the Toronto big band for the finale. (Alan Scharf)

RIGHT: Society members after the performance and before the reckoning. Roger Feather front right. Boyd Raeburn in rear. (Alan Scharf)

Charlie Parker in the hall after the gig. (Alan Scharf)

SEVEN

NOW'S THE TIME

'The Bird of Time has but a little way
To flutter – and the Bird is on the Wing.'
The Rubáiyát of Omar Khayyám.

WHEN CHARLIE PARKER returned to New York from Toronto in May 1953 he was thirty-two years old and had less than two years to live. Only a pittance of sublime music was to come before its creator surrendered to illness and calamity.

And yet the spring and summer of 1953 were golden months artistically. For the last week of May and the first week of June he played at Birdland, supported by the Bud Powell Trio (with Charles Mingus and Arthur Taylor). Recordings made from broadcasts during that fortnight caught Parker and Powell in fine fettle, improvising on such memorable compositions as Parker's 'Moose the Mooche' and 'Cheryl'. For Powell's 'Dance of the Infidels', Max Roach replaces Arthur Taylor in the drum chair, so four of the Massey Hall five are reunited.

Playing opposite Parker at Birdland was Dizzy Gillespie with his regular quintet. Evidently Parker enjoyed sitting in with them, and one such upbeat occasion was broadcast and recorded. 'The Bluest Blues', usually a vehicle for Gillespie's vocalist Joe Carroll, here becomes something of greater significance, being the last recording ever to be blessed with solos from both Gillespie and Parker. Gillespie's playing is characteristically heated, while Parker's is magnificently bluesy.

During the same busy fortnight, Parker made some recordings for Norman Granz in an elaborate setting. The idea had been Parker's. In a magazine interview back in January, he had defended his recordings with strings and announced a new ambition. 'I'd like to do a session with five or six woodwinds, a harp, a choral group, and a full rhythm section. Something on the line of Hindemith's *Kleine Kammermusik*.'[1]

The team Granz assembled in the studio on 25 May 1953 came close to meeting the Parker prescription. There was no harp, but the wind quintet (flute, clarinet, oboe, bassoon and French horn) was exactly the *Kleine Kammermusik* combination. The Dave Lambert Singers were the chorus, Charles Mingus and Max Roach the powerful engine. The problem lay in the imbalance between the restrained woodwind parts (scored by Gil Evans) and the megaphonic schmaltz delivered by Dave Lambert's choir. Much of the session was spent trying to reconcile these elements, and by the time Granz gave up and pulled the plug, only three numbers had been recorded: 'Old Folks', 'In the Still of the Night' and 'If I Love Again'. Parker's playing throughout is sublime. The syrupy 'Old Folks' is transformed into a blues by the wand of his genius, and during the two up-tempo numbers he soars above the muddle and seems to be chuckling to himself.

When Gil Evans and Dave Lambert heard the test pressings they offered to do the session again for nothing. Norman Granz declined their offer.

Parker spent the second week of June in Boston, playing at the Hi Hat Club as celebrity guest with local musicians. While he was in town he was interviewed at length on radio station WHDH. The host, John McLellan, repeatedly invited him to criticize musical styles that diverged from his own, but Parker sweetly refused to play that game. He urged McLellan to discover the virtues in Dixieland, Swing, Stan Kenton and Lennie Tristano, and named Béla Bartók as his favourite composer.

The Sunday night session at the Hi Hat Club on 14 June was broadcast by radio station WCOP, and a recording of that broadcast has been preserved. Parker politely indulges the inane banter of MC 'Symphony' Sid Torin, but his mind seems to be elsewhere. He praises the local musicians who have been allocated to support him, but when he calls them forward to take a bow, he can't remember their names. The tunes he chooses are all well worn – 'Cool Blues', 'Scrapple from the Apple', 'Laura', 'Cheryl', 'Ornithology' – and although his performance shines, the brilliance is practised rather than inspired.

*

Back in New York at the end of July, inspiration returned when he made his last great set of studio recordings. Supporting him were pianist Al Haig, bassist Percy Heath (a student of Charles Mingus) and Max Roach, his ideal drummer. They recorded one standard, plus three compositions by Parker: 'Now's the Time', 'Confirmation' and 'Chi Chi'. The last of these, an elegant blues, had been dashed off as a present for Max Roach just a few months earlier – the night before Roach's first record session as leader. Roach had gratefully recorded it, with Hank Mobley taking the saxophone part. Now Parker was ready to record it himself. He had asked Roach to bring the manuscript to the studio, but although Max hunted desperately, he was unable to find it. Never mind. There is no trumpet player to consider here, so Parker can busk it. Checking his performance against the Roach/Mobley version is revealing. First of all, Parker chooses to play 'Chi Chi' in A flat, up a fourth from the key in which he wrote it. Secondly, he picks a brighter tempo – not especially fast but well ahead of the Roach/Mobley funky walk. After Al Haig's crisp introduction, he states the intricate theme twice, then improvises six cleaver-sharp choruses, with Haig, Heath and Roach enhancing the stupendous sense of lift. During the reprise there is the slightest of reed-squeaks, so he decides to go again. Three more takes, all of them radiant and passionate, are needed before he is satisfied.

'Confirmation' is one of Parker's finest compositions, so it is surprising that this session produced his first and only studio recording of it. The harmonies are laid out in AABA song form, but the glorious melody never exactly repeats itself, and its sophistication is tempered with a powerful blues feeling. Having unfurled this ravishing theme of his, Parker makes it the basis of a sublime improvisation, exquisite in its Mozartean logic.

'Now's the Time', Parker's riffing 12-bar blues in F, was famously recorded at his first session as leader back in 1945. This 1953 version is taken much faster. With no front-line partner to share the solo space, Parker delivers an eloquent and moving testament, spread over five blues choruses, representing the summit of African-American art.

According to Max Roach, when the supposedly apolitical Parker named this piece 'Now's the Time', he was making a cryptic political statement. Decoded, the message reads 'now is the time for black Americans to claim their rightful inheritance'. But Parker would not live to see this slogan translated into the Civil Rights movement.

*

During the summer of 1953 Parker thrilled the rookie promoter Robert Reisner by agreeing to take part in the Sunday jam sessions this young man was running at his new club, the Open Door, in Greenwich Village. For a percentage of the takings Parker appeared regularly at the Open Door during the last eighteen months of his life. Here Mingus often played with him, and sometimes Bud Powell, too. A well-known photograph taken at the club shows Parker in a white suit, jamming with Mingus, Monk and Roy Haynes. Behind the musicians a bold mural depicts a pair of naked, voluptuous nymphs. When the august *Grove Dictionary of Music and Musicians* admitted an entry on jazz to its pages, this Open Door photograph was its surprise choice of illustration. Less surprisingly, the folk at Grove employed a retouch artist to make the naughty mural disappear.

Also on Parker's work schedule were regular return visits to Boston, where he would perform either at the Hi Hat Club or at the Storyville. For his engagement at the Storyville during the last week in September, he took drummer Kenny Clarke along to stiffen the local supporting cast. As usual, Boston received him warmly, although we can hear from a recorded broadcast that he was playing below his best.

NOW'S THE TIME   155

But his return visit to Montreal (after his February triumph here on TV) was a different story and a shocking experience. He had been booked by the club The Latin Quarter for seven days, starting on Monday 12 October. But after just three days the management fired him on the grounds of unacceptable behaviour. Parker appealed to the American Federation of Musicians, who had a Montreal branch, for the money due to his sidemen and himself for the whole of the contract.

The unpleasantness dragged on. The boss of the Latin Quarter, Morton Berman, wrote an aggressive letter to the union justifying the sacking. Prominent in his torrent of complaints were the charges that Parker's fellow-musicians were a bunch of amateurs, that Parker sucked lemon peel on the bandstand, and that at the end of each set he insulted the customers by stopping abruptly in the middle of a number and telling them he'd be back to finish it in thirty minutes.

The union passed Berman's letter to Parker and gave him ten days to deliver an answer. His courteous but huge reply ran to nearly 3000 words – an awful drain on the time and energy of a man just back home after gigs in Boston, Los Angeles, Seattle and Portland, and about to travel to Chicago and Baltimore. His point-by-point rebuttal of Berman's accusations included the distinguished pedigrees of all the musicians in his group. For example, the trumpeter and composer Benny Harris (responsible for writing 'Ornithology', 'Bud's Bubble' and 'Wahoo') was a respected figure in the new music, playing with Coleman Hawkins, Boyd Raeburn, Dizzy Gillespie and many others. With regard to the lemon peels, Parker explained that he had been advised to chew them regularly to alleviate a stomach condition. As for the gimmick of stopping halfway through a number and saying he'd be back, this was a standard part of his act – appreciated as humorous in nightclubs across the United States.

The union sat on its judgement for four months, during which Parker was mainly on the road, earning money to support the family and frequently sending Chan fond and reassuring telegrams. Pictures taken of him in Chicago in November come as a shock: the figure on the bandstand could be a portly, careworn, middle-aged businessman.

For what is was worth, *Down Beat* magazine voted him top Alto Sax man of 1953.

*

Parker began 1954 with a week at the Blue Note in Philadelphia. While he was there he wrote to the local branch of the union, asking them to help him recover the $350 owed to him by the promoter of a concert he played in the city over a year ago.

Back in New York he wrote to union headquarters, enclosing three contracts for engagements where he played 'but did not get paid'. He wished to file claim, he said, against the three promoters. One of these was Mr N.R. Wattam, president of the New Jazz Society in Toronto. According to Parker's letter, Wattam owed him $200 plus a percentage of the profit for services rendered on 15 May 1953 at Massey Hall. No doubt still feeling bitter about the behaviour of Morton Berman in Montreal, Parker was rounding on promoters in general. So now Dick Wattam's rubbery cheque (the one Parker's initiative had managed to turn into cash) was no longer good enough.

On 18 January Parker was back in Boston at the Hi Hat club, with which he had never had a quarrel. A set from the opening night was broadcast and recorded. On the first number, 'Ornithology', he plays with much of his old zest, but for the remainder of the set he is coasting – declining to be drawn into Symphony Sid's idiotic chatter, and leaving the bulk of the solo space to the perspiring local musicians.

During the week, he appeared as guest of honour on the Boston radio programme hosted by John McLellan, where he was quizzed by the rising star of the alto saxophone Paul Desmond, who evidently worshipped him. The conversation was recorded and has been preserved. Parker is modest about his achievements, and says he would like to travel to Europe to study. He reveals that he has been having discussions with Edgard Varèse (the avant-garde French composer who settled in New York), and that Varèse has offered to give him lessons and write something for him to perform.

Interviewed after Parker's death, Varèse remembered:

He'd come in and exclaim, 'Take me as you would a baby and teach me music. I only write in one voice. I want to have structure. I want to write orchestral scores. I'll give you any amount you wish . . . I'm a good cook. I'll cook for you.' He was so dramatic, it was funny, but he was sincere. He spoke of being tired of the environment his work relegated him to. 'I'm so steeped in this and can't get out,' he said.[2]

Regrettably, nothing came of the potentially astounding Parker/Varèse project.

On 28 January, bowing to the financial imperative, Parker secured himself a well-paid month by joining the Festival of Modern American Jazz. This was a touring package masterminded by bandleader Stan Kenton. During four weeks it would cover many thousands of miles, starting in Wichita Falls, Texas, moving through the South and up the East Coast, then crossing to the West and ending in Los Angeles. Dizzy Gillespie was also on board, but he and Parker were assigned their separate featured spots with the Kenton Orchestra. The programme made no provision for them to appear on stage together.

By working with a white orchestra like Kenton's, black artists could greatly improve their income, but sometimes the pain outweighed the gain, particularly when the band travelled in the American South. Parker disciple Dave Schildkraut, one of Kenton's white saxophonists, has described what happened when the band bus stopped in a Southern town at a restaurant that would not serve Negroes: 'Bird had to wait in the bus while the rest of us were wolfing down steaks . . . I brought him out a big steak sandwich, and he grumbled, "What, are you trying to be good to me?"'[3]

Gillespie, of course, was subjected to the same indignities but seemed less wounded. He became seriously concerned about Parker, who was drinking heavily to drown his craving for heroin. It upset Gillespie to hear his friend, fuddled with alcohol, going out on stage and playing far below his glorious best. One night he pointed out that Kenton's young alto star Lee Konitz, who had learned much from Parker, was making a better job of his solo spot than the master. That did the trick: 'Yard put down the whisky immediately. That night he came out on the stage and

I was sorry I told him because I had to follow him. Man, he ran snakes!'[4]

On 12 February 1954 the Festival of Modern American Jazz reached Toronto's Massey Hall. Here, in sharp contrast to the situation of nearly a year ago, Kenton's drawing power and public relations skills ensured the auditorium was packed.

How well Parker played that night at Massey Hall we do not know. But a fortnight later on the West Coast, at a concert in Portland, Oregon, a private recording captured him performing three numbers backed by the Kenton orchestra. What we hear is far less tortured than his 1946 'Lover Man' but troubling nevertheless. Although his instinctive musical elegance has not deserted him, he seems to lack mental and physical puff. Often his phrases trail off sadly. Alcohol is the likely villain.

The gruelling tour ended with a concert at the Shrine Auditorium in Los Angeles on 28 February. Parker had been scheduled by his agency to start an engagement at the Tiffany Club the next evening, and the manager of the club, Jack Tucker, insisted he should attend a midday rehearsal with the local musicians. Tired and unhappy, Parker called a halt after quarter of an hour and declared no more rehearsing was necessary.

That night after playing two short sets, Parker left the club during the 11.00 p.m. intermission to get a sandwich and make a long distance phone call to Chan. He was picked up by the dreaded Los Angeles Police Department and held overnight on suspicion of being a drug user. Next day, with no evidence to support a drugs charge, the LAPD booked him for being drunk and disorderly. A representative of his agency came and paid the $10 fine, escorted him back to the Tiffany Club and arranged for him to make a fresh start.

During his third night at the club, after drinking at the bar with a jazz journalist, he fell into an argument with the management and was fired. When he phoned Chan she told him their two-year-old daughter Pree, who suffered from a weak heart, was desperately ill and about to be placed in an oxygen tent. Next night, 4 March, he made his peace with the Tiffany Club and played three sets before there was another row and he was fired again. On Sunday 7 March in the early hours of the morning, news came from New York that his little girl had died in hospital. Within five minutes he had sent three telegrams to Chan, barely coherent and full of pain. The third just said, 'CHAN, HELP.'

*

Music by Béla Bartók was played at little Pree's funeral service. Her body was laid to rest in the same New York cemetery as her mother's family but in the section reserved for 'coloured folk'. Her father, bowed down with grief and guilt and afflicted by severe pain from his ulcer, vowed to make his final break with heroin.

The Kenton tour had paid well but money needs remained pressing. Parker owed hefty sums to his agents past and present, and had to meet the funeral expenses. He wrote to Norman Granz, authorizing him to sue Ross Russell of Dial Records for unpaid royalties. And he sent another reminder to the union about his long-standing claim against a defaulting Philadelphia promoter.

At the end of March his hopes of financial recovery took a nasty knock when the union wrote to tell him that his claim against Morton Berman and the Latin Quarter in Montreal had been denied. Berman was required to stump up not one cent of the $743.04 Parker alleged was due.

The day after that letter came, Parker went to the studio to record for Norman Granz with his latest quintet: Walter Bishop (piano), Jerome Darr (guitar), Teddy Kotick (bass) and Roy Haynes (drums). This was a trusty team, and the project dreamed up by Granz looked promising on paper: *Charlie Parker Plays the Cole Porter Song Book*. Four of Porter's sure-fire songs were selected and everything seemed set fair, but Parker could not respond. Although he completed the session, the recordings sound weak and insecure. A vicious combination of grief, alcohol, disillusion and failing health had maimed the songbird in him.

To pay the bills he kept working in Detroit, Philadelphia and at Robert Reisner's Open Door. On 22 April he received a letter from the American Federation of Musicians, enclosing an onslaught upon him by Jack Tucker. The manager of the Tiffany Club was claiming damages of $2,828 and swearing that if he failed to recover the money through the union, he would file a civil action. As Tucker saw it, during Parker's short visits to the bandstand he was obviously intoxicated – sweating profusely, wiping his brow with his forefinger and thrusting the sweat to the floor. Having fired him, Tucker had become stuck with advertising costs, refunded admissions, loss of prestige and loss of business. Parker appealed to the union for time to prepare his reply.

On Sunday 9 May he played the plastic saxophone at the Open Door, so his brass one must have been back in the pawnshop. He was at the Open Door again on the following Sunday, and a week after that he sent the union his painstaking rebuttal of all Jack Tucker's charges.

For the next three months he stuck at the chores, doing bread and butter bookings in New York, Philadelphia, Detroit and St Louis. Then the boss of Birdland, Oscar Goodstein, offered what should have been a plum engagement: three weeks for Charlie Parker and his Strings at the club named in his honour. Dizzy Gillespie's group was also on the bill. The headline attraction was singing star Dinah Washington – and here was Oscar Goodstein's dreadful miscalculation, because Ms Washington was another notorious drinker on the path to self-destruction.

Although the backstage Bacchanalia always outshone the show presented to the customers, the first two days passed fairly peacefully. But the third day, 29 August 1954, was a double birthday – Dinah Washington's thirtieth and Charlie Parker's thirty-fourth – and now the shenanigans spilled into the public arena. Bassist Tommy Potter, who was supporting the Parker Strings, recalled that during the intermission Parker walked out into the street, opened the door of a taxi cab and sat sideways on its floor with his feet out in the street. The driver asked him where to and he said he just wanted to sit there. After some arguing and wrestling, Parker tumbled into the vehicle, whereupon the cabbie drove to the nearest police station and handed him over.

When he returned to the club, Parker focused his discontent upon the inflexibility of the conservatory-trained members of his string ensemble. He called on them to play 'East of the Sun', but at the end of their introduction he switched to 'Dancing in the Dark' (also in their repertoire), and when they failed to cope he loudly and contemptuously dismissed the lot of them. Oscar Goodstein fired Parker.

Back home, after a row with Chan in the early hours of the morning, Parker attempted suicide by drinking iodine. Chan called the ambulance, and at 5.00 a.m. her man was rushed to Bellevue Hospital. After emergency treatment they transferred him to Bellevue's Psychiatric Division, where Bud Powell was a regular, and detained him for ten days.

Two weeks after his discharge he took part in a concert at Carnegie Hall by the so-called 'Birdland Stars of '54'. The polite review in *Down Beat* admired his professionalism but regretted he was below his best. Three days later he voluntarily re-entered Bellevue, explaining that he had become severely depressed since his release, was drinking again and feared he might do himself harm. The official findings were 'acute alcoholism and undifferentiated schizophrenia'. This time they kept him in for a fortnight, only letting him go when he agreed to return regularly for psychotherapy.

He moved with his family to a small house Chan had found in New Hope, Pennsylvania (60 miles from New York City) and commuted to Bellevue by train. According to Chan, 'Bird basked in his role as commuter. He enjoyed playing roles which he thought were part of the square, normal world.'[5] But his new life was disturbed by unpleasant news from the American Federation of Musicians. They had decided against him and in favour of Jack Tucker of the Tiffany Club. Parker was ordered to pay $500 by 5 November.

On Saturday 30 October he gave his last concert performance, at New York's Town Hall. The event was poorly advertised and sparsely attended, but according to the jazz writer Leonard Feather, Parker played magnificently. Afterwards a union patrolman came backstage and impounded a portion of his earnings.

A few days later Parker heard the sad news that the trumpeter Hot Lips Page had died of a heart attack aged forty-six. Page had been a star of the Basie band in Kansas City when Parker was a schoolboy. Parker visited the funeral parlour to pay his respects. He took with him young Jackie McLean, the alto saxophonist whose talent had been nurtured by

Bud Powell. According to McLean, Parker stood for a long time staring at the body, then spoke admiringly of the embalmer's art. Thereafter Parker took to visiting the city morgue to inspect the unidentified corpses, claiming he was looking for a missing friend.

In mid-November came a dark letter from the union pointing out that money due had not been paid and threatening expulsion. In the same month Dave Brubeck's portrait appeared on the cover of *Time* magazine. When a fan protested to Parker that *he* should have been the one honoured, he answered, 'My watch doesn't work that well.'[6]

*

On 10 December 1954 Charlie Parker made his last recordings for Norman Granz: two more Cole Porter songs to complete the album begun shakily back in March. The music by now is distressing, a painfully truthful account of himself by a great artist who has become a very sick man.

Playing as if it hurts to hold the saxophone to his lips, he delivers 'Love for Sale' – the young prostitute's pitiful lament – with an overwhelming sense of loneliness and loss. 'I Love Paris' is even more desolate. Accompanied by a sombre drumbeat, like a syncopated dead march, Parker gives a wailing account of the first, minor-key section of the song. Feeling at ease with this dirge, he repeats it (although Cole Porter did not), before moving to the major-key conclusion. And here what the composer intended as jubilant affirmation becomes, in Parker's troubled care, an extension of the tragedy. For his short solo he improvises only upon those bars in the minor key. Then at the end of the recapitulation he remains silent, leaving the others to mark the close of his final recording with more of the grimly prophetic funeral march.

*

By now Parker had lost touch with Chan and the family. A daily routine defined by railway timetables was more than he could manage. He dropped into the life of a vagrant in Greenwich Village, not caring where he laid his head.

During Christmas week 1954 his ex-employer Ross Russell came across him playing with a band of unknowns in Le Club Downbeat on 8th Avenue. His clothes were crumpled and dirty. The audience took no interest in him or his music. During the interval Russell invited Parker to his table and was shocked by his ill-health and hostility. Munching a huge white codeine pill that helped control the pain of his stomach ulcers, he attacked Russell for issuing the 'Lover Man' recording and for forcing him to sign a contract in exchange for release from Camarillo State Hospital.

While Parker was playing the next set, a club employee brought Russell a message: Parker was carrying a gun and had threatened to shoot him. Russell left the premises.

*

On New Year's Day 1955 Robert Reisner came upon Parker in Greenwich Village. Parker told him he never thought he'd live to see another year, and quoted lines he had memorized from the *Rubáiyát of Omar Khayyám*:

> Come fill the Cup, and in the fire of Spring
> Your Winter garment of Repentance fling;
> The Bird of Time has but a little way
> To flutter – and the Bird is on the Wing.[7]

Parker's temporary address was a chilly apartment on Barrow Street. Its regular occupants had carried him there after he collapsed in the street. One of these new flatmates, Ahmed Basheer (Thomas Henderson before he accepted Islam), read to Parker from the Koran and pleaded with him not to die. When Parker felt a little better they would roam the Village together or visit the cinema. They saw *Carmen Jones* four times, mainly because Max Roach had a big moment in this Hollywood version of the Bizet opera – beating out a rhythm on his drums, urged on by Pearl Bailey. 'They sure cooked that picture,' the delighted Parker told his companion.[8]

Parker last encountered the other side of his heartbeat, Dizzy Gillespie, when the two of them happened to drop into the Basin Street club on the same night. According to Gillespie's haunting memory, Parker looked fat and ill, and 'spoke about us getting together again. He said it in a way that implied *before it's too late*.'[9]

*

Five months had passed since the fiasco with the Strings, and Oscar Goodstein, manager of Birdland, felt ready to offer Parker a last chance to prove himself worthy to star in the club that bore his nickname. The comeback was to begin on Friday 4 March. The other players were to be trumpeter Kenny Dorham, drummer Art Blakey, Bud Powell and Charles Mingus.

The first night was orderly, although the danger signs were there. Jazz critic Dan Morgenstern noted that Powell was in poor shape – staring out into the audience with a fixed leer.

On the second night things went calamitously wrong. Various accounts of what happened are in circulation. What follows is taken mainly from those of Charles Mingus and Kenny Dorham. Parker came late. By the time he appeared the band was on stage and Powell was a problem. Mingus described him as 'very unruly'.[10] It seemed he had been drinking, and in his case just a small amount of alcohol had a catastrophic effect. Parker headed for the dressing room but Oscar Goodstein intercepted him and insisted on some music immediately. Parker pointed to Powell and demanded, 'What am I going to play when you give me this to play with?'[11]

He eventually mounted the platform, his resolve stiffened by whisky, but asserting his leadership turned out to be impossible. In Dorham's recollection the exchange went like this:

> Bud said, 'What do you want to play, daddy?' Bird said, 'Let's play some "Out of Nowhere".' Then Bud asked Bird, who could play in any key and any time, 'What key you want it in, daddy?' Bird snarled back, 'The key of S, mother.' Very little playing went on that night.[12]

After Powell had been helped from the stand, Parker, his comeback in ruins, seized the microphone and kept reciting the name of his Nemesis like a doom-laden mantra: 'Bud Powell, Bud Powell, Bud Powell, Bud Powell . . .'

And then, with the audience still in shock, Mingus stepped forward and made an anguished appeal: 'Ladies and gentlemen, please don't associate me with any of this. This is not jazz. These are sick people.'[13]

*

Four days later Parker left his refuge in Greenwich Village, heading for Boston where he was engaged to play at the Storyville club. But driving north through Manhattan he felt too ill to continue, so he called at the Stanhope Hotel on 5th Avenue, home of the wealthy Baroness Pannonica de Koenigswarter, a conspicuous friend to black American musicians.

We have the Baroness's account of Parker's visit. She knew immediately that something was wrong when she offered him a drink and he said no. A few minutes later he began to vomit blood, so she sent for her personal physician.

From Parker's appearance Dr Freymann assumed he was in his sixties. He could tell from his eyes he was no longer taking heroin, and in any case there were no healthy veins left to inject. He asked Parker how much he drank. Parker winked at the Baroness and confessed ironically, 'Sometimes I have a sherry before dinner.' Dr Freymann took the Baroness aside and warned her that the patient had advanced cirrhosis of the liver and bleeding ulcers, and might die at any moment.

When Parker refused to be taken to the hospital, it was agreed that he should be put to bed in the Baroness's apartment, with Nica and her daughter taking turns to watch over him. For three days they tended his needs, bringing iced water by the gallon to quench his raging thirst. The doctor paid regular calls and gave pain-killing medication. Parker liked Dr Freymann and wanted to introduce him to his music, so the Baroness played 'Just Friends' and 'April in Paris' from the album *Parker with Strings*.

On the evening of the fourth day, Saturday 12 March, Parker felt better, so he was helped to an armchair to watch the Tommy Dorsey programme on TV. The show included a juggling act, and the jugglers were throwing bricks that stuck together:

My daughter was asking how they did it, and Bird and I were being very mysterious about it. Suddenly they dropped the bricks, and we all laughed. Bird was laughing uproariously, but then he began to choke . . . I went over and took his pulse. He was unconscious. Then his pulse stopped . . . At the moment of his going there was a tremendous clap of thunder.[14]

*

Chan Parker claimed Charlie's body from the Bellevue morgue. It was removed to the funeral home where his little daughter Pree had lain, and a quiet service was planned, with music by Lennie Tristano and Charles Mingus. But Doris Parker intervened, asserting a wife's rights and threatening legal action unless the body was turned over to her. Accordingly it was moved to the Unity Funeral home, while a service was arranged to suit Doris's taste. Celebrities congregated in the grand Abyssinian Baptist Church on West 138th Street in Harlem; the organist played Arthur Sullivan's *The Lost Chord*, and the sermon by the Reverend Licorish dwelt on the sentiments that this song inspired.

Dizzy Gillespie was among the pallbearers. Norman Granz paid for the body to be flown to Kansas City, where it was interred.

*

The savage brevity of Parker's time on earth has been succeeded by a copious afterlife. While he lived, as Max Roach said, Bird gave off energy like the sun. When he died the sun exploded into brilliant fragments that embedded themselves across the world of music making. The soundtrack of the twentieth century was profoundly enriched by what he did, and the allure of his legend has spilled into the twenty-first.

The mythologizing was already under way during his lifetime. As early as 1947, *Harper's* magazine published Elliott Grennard's short story 'Sparrow's Last Jump', crudely based on Parker's disastrous 'Lover Man' session. Within days of his death the slogan 'Bird Lives' started to appear among the graffiti on New York's public surfaces. *The Legend of Charlie Parker*, a compendium of interviews with those in the know, was published in 1962 and adapted for the stage in 1965 (the tenth anniversary of his death).

Bird-like musicians have been the heroes of several novels, including *The Sound* by Ross Russell and *Night Song* by John A. Williams. A film version of *Night Song*, called *Sweet Love, Bitter*, was produced in 1967, with the comedian and civil-rights activist Dick Gregory playing the part of heroin-addicted saxophonist Richie 'Eagle' Coles.

In 1988 came the Hollywood magnum opus *Bird*, produced and directed by jazz aficionado and screen superstar Clint Eastwood. A script had been circulating for years. The original intention had been that Parker should be played by the anarchic and scandalizing comedian Richard Pryor – perfect for conveying stylish self-destruction. But in Eastwood's dimly-lit and rain-drenched picture Parker is portrayed by Forest Whitaker – a much softer presence than Pryor, with un-Parkerish weak mouth and hangdog look. *Bird* is well-intentioned, and the soundtrack includes some of Parker's finest recorded performances – most notably 'Lester Leaps In' and 'Cool Blues' from the sublime night at Rockland Palace. However, it is a pity that electronic wizardry was employed to rub out Parker's original rhythm section and insert a pristine alternative.

Chan Parker was employed by Clint Eastwood as his script consultant, and her annotated copy of the screenplay was among the eighty-three lots auctioned at Christie's of London in September 1994. This historic sale of Parker memorabilia, including letters, love poems, music manuscripts and booking contracts, drew buyers and observers from Europe, America and Japan. The top exhibit, lot 83, was the plastic saxophone used by Parker at Massey Hall. Peter King, Europe's top Parkerian saxophonist, gave a bravura demonstration on the shock-white instrument before bidding began.

It was appropriate that this sale should be held in London, because here is where the revolutionary saxophone was manufactured. Its official name, the Grafton Acrylic, derives from Grafton Way in London's West End, where its inventor Ettore Sommaruga once had his workshop. Sommaruga, an Italian immigrant, dreamed up the plastic sax while he was interned as an enemy alien during World War II.

In post-war Britain brass for musical instruments was scarce. Sommaruga patented his idea, and the production of saxophones in moulded plastic began in London in 1950. In America the Grafton Acrylic was distributed by the Gretsch company, starting in 1951. It was probably a marketing man from Gretsch who gave Parker his promotional sample. In those days you could buy a Grafton for less than $100 – half as much as a conventional brass saxophone – but it looked odd, it was brittle, and, in spite of the enthusiasm of Ornette Coleman, it failed to catch on. Nonetheless, the bidding at Christie's for this one – Charlie Parker's reserve horn – was brisk, both in person and on the telephones. The winner was the mayor of Kansas City, Missouri, who paid £93,500 ($150,000), a world record for a saxophone at auction. The mayor wanted it for the local jazz museum, because the wild and segregated city where the course of Parker's life was set has moved on and claimed him for its heritage industry. As well as the Grafton, the mayor bought the contract Parker signed for the Massey Hall engagement.

*

In the early spring of 1999, with great ceremony, a gigantic, 17-foot high representation in bronze of Parker's head was unveiled in the space at 17th and Vine that Kansas City has named Charlie Parker Memorial Plaza. Pre-eminent among the distinguished musicians who took part in the celebrations was seventy-five-year-old Max Roach – the only surviving member of the Massey Hall Quintet.

——

EIGHT

TO BE OR NOT TO BOP

'My association with Charlie Parker would have to be far above anything else that I have ever done musically, in every way.'
Dizzy Gillespie in his autobiography

ALMOST IMMEDIATELY after the May 1953 Massey Hall concert, the paths of Gillespie and Parker crossed again when they were engaged to share the bill at Birdland. Parker was backed by the Bud Powell trio, while Gillespie appeared with his regular quintet, Parker sometimes joining them. Recordings from broadcasts twice captured this informal collaboration. 'On the Sunny Side of the Street' – one of the quintet's set arrangements, built around Gillespie's droll vocal – is expanded to make room for a short solo by Parker, during which Gillespie shouts warm encouragement. And 'The Bluest Blues' – usually a feature for singer Joe Carroll – turns into a jam session where first Gillespie and then Parker take lengthy solos. Both men sound in wonderful spirits, and the occasion only becomes poignant in retrospect, as it was the last time these two great artists were recorded playing together.

During the same Birdland stint, Gillespie sometimes played with the Bud Powell Trio when Parker was not there. On the recordings made when he did so, Max Roach partnered Charles Mingus in the rhythm section. So here we have four-fifths of the Massey Hall Quintet,

169

and one of the pieces they play is 'Salt Peanuts'. In this version Roach and Powell share the part usually taken by Parker during Gillespie's vocal chorus.

The other performance we have by this quartet is of Gillespie's 'Woody 'n You' composed back in 1944 for the session fronted by Coleman Hawkins in which both Gillespie and Roach took part. Here at Birdland they choose to play Gillespie's revised version – sometimes called 'Algo Bueno' – in which the 'Woody 'n You' main theme is embroidered with Afro-Latin figures. However, the solos are in 4/4, and Gillespie's is glorious, soaring ecstatically above the superlative rhythm section.

*

No longer shouldering the cares of the Dee Gee company, Gillespie felt able to accept lengthy and well-paid engagements as a solo attraction. A juicy example, financially, was the mammoth tour by the Festival of Modern American Jazz, brainchild of Stan Kenton. The Kenton orchestra was the principal ingredient. The big-name guests, besides Gillespie, were Errol Garner and the rising saxophone star Stan Getz.

The first leg of the tour ended on the West Coast in early December 1953, and here Norman Granz booked Gillespie and Getz to record an album. And since Max Roach was fortuitously also in California, Granz booked him, too. Completing the rhythm section were three Granz regulars: bassist Ray Brown, guitarist Herb Ellis and pianist Oscar Peterson. Gillespie had long admired Peterson's keyboard athleticism, and was perfectly happy to share the front line with the technically brilliant Getz (ten years his junior).

The session follows Norman Granz's favourite recipe: familiar repertoire, loose arrangements and long, competitive solos, often at stupendous speed. Gillespie is in commanding form, but the listener is left feeling rather flat. No boundaries are tested, no discoveries made. The fault would seem to be with the rhythm section. Max Roach offers his usual range of subtle stimuli, but his work is undone by the relentless churning of Peterson's piano and Herb Ellis's guitar.

The sextet as a whole performs best on the exotic 'Siboney', and here the Gillespie/Getz partnership sounds particularly fetching. Gillespie had always been passionate about fusing jazz and Afro-Latin rhythms. Getz would go on to huge commercial success as purveyor of the bossa nova.

Norman Granz marketed the LP as *Diz and Getz* (echoing *Bird and Diz*, the snappy title of an earlier classic album). He anticipated that sales would be boosted by the continuing appearances of Gillespie and Getz with Stan Kenton's highly publicized show, shortly to resume its travels. However, Getz was arrested in Los Angeles on 19 December, convicted of heroin possession and sent to prison. His nerve-racking replacement in the Kenton package was Charlie Parker.

During the four weeks Gillespie and Parker were on tour with Kenton, they never appeared on stage together. The way each of them handled his segment in the spotlight reflected the contrasting curves of their careers. Parker, sliding downwards, was in poor health and drinking heavily. He made no announcements and toiled through his performances while the orchestra played backgrounds supplied by Kenton's arrangers. Gillespie, bouncing back up, had brought his own portfolio of big-band arrangements – 'On the Alamo', 'Oo-Shoo-Be Doo Be', 'Manteca'. He teased the audience with jolly banter and galvanized Kenton's men into creating maximum excitement behind his solo flights.

*

Gillespie was now a valued member of the Norman Granz stable of artists. In May 1954 Granz financed a costly project to keep him happy: the recording by a specially assembled big band of a suite by the Cuban composer Chico O'Farrill, all based on 'Manteca'. Gillespie played some searing trumpet solos above the large orchestral forces, but the 'Afro Suite' did not succeed commercially, and he went back to his small group.

Reviewing the group's appearance at Birdland, the 11 July 1954 issue of *Down Beat* magazine had little to say about the ensemble, preferring to give headline prominence to the startling design of Gillespie's new trumpet. Instead of pointing forwards in the traditional fashion, the bell of this eye-catching instrument swept upwards at an angle of 45 degrees.

According to the story Gillespie liked to tell, the bending of the horn was a happy accident. During a party for his wife's birthday, he had left it parked on its trumpet stand where a drunken reveller collided with it. Horror turned to delight, he said, when he experimented and discovered several advantages. The sound reached his ear more quickly and was more evenly distributed among the nightclub customers. The tone was improved. And the bell no longer pointed towards the floor when he was reading music. Convinced he had stumbled on a winner, he ordered the Martin company to make him a new one just like it, and stuck to this oddity for the rest of his life. Combined with his spectacular system of storing air in hugely inflated cheeks, his upswept trumpet created one of the most memorable trademarks in the business.

Gillespie's quintet appeared at Birdland again in August as part of a triple bill, with Charlie Parker and Strings and singing star Dinah Washington. And this time it was Parker, not Gillespie, who garnered the headlines – for entirely the wrong reasons. After excessive carousing on his thirty-fourth birthday, Parker was expelled from the club. This grim farce was Gillespie's last sight of his dear friend in performance.

*

On the next recording devised by Granz, Gillespie did battle with his boyhood hero Roy Eldridge, combative king of the swing trumpeters. There was no Max Roach on hand this time. Instead Granz assembled an entirely mainstream rhythm section, with drummer Louis Bellson joining the Oscar Peterson trio. Although this conservative environment seems heavily tilted in Eldridge's favour, Gillespie outshines his master by a considerable wattage. Even on the swing and Dixieland favourite 'I've Found a New Baby', he swings harder and is far more inventive.

From the mass of material they recorded, Granz was able to compile two money-spinning LPs, *Trumpet Battle* and *The Trumpet Kings*. Sales of these enjoyed the cross-promotional benefit of his Jazz at the

Philharmonic tours, where the friendly wars between the two trum-peters were re-fought nightly.

Enjoying their new financial security, Gillespie and his wife Lorraine had moved from their Harlem apartment to a house in Corona, Long Island, and it was here in the early spring of 1955 that he received the news of Charlie Parker's death. According to Lorraine, she saw Dizzy give way to grief only twice: 'when his mother died, and when Charlie Parker died. When Charlie Parker died he just went on downstairs to the basement, just went down there crying. He never said a word. I knew what he was crying for.'

Gillespie remembered with pain and regret his last, casual encounter with Parker at the Basin Street East club, shortly before Parker's death. Parker had urged that they should play together again. Looking back, Gillespie could see that his friend had been pleading for salvation. But 'I didn't know what to do. I just didn't know what to say to that man.'

Now he busied himself helping to straighten the muddle that followed Parker's death. Doris had overturned Chan's funeral arrangements, and there was a proposal, but no money, to send the body to Kansas City where Parker's mother was waiting. Gillespie contacted Norman Granz, who said if Parker's mother wished it, then he would willingly pay the transportation expenses. So after a service in Harlem's Abyssinian Baptist Church, where Gillespie was one of the pallbearers, Parker's body was flown to his home town for burial in the local cemetery.

*

For much of 1955 Gillespie was a well-paid employee of Norman Granz and his Jazz at the Philharmonic. Then he formed a sextet, starting in 1956 with engagements at Birdland and at the Showboat in Washington, DC. It was while they were in the nation's capital that the black con-gressman and clergyman Adam Clayton Powell, Jr. summoned Gillespie to an extraordinary press conference. The charismatic Clayton Powell had shot to fame with fiery sermons from the pulpit of that same Abyssinian Baptist Church in Harlem where they had held Charlie Parker's funeral service. In 1944 he had been elected to Congress. Now he was pleased to announce to Washington's assembled journalists that, on his recommendation, the US State Department had agreed to finance an overseas tour by a Gillespie big band; it was a pioneering propaganda mission to promote 'American cultural values'.

Gillespie was clear about the way he was being used. No one knew better than he that an orchestra consisting mainly of black musicians, with only one or two white members, under a black leader concealed more than it revealed about the nature of American society. Nevertheless, the opportunity was too seductive to resist.

The start date was in mid-April, and since Gillespie would be away in Europe with Jazz at the Philharmonic during the preceding months, trumpeter and arranger Quincy Jones was hired to assemble and rehearse the players. They flew to Rome and linked up with their leader on 15 April 1956, then on to Iran where the goodwill tour began. Thereafter, Gillespie and the band entertained audiences in Pakistan, Syria, the Lebanon, Turkey, Yugoslavia and Greece. At the end the State Department pronounced itself more than satisfied with the foreign relations dividend, although Embassy diplomats along the way had been offended by Gillespie's unorthodox style of statesmanship.

In Ankara he refused to play at the swanky Turkish-American Club unless they allowed the street children to come in. In Damascus, during Ramadan, as soon as the sun set behind the concert hall, he stopped the music, yelled 'Food!' and led the charge towards the buffet. In Athens students who had been stoning the American Embassy in protest against US policy in Cyprus came to his concert and danced in the aisles. A headline proclaimed, 'Greek Students Lay Down Rocks And Roll With Diz!'

In August of the same year the State Department found him a new mission: to tour Ecuador, Argentina, Uruguay and Brazil. The result was mutual bliss. While he bathed in the waves of South American enthusiasm, Gillespie could also experience at source the Afro-Latin rhythms he had loved all his life. Aware of the success of Debut with the Massey Hall recording, he had purchased a portable Ampex tape machine. And he persuaded his friend and former partner in the defunct Dee Gee company, Dave Usher, to take a holiday from the oil business and come along and record the tour. Usher obliged, but because of Gillespie's con-tract with Norman Granz, the tapes went into store. They were finally issued in 1999.

For Granz the existence of this well-drilled, state-subsidised orchestra was a prize opportunity. In the interval between the Middle East and South America tours he booked them into a New York studio and recorded seventeen numbers. The music on this album is enjoyable, but the sense of wild adventure that pervaded the earliest Gillespie big band recordings has gone, and many of the highlights have a retrospective character. Quincy Jones's arrangement of 'A Night in Tunisia', for exam-ple, sticks close to the version Gillespie recorded with the Boyd Raeburn orchestra in 1944.

The most exhilarating of the seventeen performances is Gillespie's 'Groovin' High', which looks back to the 1945 recording he made with Charlie Parker. Observing the letter as well as the spirit of that classic, the opening theme is played here by just a quintet, and Parker's part is taken by Phil Woods, one of his most devoted followers. The full orchestra joins in behind the solos – first from Woods then from Gillespie, who is in tremendous lip – and the final effect is a heady mix of nostalgia and fresh excitement.

*

After the South American trip, the State Department had nothing more to offer, and Gillespie struggled to retain his assembly of fine musicians. A modicum of work was found in the clubs in the New York area but the economics were grim.

In the spring of 1957 Granz brought them to the studio to make another batch of recordings, but the best evidence of their power to excite is found on the 'live' album made at July's Newport Jazz Festival.

The occasion is dominated by Gillespie's huge personality. He tickles the crowd with his announcements, and takes a leading role in the per-formance of all six numbers. Four of these are 12-bar blues, including the tearaway opener 'Dizzy's Blues', with its long and nimble Gillespie trum-pet solo.

His new arrangement of 'Manteca' preserves the essence of his thrilling 1947 recording, but adds an ironic touch: a slogan for the band to chant along with the opening ostinato, 'I'll never go back to Georgia!'

Following 'Manteca', and contrasting with it utterly, comes 'I Remember Clifford' – composed by band member Benny Golson in memory of Clifford Brown, the phenomenal trumpeter who had been co-leading the Max Roach–Clifford Brown Quintet when he was killed in a car crash at the age of twenty-five. Gillespie had given Brown every encouragement during his short life. Now he plays a deeply expressive solo on Golson's sombre and beautiful ballad.

*

The Lenox School of Jazz, an annual summer programme of jazz education, came into being in August 1957. The location was Music Inn – a New England resort set in lovely countryside, with its own woods and lake. Nearby was Tanglewood, summer home of the Boston Symphony Orchestra.

Sufficient sponsorship had been found to invite some of the world's greatest jazz musicians to this rural idyll, where they would spend three weeks working with promising youngsters. Long known in the jazz world as an unselfish and inspirational guide, Gillespie was one of the first stars to be signed up. Three of his former protégés were also enlisted: John Lewis (who became the course director), Milt Jackson and Max Roach.

One of the pupils, pianist Ron Riddle, recalled how stimulating Gillespie's ensemble class could be:

> Once, in the middle of a chorus of 'Indiana', Mr Gillespie suddenly
> stopped playing and gave me a piercing look. 'NEVER play that chord!' he
> said. Then he parked his incredible horn and took a seat at the piano.
> What followed was an amazingly lucid 15-minute lecture-demonstration.[1]

Gillespie's own memories of the Lenox School were full of fondness, tinged with sadness that Charlie Parker had not lived to see it.

*

Back in the cruel world of commerce, his big band survived until the end of the year, then succumbed to the laws of the market. Fortunately, touring as a star of Norman Granz's Jazz at the Philharmonic remained a lucrative option, and Granz, wary of big band economics, had persisted with his policy of recording his star trumpeter in diverse small-group environments.

In October 1956 he teamed him with Stan Getz for a second album. The rest of the line-up reads like a Gillespie class reunion. The bassist and the drummer, Ray Brown and Stan Levey, earned their spurs with the Gillespie–Parker Sextet in California. The pianist, John Lewis, blossomed in the 1946 Gillespie big band. The alto saxophonist, Sonny Stitt, substituted for Parker in the 1946 Gillespie Sextet. The odd man out is Granz's house guitarist Herb Ellis.

Entitled *For Musicians Only*, the album consists of four long tracks, with wide-open spaces for all the soloists. Two of the chosen vehicles are key texts from the new-music revolution. Gillespie's 'Bebop' was composed in 1944 and epitomized the upheaval. The version on *For Musicians Only* is even faster than his 1945 recording, but makes less impact. What was searing has become routine: storming the barricades, recollected in tranquillity. The final item on the new album was made immortal by its inclusion at Massey Hall. Variously known as 'Wee', 'Allen's Alley' and 'Big Noise', it is listed on the *For Musicians Only* record sleeve, bafflingly, as 'We (My Honey and Me)'. However, Gillespie, Getz and Stitt all deliver flawless, virtuosic solos.

The most idiosyncratic of the albums fostered by Granz was the one that paired Gillespie with Stuff Smith, wild man of the jazz violin, nicknamed 'the palpitating Paganini'. Although strange, this mating was not new: Gillespie had used Smith to spice up some of his Dee Gee recordings back in 1951. The novelty on this Granz album is 'Rio Pakistan', a Gillespie composition based on the exotic scales he heard played by the local string players when he visited Karachi.

Three of the best albums of the period were produced during a flurry of recording activity at the end of 1957. The most elaborate of these involved a specially assembled octet, playing arrangements and compositions by two of its brightest members, the young saxophonists Benny Golson and Gigi Gryce. Gillespie was the star soloist on this carefully structured LP, which Granz chose to call *The Greatest Trumpet of Them All*.

The other two albums (*Duets* and *Sonny Side Up*) were recorded at impromptu blowing sessions; it was standard Granz territory but this time with none of Granz's standard supporting cast. Pianist Ray Bryant was a young modernist with deep roots in the blues and gospel music. The bassist was Bryant's like-minded brother Tom. Charlie Persip (school of Max Roach) played the drums. Sonny Stitt and Sonny Rollins confronted one another on tenor saxophones. Inspired by this tough yet soulful environment, Gillespie gave the very best of himself, not just at the fastest of fast tempos, but also on the slowest of slow blues.

*

For the next two years Gillespie worked steadily, dividing his time between leading a small group and touring with the Norman Granz road shows. There were, however, several notable breaks with this routine.

In January 1959 his group appeared on the *Timex* TV show. During their comic 'Umbrella Man' routine (a hangover from the desperate days of Dee Gee records) they were joined by Louis Armstrong. This, the first public meeting of Dizzy and Satchmo, has been preserved on video. Gillespie sings and rolls his eyes, there is an exchange of trumpet fire, and the performance ends mirthfully, with Gillespie crooning the punch line, 'looks like rain', and Armstrong pretending he's being showered in spittle.

In the summer of 1959 the reconstructed Gillespie big band played at the Randall's Island Festival in New York. Adding a grave note to the proceedings, Gillespie presented a cheque for $1,000 to New York's Special Committee on Narcotics. He wanted jazz to be identified with positive forces and looked forward to a clean new world where a genius like Charlie Parker could be saved from descent into drug ruin.

It was 1959 when Gillespie's mother died. While he was mourning her loss he received an invitation from the mayor of his home town, Cheraw,

South Carolina, to honour them with an official visit. On the big day two bands paraded and Mayor Bennett made a speech welcoming Cheraw's most famous son, before Gillespie and his group gave a concert at the High School. The audience was racially mixed – a Cheraw first. Gillespie's old music teacher, Alice V. Wilson, was proud to be there but disappointed that the older generation of white citizens stayed away.

Gillespie used the momentum of the occasion to call at the big house of the family that had owned more slaves that any other in the district. His mother used to work here, and the only room in the house he knew was the kitchen. This time he came in by the front door, and the elderly owner, James A. Powe, was pleased to tell him about his mother's ancestors. Gillespie's great-grandmother had been purchased by Powe's father at the slave market in Charleston. The Powes named her Nora and trained her to be their house servant. The father of Nora's two children was white. So it seemed Gillespie and the present Mr Powe had to be related. At this revelation, says Gillespie in his autobiography, 'I reared back in my seat on the sofa laughing.'

*

In 1960 Gillespie's music enjoyed a rejuvenating boost when the Argentinean pianist-composer Lalo Schifrin joined his group. Gillespie had heard Schifrin playing in Buenos Aires in 1956, during the big band tour, and had been so impressed that he promised the young man a job if ever he came to New York. Four years later Schifrin arrived and Gillespie welcomed him.

Schifrin had studied at the Paris Conservatoire and was directing the Argentinean Radio Orchestra as well as running the Bebop Club of Buenos Aires when Gillespie discovered him. The first large-scale consequence of his engagement was *Gillespiana*: a suite in five movements, which he composed to celebrate the leader's multi-faceted talent and trumpet sovereignty. Norman Granz swiftly set up a recording.

Gillespiana is in concerto grosso form, with the Gillespie quintet (including Schifrin on piano) pitted against an orchestra of brass and percussion. Each of the movements has a distinctive character, with the one at the centre, 'Panamericana', containing the essence of Gillespie à la Schifrin: a joyous blending of rhythms and sonorities from the worlds of jazz and Latin America.

In March 1961 the same musicians performed *Gillespiana* at Carnegie Hall, and completed the concert with a set of arrangements by Schifrin of hallowed Gillespie tunes. Topping these was 'Tunisian Fantasy', an elaborate homage to 'A Night in Tunisia'.

Later the same year the Gillespie Quintet with Schifrin toured South America. Argentina of course welcomed them warmly, but the most fruitful time was spent in Rio de Janeiro, Brazil. They visited the Samba School, swapped ideas with local composers, and brought back to the USA the happy hybrid that crossed jazz with the samba beat. This fresh style swept the world as the bossa nova.

At the Monterey Festival in September the Quintet played several songs in the new idiom. One of these, 'Desafinado', was snapped up by Stan Getz, whose beguiling recording became a massive hit.

Commercial success on such a scale eluded Gillespie, but the bossa nova stayed in his quintet's repertoire. In May 1962 they issued an album of Braziliana, and in July they were recorded in concert at the Jazz Festival in Juan-les-Pins. The album, called *Dizzy on the French Riviera*, must be one of the sunniest ever made.

Its warm, sand-between-the-toes feeling is established right at the start, with the gentle sounds of Mediterranean sea wash and children playing at the water's edge. Afro-Latin percussion and exultant whooping slowly penetrate this idyll, until we find ourselves surrounded by Gillespie and his merry band. The regular quintet members, besides Lalo Schifrin, are bassist Chris White, drummer Rudy Collins and saxophonist Leo Wright, all of them in their twenties. The local reinforcements are the percussionist Pepito Riestria and the gypsy guitarist Tzigane Elek Bacsik (cousin of Django Reinhardt).

The opening number is the bossa nova 'Chega de Saudade' ('No More Blues') by Antonio Carlos Jobim, two long, curvaceous melodies for the price of one. The Parkerian alto of Leo Wright unveils the first of these. Gillespie does the same for the second, and as soon as he takes over, drummer Rudy Collins obediently applies himself to an enormous cymbal – the treasured property of his boss. Collins found this *objet trouvé* overwhelmingly loud, but Gillespie loved the glorious impurity of its tone. Riding above the bossa nova rhythm and the mega-cymbal, his effortless solo on 'No More Blues' combines the maturity of middle age (he's forty-four) with a childlike, bubbling joy. And when it's over he's still bounding with infectious enthusiasm, encouraging the others by smiting himself expertly on elbow and knee with a tambourine.

'No More Blues' has set the tone for a mainly polyrhythmic pro-gramme – including 'Desafinado', 'Pau de Arara' and the closer 'For the Gypsies', which gradually dissolves into the sounds at the water's edge where we began.

Shuffling off the concert platform in his bare feet, Gillespie turned to a friend and said, 'Man, it's just heaven here. If you have to die, this is the way to go.'[2]

*

Lalo Schifrin stayed for just a few more months. His last grand gesture was 'The New Continent', a fully composed suite (with movements enti-tled 'The Sword', 'The Legend of Atlantis' and so on) to be performed by Gillespie in front of an enlarged and brassy jazz band. They recorded it in Los Angeles in 1962, using the cream of Hollywood's session musi-cians. Following this impressive exercise, Schifrin said farewell to Gillespie and joined the well-paid ranks of composers for the silver screen.

As well as losing Schifrin, Gillespie also had to manage without the business brain of Norman Granz, who had sold his record company. This was a heavy blow, although its effect was not immediately apparent. Another company, Philips, looked after him well at first. *Dizzy on the French Riviera* was issued by them, and they followed it up with another elaborate production.

The idea for this one, *Dizzy Gillespie & the Double Six of Paris*, had been hatched during those balmy Mediterranean days. Mimi Perrin, leader of the acrobatic French vocal group the Double Six, had been a member of the adoring circle around Gillespie in Juan-les-Pins. She and her virtuosic ensemble were keen to take some of the classic recordings by their American hero and translate them into song. Lalo Schifrin undertook to write the choral arrangements and completed them before he left the master's employ.

The first part of the intricate recording process was achieved in a Paris studio in July 1963, and is of added interest to us because it involved Bud Powell. Powell was now a Paris resident, and when he felt well enough he played in a nightclub with fellow expatriate Kenny Clarke on drums and Frenchman Pierre Michelot on bass. This was the trio that worked with Gillespie to lay down the album's foundation. At later sessions Mimi Perrin and her choir were added to the tape.

Dizzy Gillespie & the Double Six of Paris consists largely of early Gillespie compositions, some of them first recorded by his 1946 big band, others during his glory days with Charlie Parker. The new versions observe the spirit and often the letter of the originals, and the result is weirdly nostalgic, a fervent memorial service to a hero who is himself a member of the congregation.

*

Gillespie scholars have tut-tutted over what happened to his music during the years that followed. It seems he felt creatively exhausted, and continued playing because he needed the money and it was the only job he knew. Sometimes he would admit to colleagues that he was no longer interested in innovation. But even if he never played or wrote another note, his place in music history was secure. There were those among his admirers who thought he should enter politics.

On 21 October 1963, Gillespie's forty-sixth birthday, they held a 'Dizzy for President' ball in San Francisco. The liberal journalist Ralph Gleason was chief organizer of this fund-raising event, whence flowed a lively but earnest campaign, with badges, bumper stickers, balloons and a campaign song, 'Vote Dizzy!' (to the tune of 'Salt Peanuts').

The campaign was linked to the Civil Rights movement, and many of its supporters, black and white, had been radicalized by the horrific racist backlash against desegregation in the Southern States. In September the bombing of a Negro church in Birmingham, Alabama, had killed four schoolgirls.

In November President Kennedy was assassinated, so the front-runners in the 1964 election were to be the Texan Democrat Lyndon Johnson and the Republican reactionary Barry Goldwater. Fearing that the issues he cared about would now be ignored, Gillespie devoted more time than he had intended to the dissemination of his manifesto. He rehearsed a speech in which he listed his key concerns: civil rights, to be gained if necessary through mass boycotts; the diplomatic recognition of China; and an end to the war in Vietnam. He also promised that life for Americans under their first trumpeter-President would be fun. The White House would be renamed the Blues House, and top government jobs would go to qualified musicians instead of political hacks. Max Roach 'argued for the position of Minister of War, but since we're not going to have any, I convinced him to be Minister of Defence'. Charles Mingus had been lined up for Minister of Peace, 'because he'll take a piece of your head faster than anybody I know'. Other senior positions would be filled by Duke Ellington (Minister of State), Louis Armstrong (Minister of Agriculture) and Thelonious Monk (Roving Ambassador Plenipotentiary). Miles Davis would head the CIA. There were no obvious candidates for the job of first black astronaut, so Gillespie volunteered to rocket into space himself.

People across America wrote to ask how they could help. Since there was no Gillespie party machine, they were invited to sign a petition to the State of California, pleading that the name of John Birks Gillespie be entered as an independent presidential candidate. Predictably, California was not minded to grant their request.

On 4 April 1968 the hopes of those striving for a more harmonious America were dashed when Dr Martin Luther King was assassinated. But, as he later admitted, Gillespie on that fateful day was so drunk that the national tragedy passed him by. The day before he had given a concert at his old college, Laurinburg, North Carolina. Then on the day itself he had driven with his pianist, Mike Longo, down to Cheraw to drink home-made wine with friends and relations. By the time rumours of Dr King's death began to circulate, he was too far gone to take them in. At 2.00 in the morning his thoughts became fixed on moonshine whisky. He guided Longo to the remote shack where it was distilled and woke the bootlegger. After several hours of reckless consumption, he gave way to an evil urge to snatch the wig worn by his host's wife. In exchange, she bashed his face, broke his glasses, ripped his shirt and sank her teeth into his flesh. Mike Longo was left to load his bleeding and stupefied boss into the car, drive to a filling station and ask for directions back to Laurinburg. News of the slaying of King was spreading and provoking outrage, and the darkness was noisy with police sirens. He prayed no one would demand to know why a white man like him was in charge of a battered black man on such a terrible night.

Reflecting soberly upon this and other alcohol-fuelled follies, Gillespie recognized that he must climb from the degrading circle of boredom, depression and binge-drinking into which he had descended. His guide towards redemption was Beth McKintey, a missionary for the Baha'i faith. She first approached him when he was playing in a club in Milwaukee, and asked if they might discuss Charlie Parker. Here was a subject he loved and he talked freely. During their many subsequent meetings Beth McKintey caused him to review the unfolding of his own life and gave him pamphlets that set out the Baha'i beliefs.

Baha'i theology, which evolved in the Middle East in the nineteenth century, viewed all the world's great religions as part of a seamless continuum and argued for the oneness of mankind. Touched by this profoundly anti-racist message, Gillespie became a fervent member of the universal Baha'i congregation.

He renounced alcohol abuse and liked to say that the Baha'i faith had cured him of his 'dizziness', but in January 1972, when he was playing at the Village Vanguard in New York, he accepted some mysterious refreshment offered by a fan and collapsed on stage. At the hospital they had to restart his heart. After that he renewed his vow to make the most of his gifts from God.

*

To keep up with the times he altered the line-up of his group, dropping the saxophone and bringing in a guitar and an electric bass. But he sounded happiest and most convincing on those occasions where, by public demand, he revisited former glories.

In 1968 he toured Europe with his Reunion Big Band, celebrating the 20th anniversary of his triumphant visit with the orchestra of 1948. The Reunion Band was fêted in eight European countries, and its well-drilled act was recorded in concert in Berlin's Philharmonic Hall. They opened with the volcanic 'Things to Come', Gillespie's revolutionary anthem from the 1940s, and closed with a new variant he had written, the relaxed 'The Things are Here', confirming that the revolution had long since been accomplished.

In 1971 the promoter George Wein organized a touring package he called Giants of Jazz, which teamed Gillespie with other former revolutionaries, including Sonny Stitt, Art Blakey and Thelonious Monk. Their concert repertoire included 'Blue 'n Boogie', 'Tin Tin Deo' and ''Round Midnight'. European audiences were ecstatic.

In 1973 Norman Granz emerged from his European retreat and formed a new record company, Pablo (named after Pablo Picasso, many of whose paintings he now owned). Although the name was new, Pablo turned out to be a conservative, revivalist brand, picking up where Granz had left off in 1961. Gillespie jumped at the chance to work for Granz again. One of his first assignments as a Pablo artist was to record an album of duets with Oscar Peterson.

The session took place in London, and to give himself the edge, Gillespie arrived early and took a nap before Peterson appeared. 'Ain't no use trying to get your rest now, brother, you're in trouble today,' was Peterson's jovial reaction when he walked into the studio. This was the autumn of 1974. Gillespie's chops were softer than they used to be and Peterson was troubled with arthritis, but these fiercely combative veterans spent two days putting each other to the test. Among the highlights were 'Dizzy Atmosphere' at its usual dizzy speed, and 'Blues for Bird', their joint homage to Charlie Parker.

Also during this European visit, Gillespie attended a large-scale Bird event: a festival in Portugal they called The Musical Life of Charlie Parker. Here he brought delight by performing with an ad hoc assembly of seasoned ornithologists, including Red Rodney and Sonny Stitt.

*

Back in the USA the honours piled up: a Grammy Award for the album with Oscar Peterson; the Handel Medallion, presented by Mayor Lindsay on behalf of New York City; the Duke Ellington Fellowship at Yale; and, the one which made him most proud, the Paul Robeson Award from Rutgers University for his achievements as an African-American.

In 1976 he was invited by his home state, South Carolina, to come and address an extraordinary session of its Legislature. Although he was flattered and touched by this gesture, he made a tough speech, based on a Baha'i text called '200 Years of Imperishable Hope'. Having outlined the history of racism in America, he detected shoots of promise in the South and looked forward to the transformation of the nation.

Jimmy Carter, the peanut farmer from Georgia, was elected US President in 1977. During his first year in office he invited Gillespie to come and give a concert at the White House with Earl Hines and Sarah Vaughan, and in 1978 Gillespie was back again, as one of the performers at a gala on the south lawn to celebrate twenty-five years of the Newport Jazz Festival. Gillespie and Max Roach were high on the star-studded bill. They played duets until Gillespie insisted that Carter must join them to form a trio. Surprised but compliant, the liberal President went into a huddle with the two master musicians, who explained his duties to him. The piece they were about to play would be fast, but all Carter had to do was shout 'Salt Peanuts!' twice, whenever Max pointed a drumstick at him. Carter did as he was bid, and although the standard of performance fell short of the 'Salt Peanuts' at Massey Hall, having a peanut-farming President as vocalist was certainly a coup.

Sitting in a wheelchair amongst the celebrity audience was Charles Mingus, now in the closing stages of a paralyzing illness. Within six months Mingus was dead. Gillespie played a prominent part in the 'Salute to Mingus' valedictory concert in Greenwich Village.

That same year, 1979, after a five-year gestation period, Gillespie's autobiography was published. He called it *Dizzy: To Be or Not To Bop*, unable to resist the jokey Shakespearean reference. Written in collaboration with his friend the academic Al Fraser, the hefty tome blends Gillespie's recollections with the points of view of friends, relatives and fellow artists. Most affecting are the elegiac passages describing the golden moment when his genius twined with Charlie Parker's.

*

Helping Gillespie sustain his zest during the 1970s and 80s was the young Californian trumpeter Jon Faddis, whom he called his 'prodigy-protégé'. In 1968 when Faddis was fifteen years old he joined Gillespie on stage and played the trumpet coda to 'A Night in Tunisia'. Thereafter he was often employed to share Gillespie's load on big occasions.

In 1987 at the age of seventy Gillespie formed a new big band that played classics like 'Emanon', 'Manteca' and 'Things to Come', adding electric guitar and bass guitar for a topical jazz-rock touch. Faddis was a crucial member of the trumpet section, there to look after the highest notes and take over some of his boss's solo spots. The band's pièce de résistance was 'A Night in Tunisia', which by now had a double coda. First a modest one from Gillespie, alluding to his 1940s original, then a massively virile one from Faddis. During the pauses in Faddis's macho display Gillespie would make little jokes – an old man's rueful commentary upon the pitiless passage of time.

*

Two years later he signed up for the sternest of tests: a performance with no understudy, no big-band safety net, supported only by the strong arms of the drummer he had discovered at Clark Monroe's Uptown House in Harlem nearly half a century earlier.

Max Roach was now sixty-five, a master musician, whose body of recorded work included a series of marathon free-form duets with members of the avant-garde. Impressed by these, the organizers of the 1989 Festival at the Maison de la Culture in Paris proposed a similarly unstructured performance with his former boss as part of the build-up to the 200th anniversary of the French Revolution. The concert was set for 23 March, in the middle of a Gillespie world tour, so there was little time for planning and preparation, as Roach remembered:

> We didn't have a moment alone together, excepting the day of the concert, when the car picked us up. We looked at each other and Diz said, 'There's no piano and no bass! What about the changes?' I explained to him what happened with Braxton and with Archie Shepp. Not that he didn't know it. Dizzy really is like a fox. He said, 'Ooh, you mean I'm free?'[3]

The concert has been issued on two CDs. For two hours, in front of a spellbound audience including many young trumpeters keen to see how he will manage, Gillespie puts himself through his septuagenarian paces, fortified by Roach's uplifting and sensitive presence. The modules of the performance flow freely one into the next, but the duo eschews the avant-garde extremes. Tonality is never abandoned and sometimes the atmosphere is powerfully nostalgic. One module evokes Thelonious Monk's ''Round Midnight', and two more revive classics that were played at Massey Hall: 'Wee' (or 'Allen's Alley' or 'Big Noise') and 'Salt Peanuts', with Roach playing the Charlie Parker part during the chorus where Gillespie sings.

Three months after this marathon, in July 1989, Gillespie and Roach were back in Paris for further celebrations of the bicentennial of the Revolution. The all-star concert in which they took part was dedicated, with commendable Gallic logic, to that arch-revolutionary Charlie Parker.

*

Gillespie entered the 1990s at the head of the United Nations Orchestra, his latest big band, whose personnel exemplified the oneness principle of his Baha'i religion. Sitting alongside the US veterans were members from

Brazil, Cuba, the Dominican Republic, Panama and Puerto Rico. A young Cuban virtuoso, Arturo Sandoval, took over the duties of Jon Faddis, and the band travelled widely. But by the start of 1992 Gillespie was too ill to continue.

Cancer had claimed him. He died on 6 January 1993. At his memorial service in St Patrick's Cathedral, New York, musicians saluted his spirit with a performance of 'A Night in Tunisia'.

NINE

GLASS ENCLOSURE

'*Bud was like a very delicate piece of china.*'
Elvin Jones[1]

ESCORTED BACK to New York by Oscar Goodstein after the Massey Hall adventure, Powell spent the summer of 1953 working at Birdland. Here his Trio (with Charles Mingus and drummer Arthur Taylor) not only starred in its own right but also acted as a rhythm section for others. A highlight of their season was the two weeks when Charlie Parker joined them; luckily for fans, some recordings were made.

The way Powell sparkles on Parker's 'Cheryl' is familiar – he had played brilliantly on Parker's 1947 recording of this tune – but his contribution to 'Moose the Mooche' is a new delight. The twisty theme is negotiated at hair-raising speed, and he shows the clarity of his mind and the steel in his fingers by playing it in unison with Parker. Then he adds a ferocious solo, trailing sparks.

On his own composition, 'Dance of the Infidels', he and Parker both play long, masterful solos, and the whole performance has a tremendous spring in its step, with Max Roach sitting in on drums. And Roach is there again when Dizzy Gillespie guests with the Trio, playing 'Salt Peanuts' and 'Woody 'n You'. Tantalizingly, when Gillespie is in, Parker is out, so the full Massey Hall line-up is never repli-cated.

When there were no hornmen to be accommodated, Powell would lead his Trio through some practised routines: arrangements of songs like 'I've Got You Under My Skin' and 'Autumn in New York'. The rapport between Powell and Mingus was uncanny, and their shared ability to generate colossal swing produced performances, such as 'I Want to Be Happy', with the power to transcend the murk of the low-fi recordings and overwhelm us with joy.

*

By the middle of August, when the Trio made its next album for Blue Note, Charles Mingus had moved on. His replacement, George Duvivier, obliged record producer Alfred Lion by committing to paper the extraor-dinary music drama that had been gathering in Powell's mind.

Lion had heard excerpts when he visited the apartment where Goodstein kept Powell confined. Asked what the music was called, Powell scanned the room and answered, 'Glass Enclosure'. This haunting, claus-trophobic work is intensely agitated, both harmonically and rhythmically. It allows no scope for improvisation and is like nothing else in the Powell œuvre, yet in its dark, unsettling character it is quintessen-tial Powell.

The following month he recorded eight pieces for Roost Records: five popular ballads and three jazz standards, including Gillespie's 'Woody 'n You'. What came out is not great Bud Powell, but it is fine piano music by any standards except those he set himself, and it conveys with savage truthfulness a despairing state of mind. Harsh chords are hit spitefully hard. Promising melodic ideas are hacked down in their prime.

During the winter of 1953 the Trio kept working at Birdland, but Powell was deeply unhappy. He told Goodstein he was playing badly, and between sets he would go off and hide. Early in 1954 Goodstein sent him to the West Coast for a long residency at the Haig in Los Angeles, where bassist Curtis Counce was paid extra to act as his minder. There were no offstage disasters, but Powell in performance often became agitated and unable to improvise. The engagement was cut short. Back in New York he was sent to hospital for more psychiatric treatment. His spirit, however, was not entirely broken and the trajectory of his creative life was not exclusively downwards.

In June 1954 he recorded two new compositions of his own and six personal readings of popular ballads with his Trio for Norman Granz. His rendition of 'It Never Entered My Mind' is particularly gorgeous, made so by the purity of his chosen voicings and the mirror-calmness of his delivery. On the other ballads the heaviness of his dark chords is offset by confident, feathery decoration. One of his new pieces, 'Fantasy in Blue', is startling in its originality: a hypnotic mantra that makes no harmonic progress. The other new work is more conventional – a cheerful ditty that he called 'Buttercup', in honour of the new lady in his life.

The buxom Altevia Edwards, nicknamed Buttercup, claimed to be a long-standing friend of the Powell family. She said she realized her destiny lay with Bud when she visited him in hospital and found him trussed in a straightjacket and so disturbed he didn't recognize his own mother. Having secured his release, she moved into an apartment with him, and eventually replaced Oscar Goodstein as his guardian.

Unfortunately, she was unable to wean him from alcohol. And, as witnesses constantly averred, booze in even the smallest quantity had devastating consequences. It was probably an ingredient in the artistic shambles of 16 December 1954 when Powell came to record again for Norman Granz. On this occasion, despite the efforts of Percy Heath on bass and acutely sensitive support from Max Roach, little that was worthy of Powell was produced.

Granz stumped up for more recording sessions on three consecutive days in January 1955, and here again the results are patchy. On the first day, with Lloyd Trotman on bass and Art Blakey on drums, Powell is in charge of his faculties but fixed on playing in a retrospective style – less like himself than like Earl Hines or Teddy Wilson. On day two it seems he hit the bottle before reaching the studio. The result is a disaster. It is as if the real Bud Powell is somewhere else, listening to the struggles of this keyboard novice and vainly willing him to do well. On day three, this time with Percy Heath and Kenny Clarke, Powell has recovered slightly, but his performances still make for grim listening.

*

In March 1955, still in the slough of despondence, and still dosing himself with alcohol, Powell was booked to form part of the quintet with which Charlie Parker would make his Birdland comeback. The consequence was predictably catastrophic.

On the first night, according to jazz critic Dan Morgenstern, Powell could not focus on the music. During the playing of 'The Man I Love' he kept repeating the first sixteen bars and failing to go on to the middle eight, oblivious to Parker's urgent signals.

During an intermission while Parker was sitting with friends, including the blind pianist Lennie Tristano, Powell approached, babbling insults. Tristano recalled the incident with horror:

> Bud said, 'You know, Bird, you ain't shit. You don't kill me. You ain't
> playing shit now,' and went on putting him down unmercifully. I said,
> 'Bud, don't talk that way: Bird's your poppa.' Bird said, 'Lennie, don't
> pay any attention. I dig the way he plays.'[2]

On the second night Parker arrived to find Powell already incapacitated by drink and flailing senselessly at the keyboard. Bitter words were exchanged and Parker's comeback ended in disaster and disgrace. A week later he was dead.

*

The Powell–Buttercup ménage endured and Powell kept working.

In April he spent two days in the studio, backed by George Duvivier and Arthur Taylor, making recordings for Norman Granz. The results are more coherent than his January efforts, but the muse that burned back in the 1940s and early 1950s is almost out.

Although he would never talk about Charlie Parker, he concluded these April recordings with a pair of musical salutes. First 'Star Eyes', a pretty pop song that Parker made his own. Then 'Confirmation', one of Parker's subtlest compositions.

After that he made no more commercial recordings for more than a year, but stayed active on the club circuit. In the autumn of 1955 he was working in Cleveland in a trio with Charles Mingus and drummer Elvin Jones. When Mingus left to lead his own band, he was replaced by Parker's long-time bassist Tommy Potter. This version of the Powell Trio worked on and off for the next eighteen months. It was a worrying time for Elvin Jones, who reported, 'Bud was very shaky, very sick . . . Once, when people poured some wine in him, he was found the next morning in an alley in his underwear with even his shirt and tie stolen.'[3]

The next time Powell came to the attention of the press was in March 1956, and the story was a sensational one. He was arrested while performing at a theatre in Newark, New Jersey, and jailed in consequence of a paternity suit filed by Altevia Edwards (Buttercup). He was released on bail, and when the matter came to court Oscar Goodstein testified on his behalf that electric shock treatment for his mental illness had rendered him sterile. Despite the unpleasantness of the proceedings, Powell and Buttercup stayed together, and Powell accepted the baby boy, called John, as the third member of their household.

On 26 June 1956 Powell's younger brother, Richie, was killed in a car crash, just as he was achieving recognition as a pianist with the fêted Max Roach–Clifford Brown Quintet. Brown died in the same accident. Bud preferred not to speak of it.

In September he made his last recordings for Granz, sounding fit and proud. Gillespie's 'Bebop' is delineated at colossal speed. The equally fast 'I Know that You Know' is peppered with sensational four-bar breaks. Ballads like 'I Should Care' are extravagantly embellished. Charlie Parker's 'Now's the Time' is led through weird, atonal territory.

Chaperoned by Buttercup, Powell was added to the touring package called 'Birdland '56' (including Miles Davis and Lester Young) which spent three November weeks in Europe. The tour began in Paris, and many fans from England crossed the Channel in pursuit. Among them was Alun Morgan, who found the American stars at the bar of the Club

Saint Germain on the night before the show. Morgan, a Powell devotee, was thrilled when his hero detached himself from the crowd of drinkers and sat at the club piano. But what followed came as a horrible shock:

> For the next three minutes we heard a painfully badly played version of 'Nice Work if You Can Get It', in the course of which Bud's hands seemed to be seized with some paralysis, for fingering mistakes were legion. Back at the bar, Bud seemed hurt and dazed.[4]

It was Miles Davis who dispelled the tension, flinging an arm around Powell's shoulders and advising kindly, 'You know man, you shouldn't try to play when you're juiced like that.'[5]

The concert next night was at the Salle Pleyel, the scene of past triumphs for Dizzy Gillespie and Charlie Parker. Powell's contribution was a short set of unaccompanied piano pieces. Opinions varied concerning the quality of his performance. Alun Morgan found the playing chaotic. Mike Butcher, reviewing the concert for *Jazz Journal*, described 'the art of a mentally sick man who bares his soul for us to take or leave'.[6] Francis Paudras, the young French graphics designer and amateur pianist who would devote much of his life to the Powell cause, hailed 'the magical sounds that poured forth'.[7]

During the rest of the European tour, the French musicians who played supporting roles on the Birdland bill felt privileged to listen to Powell perform every night. On some evenings he was disappointing, on others he thrilled them. Bassist Pierre Michelot noted that, socially, Powell was very subdued under Buttercup's wing, but that 'the music that was coming out of his soul was like nothing I'd ever heard'.[8]

*

Shortly before and again shortly after the European tour, Powell recorded for RCA Victor. The results give us an idea of what the Europeans must have heard from him on his good nights. Sometimes the playing is imprecise, but the flaws in execution are overwhelmed by the power and urgency of his message. On two of the toughest pieces – 'Salt Peanuts' and 'Shaw 'Nuff' – he takes risks and swings like hell. And his account of his own fine composition 'Oblivion' is a fierce alternative to the perfection of his 1951 recording.

In August 1957 he recorded again for Blue Note, but the result is not in the same class as his previous albums for the label. The minor-key swinger 'Blue Pearl' (named for his mother) is the only new Powell composition. The other three tracks by his Trio dwell on familiar chord sequences. Longest by far is 'Some Soul', a slow 12-bar blues that hints at but fails to emulate Charlie Parker's masterpiece 'Parker's Mood'.

Anticipating that Powell might not have the strength to sustain a whole album with just bass and drums, Blue Note boss Alfred Lion had enrolled trombonist Curtis Fuller to come and share the load. Fuller plays on three numbers: two standards and Charlie Parker's 'Moose the Mooche'. At Birdland in 1953 Powell zipped through this tricky theme in unison with its composer. Here it is taken at a funereal pace, presumably for Fuller's benefit; even so, piano and trombone fail to reach perfect agreement.

*

A year after his first visit to Paris, Powell was back again to play for three weeks at the Club Saint Germain, with the solid French bassist Pierre Michelot and the distinguished expatriate drummer Kenny Clarke. Francis Paudras was among the adoring crowd that gathered on opening night. He noted that Powell 'was welcomed like a diva'. And as for the music, 'The intensity of his playing was such that he had trouble breathing . . . At times it was unbearable.'[9]

When the contract was up, Powell returned to the States, where uncritical fan worship and gainful employment were less easy to find. In May 1958 he made his next album for Blue Note, with the powerful rhythm team of Sam Jones (bass) and Philly Joe Jones (drums). Although his improvising was below full strength, he came to the studio with eight new compositions, ranging from slow blues through Afro-Latin to the wistful ballad 'Time Waits'. His personal favourite among these was 'John's Abbey' (named for his young son), a brisk, boppish 32-bar theme, similar in its intricacy to Parker's 'Moose the Mooche'.

To support Buttercup and the baby he took what work he could find in the New York clubs, where his reputation for trouble went before him. His employment prospects were not helped by a report in the August 1958 issue of *Jazz Journal* about his attempts to sit in during a Birdland tribute to Lester Young. According to writer Dan Morgenstern, Powell, previously such a stickler for sartorial formality, wore a blotchy beard and showed distressing signs of neglect.

But the artist inside him had not died. At the end of December he made another trio album for Blue Note, a set of sharp-witted perform-ances built on fresh compositions. Gone is the seed-scattering ardour of his salad days, but he is technically adroit and full of musical cunning. The album, called *The Scene Changes*, was his last in the USA for nearly six years. He spent the start of 1959 in hospital, and after his release Buttercup took him and young John to reside in Paris, where a warm welcome and a job were waiting.

*

In March he opened at the Blue Note club, with Pierre Michelot on bass and Kenny Clarke on drums. The trio became known and loved by the French as *Les Trois Patrons* (The Three Bosses).

In July he moved to Le Chat Qui Pêche, a damp and smoky cellar for die-hard jazz fans. Here his American accompanists were Chuck Israels on bass and J.T. Hogan on the drums; the music they produced was relentlessly hard driving. Crouched outside in the street night after night, listening to it all through an orifice at pavement level, was the devoted Francis Paudras, unable to afford the price of admission.

In October, when Powell, Michelot and Clarke were working at the Club Saint Germain, they were visited by French television cameras. The tape of that telecast is eloquent. Illness has turned Powell into a heavy man, far removed from the slender waif seen in photographs taken ten years earlier. He's formally dressed in dark suit and tie, and the tight collar of his shirt digs into the folds of his neck, creating a Buddha-like effect. He sits bolt upright at the piano, staring ahead, entirely detached, it would seem, from his busy hands. These are working in a relaxed and unshowy way, using an extraordinary combination of techniques: the arched hand-shape that is *de rigueur* for European recitalists; and the flat-fingered jabbing of Thelonious Monk.

The first musical offering is Powell's recent composition 'Crossin' the Channel'. The scampering theme is delivered by both hands in unison, and the ensuing improvisation is in the mature Powell manner: right hand fleet and cool; left hand less percussive, more insinuating and higher up the keyboard than it used to be. The other number played by the trio is Oscar Pettiford's 'Blues in the Closet', utterly relaxed and intensely swinging.

In December, French television were to broadcast more by Les Trois Patrons, this time from the Blue Note club. Here Powell showed off his good health by playing 'Get Happy' as fast as ever, and following it with the finger-busting 'John's Abbey'.

To round off a fruitful first Parisian year, on 18 December he made a guest appearance on the stage of the Théâtre des Champs-Elysées, where he joined the concert being given by Art Blakey's Jazz Messengers. In his honour the Blakey band played two of his most famous compositions, 'Dance of the Infidels' and 'Bouncing with Bud', and insisted he should take the lion's share of the solo space. Although lacking ferocity, his long improvisations delight with the sharpness of their timing.

*

At the start of 1960 Powell was out of work. Shocked to learn that he had been spotted begging on the Boulevard Saint Germain, Francis Paudras and his girlfriend Nicole rode to the rescue. They picked him up, took him to a café, met his request for red wine and kept him company until nightfall. Then they escorted him to the Hotel Louisiane, where he lived with Buttercup and John. Buttercup granted their request to come and collect him and take him home with them for lunch next day.

When Paudras arrived, Powell was waiting for him at the hotel-room door, already wrapped in his overcoat and beret. As they left, Buttercup issued her instructions. Bud was to be given no alcohol and must be returned on time. She also gave Paudras three pink pills to be swallowed by Bud in the middle of the afternoon.

As Paudras describes it in his book,[10] the lunch in the little apartment he shared with Nicole on the Rue Boursault was idyllic. Powell dug deeply into Nicole's French cooking, then chose a sequence of Tatum records from Paudras' collection. Finally he sat down at the baby grand piano and played an intensely romantic version of 'April in Paris', which the ecstatic Paudras recorded on his Ferrograph.

Luncheon chez Paudras became a regular part of Powell's life. When the Blue Note club engaged him again, Paudras would take him home in the early evening so Buttercup could look him over before he went to work. At the club Paudras would station himself on the stage behind the piano. It worried him that Powell seemed to be struggling to stay awake. Suspecting that the pills dished out by Buttercup might be the cause of the lethargy, he sent one for analysis. It turned out to contain Largactyl, a powerful tranquillizer, commonly used as an antipsychotic but normally administered only under medical supervision. How Buttercup was able to obtain it remained a mystery.

According to the Paudras book, when he and Nicole went to collect Powell for lunch one day, they found him tied to a table leg with young John dancing around him. After they had removed him from this horrible scene, he admitted to them that Buttercup was not his wife and Johnny was not his son.

*

In April 1960 Powell joined Kenny Clarke and the master-bassist Oscar Pettiford for a concert in Germany. Here, for the benefit of the capacity audience in Essen's huge Grugahalle, this trio of groundbreakers recalled the revolutionary repertoire of their New York heyday, starting with Dizzy Gillespie's 'Shaw 'Nuff' and ending with 'Salt Peanuts'.

For the second half of the concert the trio was joined by Coleman Hawkins. The first and most noteworthy of the quartet performances is 'All the Things You Are', prefaced by Gillespie's evergreen introduction. During Hawkins's forceful solo, Powell provides a discreet accompaniment very different from the dense backcloth he wove at Massey Hall. And when it's Powell's turn to improvise he does so neatly and economically – a pencil sketch rather than a painting in oils.

Three months later at the Jazz Festival in Antibes, Powell was reunited with another master bass player. In the years since Charles Mingus last performed as a member of the Bud Powell Trio, he had established himself as one of America's most important composers and bandleaders. The quintet he brought to Antibes, including Eric Dolphy and Booker Ervin, played in a much freer style than Powell was used to, but common ground was found when he joined them on stage for a performance of 'I'll Remember April' (famously recorded by Powell many years earlier). In spite of the sympathetic context, his long solo here sounds fragile and his ideas fade before reaching full bloom.

Back in Paris, Francis Paudras became more and more upset by the oppressive regime at the Hotel Louisiane.

The picture brightened in the spring and summer of 1961, when Thelonious Monk was touring Europe. Paudras and Powell went to a Monk concert together, and Paudras came to appreciate the powerful bond between these two great artists.

In December, backed by Pierre Michelot and Kenny Clarke, Powell made an album that was issued as *A Portrait of Thelonious*. Among the Monk compositions lovingly rendered is 'Off Minor', previously recorded by Powell a dozen years earlier during the landmark session with Curley Russell and Max Roach. The change in approach is striking. The first interpretation was warm, rounded and rich. The new one is sparse and spiky, much closer to the Monk essence.

In the spring of 1962, accompanied by Buttercup, Powell left France on a European concert tour. According to press rumours, things went awry in Switzerland, where he suffered severe mental health problems. Nevertheless, he moved on to Sweden and played for four weeks with a local rhythm section at the brand new Golden Circle club in Stockholm. Abbe Johansson, the club manager, found him extremely withdrawn, and blamed the condition on the electric shock treatments Powell had endured in a Swiss hospital.

The five albums recorded at the Golden Circle are not great Bud Powell, but serve as a testament to his suffering. Sometimes the choice of material is telling. 'Relaxin' at Camarillo', for example, the tortuous blues written by Charlie Parker after his release from mental hospital. And 'I Remember Clifford', Benny Golson's elegy for Clifford Brown, the young trumpeter who died in the same car crash that killed Powell's brother Richie.

*

One day when Paudras went to pick Powell up from the Hotel Louisiane he found that Buttercup had moved him out of her quarters and into a little room that she kept locked. Paudras was obliged to talk to him through the door. After several more visits in the same humiliating circumstances, Paudras was phoned by Buttercup, whose hostility had turned to panic. Powell had escaped on to the roof, and thence into the home of a terrified woman who alerted the law. He was now under arrest and the gendarmes would not release him to Buttercup, although he was contracted to play that night. Paudras came to the police station and persuaded them to let his friend go.

After that he was allowed access to Powell whenever he visited the hotel, but to make sure there was no absconding, Buttercup adopted the crude expedient of confiscating her breadwinner's trousers. These were only returned to him when it was time to go to work.

The boss of the Blue Note would send a car to pick him up and then make sure he was delivered back into Buttercup's custody at the end of the last set. But in spite of the tight security, Powell escaped from the club one night and vanished.

It took Paudras three days to track him down. He found him in the Laënnec Hospital, in a large ward for infectious diseases filled mainly with immigrants from North Africa. Powell would not communicate or cooperate, and was being kept under observation. Paudras visited him each day. Then one day Powell was gone, transferred without warning. After a struggle with the hospital bureaucracy Paudras was allowed to visit him in his padded cell in the psychiatric wing. He patiently explained Powell's genius and his suffering to the young doctor on the case, and at last it was agreed that Powell could be released into his care. When Buttercup was telephoned and asked if her charge could go and live with Paudras, she raised no objection.

*

Powell had lost his job at the Blue Note club, but with Paudras and Nicole on the rue Boursault he found peace and began to regain his strength. His hosts did not entirely abandon their habit of taking wine with meals, but they set their guest a good example by drinking very little and made the happy discovery that his demands for more booze could be satisfied with alcohol-free beer. On doctor's advice, the dose of Largactyl was gradually reduced. There was no sleeping accommodation for him in the tiny apartment, so Paudras rented a bedroom for him in the small hotel next door.

By the start of 1963 Powell was transformed. Paudras took him to sit in at the Blue Note club, where his performance and his demeanour overcame the owner's bad memories and he was rehired (although his earnings were collected nightly by Buttercup).

When the news of his return to health reached America, Frank Sinatra's Reprise record company commissioned Duke Ellington, no less, to supervise the production of a Powell trio album in Paris. The album (released as *Bud Powell in Paris*) consists mainly of familiar tunes, including Ellington's 'Satin Doll'. According to Paudras, Ellington was delighted with the performances, during which he did little dance steps behind Powell, whispering 'Play, genius, play!'[11] Buttercup came to collect the cheque.

Paudras's career as a graphics designer was flourishing, so he and Nicole were able to take a larger apartment where Powell could have his own room. The new address, 64 rue de Clichy, became a Mecca for American musicians living in Paris or just passing through. Those who marvelled at the reinvigorated Bud Powell included Dexter Gordon, Johnny Griffin, Sonny Rollins, Sonny Stitt, Arthur Taylor, Hank Mobley and Max Roach.

Dexter Gordon, with whom Powell had once made some brilliant recordings, was now a European resident after hard times in the USA. He and Powell, escorted by Paudras, would stroll through the streets of Paris on fine spring nights, reviewing their lives. In May, Gordon recorded an album with Powell, Michelot and Clarke that looked fondly back. They opened with Charlie Parker's 'Scrapple from the Apple', moved through a selection of standard tunes, and closed with a worthy performance (but not in the Massey Hall class) of Gillespie's 'A Night in Tunisia'.

When Gillespie himself came to Paris and gave a concert with his quintet at the Palais des Sports, Paudras and Powell were in the audience and went backstage afterwards. At home the following day, still excited, Powell sat Paudras down at the piano and insisted on teaching him several neat devices he had learned from Gillespie in person many years before. First, Gillespie's way of introducing 'All the Things You Are', then his introduction and coda for "Round Midnight".

To make the most of Gillespie's Paris sojourn, his record company brought him together with the French scat singers the Double Six and the top trio in the French capital, Les Trois Patrons. The backward-looking repertoire chosen for the album they made – including 'Anthropology', 'Blue 'n Boogie', 'Groovin' High' and 'Hot House' – suited Powell comfortably.

*

The new Paudras apartment was at the top of five flights of stairs, which Powell climbed with increasing difficulty. He started to lose weight, and soon any physical effort exhausted him. Paudras took him for a check-up and was shocked to be told that Powell was suffering from tuberculosis. Tests revealed that the disease was at an advanced stage and had eaten a huge hole in one of his lungs. Suspecting he might be sent to hospital, Powell fled and was missing for three days. When Paudras found him he was so exhausted and ill that he submitted to the inevitable. The Hospital Foch took him in on 17 September 1963, and Paudras guaranteed to meet the bills.

When word of the desperate situation reached Oscar Goodstein in New York, he moved fast. He sent money towards medical expenses to the American Embassy, and when this was seized by Buttercup, he adopted Paudras as his man in Paris. A benefit concert was held at Birdland, starring Thelonious Monk and Dizzy Gillespie, and the proceeds were sent via Paudras to the Hospital Foch.

In November, Powell was transferred to the sanatorium at Bouffémont. His holed lung had mended well enough to avoid surgery, and he continued to make such good progress that they allowed him to spend Christmas at home with Paudras. During the early months of 1964 they let him come home at the weekends, but the expenses were piling up. At Oscar Goodstein's suggestion Paudras organized a benefit concert featuring French and American musicians: an effective fundraiser that lasted six hours.

By the early summer Powell was fit enough to play in public again. He returned to the Blue Note but with a clause in his contract that said he was under doctor's orders to play only the first set, then go home and early to bed each night.

Encouraged by what he was hearing about Powell's recovery, Oscar Goodstein made an offer he was sure could not be refused. If Paudras would bring Powell to New York, Goodstein would pay their single airfares as an advance against earnings. Then he would put Powell into Birdland for ten or twelve weeks, at $500 per week. When Paudras hesitated, Goodstein bombarded him with letters, stressing the glories that would attend Powell's triumphant return. A date was set for the transatlantic flight.

Meanwhile, anxious that the convalescent Powell should not be stuck in sweltering Paris in August, Paudras and Nicole took him for a seaside holiday to a Normandy village aptly named Edenville. A friend of Paudras who ran the local restaurant turned part of it into a nightclub, with a piano. Powell relished the cuisine and gave a generous performance each evening, accompanied by keen young Frenchmen on bass and drums. The exiled American saxophonist Johnny Griffin came to stay for a few days, each of which ended in a lengthy jam session. Paudras made tapes. 'Salt Peanuts', 'Hot House', 'Wee' ('Big Noise') and '52nd Street Theme' are all here, and Powell has found something like his Massey Hall form. But the idyll at Edenville was short. On 16 August 1964 he and Paudras flew to America.

*

Oscar Goodstein met them at New York's Kennedy Airport and escorted them to the hotel near Birdland where he had booked them a room. The hotel would be paid directly by him, he said, and so would the Italian restaurant across the street where they could take their meals. All these costs would be deducted from Powell's Birdland earnings.

New York in August was oppressively hot, and the twin-bedded hotel room had no air-conditioning. Paudras thought Powell deserved better than this, but was reluctant to cross Goodstein so soon. The dynamic businessman instructed them to meet him in his office first thing in the morning.

When they arrived, Goodstein said there was much to be done. Before Powell could work in New York, he must be granted a cabaret card, and prior to that, things must be squared with the musicians' union. He took them to the union office, where it was established that before he could be employed, Powell must pay his back dues for all the years he was away in Paris. Paudras watched as Goodstein handed over about $900, explaining that he would recover the money from Powell later.

Next Goodstein sent Paudras and Powell to see Maxwell T. Cohen, who had acted as Powell's lawyer since the early 1950s. Cohen gave them a letter of introduction to the Liquor Authority, which had the power to grant or withhold the vital cabaret card. Paudras found Cohen likeable but was dismayed by the erosion of Powell's future earnings. Goodstein had given him a $700 cheque to pass on to Cohen, for past services on Powell's behalf.

The official they had to deal with at the Liquor Authority, a Mr Gillespie, could not have been less like his illustrious musician namesake. Viewing Powell with undisguised contempt, he ordered him to go away and submit to a narcotics test, a complete medical examination, a police assessment and fingerprinting.

The waiting room for the narcotics test was like the antechamber to hell: full of junkies in agony. By the time the suggestible Powell was seen by the doctor, he had been seized by psychosomatic withdrawal symptoms. Although the test proved negative, the doctor remained scornful and suspicious.

The general medical was a formality, but the visit to the police was torture. Powell sweated profusely under their aggressive questioning, and smudged his face with ink as he tried to wipe his brow during the fingerprinting session. Back at the hotel he said he would take a short walk before dinner. When he returned he was drunk.

Now the hurdles set up by the Liquor Authority had been cleared, Paudras was looking forward to the issue of the cabaret card. Instead he was summoned to another meeting with Mr Gillespie, who angrily accused him of withholding vital information. Surely he must have known that Powell had once attempted suicide, which was a criminal offence? Checking with Maxwell Cohen, Paudras discovered that Powell had slit open his left armpit with a razor and nearly died from loss of blood. Mr Gillespie was persuaded not to use this incident to disqualify Powell from working, and the card was grudgingly granted.

*

The opening night was emotional. Escorted by Paudras, Powell walked the short distance from the hotel to Birdland and then passed through the applauding guard of honour of musicians at the entrance. Inside the packed club, according to *Newsweek*, those giving him a prolonged standing ovation included Charles Mingus and Max Roach.

Waiting on the platform were the two young accompanists allocated by Goodstein: bassist John Ore and drummer Horace Arnold. When the applause finally quietened, Powell sat down and struck a fast tempo. Clapping and cheers broke out again to acknowledge his choice of tune, 'The Best Thing for You Would Be Me'.

Press reviews of the evening were positive. *Time* magazine welcomed Powell's performance as 'a giant step up from limbo'. *Down Beat* reported 'moments of inspired music-making'. Oscar Goodstein was ecstatic.

Paudras was vexed that this cardinal occasion had not been preserved for posterity. He installed his recording gear at Birdland and taped every subsequent evening. Some of his tapes are now in circulation, and on the evidence of these, Powell's playing was fitful. For example, Monk's ''Round Midnight', complete with the Dizzy Gillespie introduction and coda, is presented with solemn majesty, but Powell's own 'Hallucinations' is sluggish and heavy-handed compared with his masterpiece recording of 1951.

When Powell began complaining about the inexperience of the young drummer, Goodstein insisted he could not afford any of the better-known musicians. A solution was offered by Max Roach, who recommended a promising student of his, J.C. Moses. After an audition at Birdland, Moses was hired.

Roach and his wife, the singer Abbey Lincoln, invited Powell and Paudras to visit them at home. When the pianist and the Frenchman arrived at the apartment on Central Park West, they walked into a surprise party, packed with musicians, writers and painters assembled to welcome Powell royally. The call Paudras and Powell paid on the reclusive Thelonious Monk was another occasion for joy.

Seizing the upbeat mood, Goodstein contacted Alfred Lion and Francis Wolf, suggesting Powell should make another album for Blue Note. The parties met at Birdland, where terms were agreed. Afterwards Lyon suggested they all go out for a meal, but Powell had vanished. Wolf admitted Bud had asked him for money and that he had handed over $20. Paudras scoured the neighbourhood bars, then went back to the hotel and sent out distress calls until he fell asleep.

His phone rang at 5.00 a.m. It was William Powell, Bud's father, saying that Bud was at his home, drunk and unwelcome, and that Paudras should come and remove him. Paudras took a taxi to the Harlem address. William roused Bud from his stupor and told him he must go. Paudras wondered what had passed between them. Despite his pressing, William never came to Birdland to hear his son.

*

Rehearsals for the Blue Note album, with Paul Chambers and Roy Haynes, took place at Birdland in the afternoons. Drawn by his love of Powell, Charles Mingus joined them each day and strove to spread good cheer. But after the scene with his father, Powell had slumped. One afternoon he announced suddenly and finally that the Blue Note project was off.

His spirits revived when his first girlfriend, Frances Barnes, came to see him at the club one night, bringing their daughter Celia. He had last seen Celia when she was a baby. Now she was a shy teenager. While she and her mother sat in the Birdland audience, he played the beautiful song he had composed for her fifteen years ago.

A few nights later he disappeared again. Birdland had to manage without him while Paudras searched and Goodstein raged. In the end Powell was found at the home of a friend from his youth, the pianist Elmo Hope. Tracking down Hope had exhausted him, but he had become set on a reunion with the man who had visited him faithfully when he was locked away in Creedmoor hospital. Paudras took him back to the hotel, and after a few days rest he went back to Birdland and played each night until the end of his contract.

When the engagement was over, Goodstein advised Paudras that expenses had consumed all Powell's earnings. 'Poor Francis,' he said, 'you owe me $42. But forget it. It's on me!'[12] They could not afford either to remain at the hotel or fly back to France, so Paudras and Powell accepted a kind invitation from Ornette Coleman, standard bearer of the avant-garde, to share his basement apartment in Greenwich Village. A profound admirer of Powell's music, Coleman had come to pay his respects as soon as he heard Powell was back in New York. He became a constant friend.

Delightfully for Paudras and Powell, each new day in the basement began with the sound of Coleman doing his musical exercises. He would take a set of tunes by Charlie Parker and play them at double speed on his white plastic alto saxophone, a Grafton Acrylic, identical to the one used by Parker at Massey Hall.

In October the New York weather turned cold and Paudras began to worry that Coleman's freezing basement, with its bare stone walls, might be bad for Powell's health. Baroness Nica de Koenigswarter came to the rescue. Always concerned for musicians in need, the wealthy baroness who had nursed Charlie Parker in her Manhattan apartment now proposed that Powell and Paudras should come to live in her mansion across the river in New Jersey. Oscar Goodstein, meanwhile, had set up a recording session for Powell with the Roulette label, the proceeds of which would pay for tickets back to France.

Everything seemed to be proceeding smoothly, until one night Powell wandered off on his own and discovered the baroness's well-stocked wine cellar. Paudras found him drunk and put him to bed. In the morning he was gone. The session with Roulette had to be cancelled. After three desperate days of cold weather and rain, a policeman found Powell collapsed in a doorway in Greenwich Village. Back at the baroness's he slept for two days and then behaved as if nothing had happened.

The recording session was rescheduled for 22 October. In the studio on that day Powell was joined by bassist John Ore and drummer J.C. Moses. While Moses was setting up his kit, Powell slipped away and helped himself to drinks at a party that was happening next door. By the time Paudras found him his walk was unsteady and his eyes were dull.

The album that emerged from that session, issued by Roulette as *The Return of Bud Powell*, caused Paudras great sadness. Powell's genius is still there deep down, but on the surface, at fast tempos, there are weak-knuckled flaws you would not accept from far inferior players. It is on the ballads where his emotional power conquers all. 'Someone to Watch Over Me' is reminiscent of Charlie Parker's haunted and gasping 'Lover Man', although Powell is not *in extremis* like Parker was. His harmonization is ravishing, and his dramatic timing suffuses the Gershwin song with a sense of tragedy.

The return flight to France was booked for 27 October. On the eve of departure Frances Barnes and Celia came to Nica de Koenigswarter's house and took Powell away to spend the night with them. He promised he would meet Paudras at the airport in the morning. He never came. Paudras, who had no money and whose wife had given birth to their first child while he was away, agonized and then took off.

*

Those who went to visit Powell in Brooklyn, where he lived with Frances and Celia, reported that he kept a bottle of whisky at home and did the daily rounds of the neighbourhood bars.

In March 1965 he took part in the Carnegie Hall concert to mark the tenth anniversary of the death of Charlie Parker. The other musicians, including Dizzy Gillespie, were shocked at his deterioration. According to the commentator Ira Gitler, 'he was bloated and his eyes had a lost look as he slowly shuffled to the piano. It was difficult to look at or listen to Bud that night.'[13]

In November he was consigned to Kings County Hospital, a huge institution in Brooklyn for the mentally ill, after he dragged Frances to the police station, swearing he saw her murder a rat.

He died on 31 July 1966, two months before his forty-second birthday. The death certificate gave the causes as tuberculosis, malnutrition and alcoholism. Thousands lined the streets when his funeral procession passed through Harlem, with a band on a truck playing ''Round Midnight' and 'Dance of the Infidels'.

*

In 1979 Paudras signed a legal document, witnessed by his trusted friend Max Roach, bequeathing his vast store of Powell tapes to Bud's daughter Celia.

In 1986 he published *La Danse des Infidèles*, his account of his devotion to Powell's genius. In the same year Bertrand Tavernier's feature film *'Round Midnight* was released. An opening title announces that the story is 'inspired by incidents in the lives of Francis Paudras and Bud Powell', but the leading character turns out to be an amalgam of Powell and another doomed black American genius, Lester Young. Although embarrassingly twee around the edges, the movie is saved by the riveting central performance of non-actor Dexter Gordon, Powell's one-time confrère – another of those African-American musicians who suffered in their homeland and found solace abroad.

TEN

———

MEDITATIONS FOR A PAIR
OF WIRE CUTTERS

'His life was beyond music. His life was art.'
Randy Brecker[1]

AS WELL AS nursing the Debut label, Charles Mingus spent the summer of 1953 as a busy freelance. Three days after the flight home from the Massey Hall concert he was the piano player, with Percy Heath on bass and Max Roach on drums, when Miles Davis recorded 'Smooch' (another name for 'Weird Nightmare') for the Prestige label. A week after that his bass and Roach's drums laid a solid foundation for Charlie Parker's experimental recording with woodwind and voices. The sponsor of the session, Norman Granz, had Parker under contract, so it made sense to offer him the chance to buy the Massey Hall tapes. When negotiations broke down, Mingus felt entitled to issue this important material on Debut.

His regular gig during May and June was at Birdland with the Bud Powell Trio. Here his lightning reflexes, powerful swing and awesome instrumental command allowed him to weave wondrous responses to Powell's lines, or take rhapsodic, guitar-like solos, scorning the servitude of keeping a steady beat that was the average bass man's lot.

For two joyful weeks Charlie Parker joined the Trio, and between sets

211

Mingus would savour the conversations with him. Years later he liked to recall the evening when they talked of reincarnation:

> I made a view on it and Bird said, 'Mingus, that's something to think about. I'll give my views, let's discuss it on the bandstand.' When I got to the bandstand, man, what he played – it totalled up everything we was talking about! . . . I'm saying *Bird* started this. I never heard it in Duke. I heard Duke's emotions and feelings, but I never heard him communicate a definite thought, or words.[2]

*

In that same exhilarating New York summer of 1953, Mingus played with Charlie Parker on Sunday afternoons at the Open Door in Greenwich Village, and put on concerts with Max Roach at the Putnam Central Club in Brooklyn.

In September, Roach took a tempting engagement on the West Coast: six months as resident drummer at the Lighthouse club in Hermosa Beach. He had just bought a new car, and Mingus offered to share the driving across America.

They broke their 3000-mile journey in East St Louis, where they were welcomed by Miles Davis, who was resting at home with his prosperous family. Mingus and Roach were amazed at the luxury and the extent of the Davis spread: the maid, the cook, the herds of livestock. Roach still remembers the silk pyjamas, and likes to recount a story that illustrates Miles's style of humour. As he tells it, Mingus, whose skin was very fair, was constantly raging against white people. After one of these tirades Miles, whose skin was very dark, solemnly assured him that the Davis family kept a careful watch over its herd of prize-winning all-black cattle. If a calf was born with even a speck of white, it was instantly slaughtered. Mingus was appalled and condemned the Davis family as heartless racists.

Miles decided to join his two friends on the road for the remainder of their long drive. According to his autobiography, he and Mingus fought non-stop all the way to California, with Roach as referee.[3] After a short stop in Los Angeles, where he visited his family, Mingus flew back to New York using the ticket Roach had been given.

During the autumn and winter the Debut company released, in stages, the Massey Hall recordings. The reviews were enthusiastic, sales were good, and leasing deals were struck with European companies. Debut invested its funds in producing records by deserving artists. Paul Bley, Kenny Dorham, Thad Jones and Teo Macero were among those given their first chance to record under their own name. Mingus himself played bass for many of the sessions, including one where the pioneering bass fiddler Oscar Pettiford played the cello.

In January 1954 Mingus was booked to play for four weeks in Miami Beach, Florida, with another idol of his, Art Tatum. Tatum's decorative brilliance thrilled him, but he offered this reservation: 'Tatum knew every tune written, and I think it got in the way of his composition, because he wasn't a Bud Powell. He wasn't as melodically inventive as Bud . . . Bud and Bird to me should go down as composers.'[4]

Back in New York he promoted his latest cause, the Jazz Composers' Workshop: a loose grouping of musicians with whom he could give performances that were frankly experimental. When he brought them to the studio, at the end of October, it was not for Debut but for the more senior Savoy record company. The six recordings they made are a display board for Mingus the composer and leader. Contrapuntal ensembles and collective improvisation loom large, and one of the compositions shows aspects of his writing at its best. This is 'Eulogy for Rudy Williams', inspired by the recent death of the underrated saxophonist. The poignant theme is picked out in rich Ellingtonian colours, the lithe Mingus bass moves matters irresistibly forwards, and the solos are intensified by dramatic occurrences in the ensemble.

On 5 December the Mingus team gave a New York concert billed as 'Developments in Modern Jazz', where each musical item was followed by a debate with the audience.

*

Early in March 1955 Mingus made one of his increasingly rare public appearances as a sideman. Never has such an occasion been more traumatic. He had been booked, along with Bud Powell, drummer Art Blakey and trumpeter Kenny Dorham, to support Charlie Parker during his last-chance appearance at Birdland. The second night of the engagement ended in shameful disorder, with Parker despairing theatrically over the drunken Powell. Mingus felt compelled to make a public announcement disassociating himself from such sick behaviour. In one account he gave of the horrible incident, he remembered that Parker returned to Birdland later that same evening, 'put a wet cheek next to mine, and said "Mingus, I'm goin' someplace, pretty soon, where I'm not gonna bother anybody."'[5]

A week later Parker was dead and his common-law wife Chan was arranging a quiet funeral service at which Mingus and Lennie Tristano would play. When Doris Parker overturned these plans, a committee was formed, including Mingus and Dizzy Gillespie, to try to bring calm to the chaos Parker had left behind.

Chan and Doris both attended the elaborate ceremony in Harlem's Abyssinian Baptist Church. When the service was over Mingus whispered urgently to Chan that she should not grieve, because the real Charlie Parker could never die.

*

Still battling for Debut records, Mingus persuaded the highly marketable Miles Davis to come and record for them. The other players at the July session were Teddy Charles (vibes), Britt Woodman (trombone), drummer Elvin Jones and Mingus himself. An illustrious line-up, but the results were disappointing, probably because Miles's mind was on career moves of his own. According to Elvin Jones, 'If they had just printed the conversations in the studio that would have been a best-seller.'[6]

Soon afterwards Mingus dissolved his working band and went to Cleveland with Elvin Jones to play in a trio with Bud Powell. In October he was back in New York, leading a group at the Café Bohemia. By now the democratic title Jazz Composers' Workshop had been significantly altered to the Charles Mingus Jazz Workshop.

During the summer of 1955 America had been horrified by the lynching in Mississippi of a fourteen-year-old black boy, Emmett Till, accused of saying 'Bye, baby' to a white woman in a small-town grocery store. This barbaric act was still reverberating when the Workshop opened at the Café Bohemia and premiered 'Work Song'. This is the first Mingus composition with a politically resonant title. According to the group's pianist, Mal Waldron, it was inspired by the folk protest-song that has the line 'Swing that hammer over your shoulder: get bolder and *bolder*.'[7] In December, when an evening of performances at the Café Bohemia was recorded for Debut, 'Work Song' was among them. So was 'Haitian Fight Song', a canonic, minor-key blues Mingus said he could only play right when he was thinking about prejudice and hate. Another outstanding Mingus composition, 'Jump Monk', is entirely non-political: a brilliant, cascading theme, which combines Monkish eccentricities with brutal straightforwardness.

Adding lustre to an already shining evening, Max Roach (taking a break from leading his own quintet) replaced the group's drummer Willie Jones for three numbers. The wing-heeled 'I'll Remember April' is the most conventional. 'Drums' is an atmospheric mini-concerto, in which Mingus's bowed bass slowly leads the horns through penumbral terrain, while Roach romps and races in a world of light. For 'Percussion Discussion' the other group members retire, leaving the stage to the giant musical personalities of Mingus and Roach, who conduct a fierce and dazzling musical debate. At the post-production stage Mingus added a second bass part – not to correct a technical defect, as with Massey Hall, but simply for the joy of dancing among the arguments already spun.

*

By the start of 1956 Mingus had acquired an agent and a contract to record with the thrusting Atlantic record company. And for its first Atlantic session (30 January) his Jazz Workshop had two new saxophonists: J.R. Monterose and one-time Bud Powell favourite Jackie McLean.

The title track of the album they made, *Pithecanthropus Erectus*, is a landmark in American music – Mingus's considered response to the challenge of combining structure with freedom. In his programme note

Mingus explains that his starting point was the humanoid fossil found in Africa, and goes on to identify the music's four sections. These are Evolution, Superiority Complex, Decline and Destruction. Two of them rest on a fixed harmonic sequence; the other two flow freely from a pair of alternating chords. The entire pattern is set out by the ensemble, then used as a basis for the solos. Racking up the intensity are the outbursts of collective improvisation and the vocalized tone of the horns, sometimes urged on by Mingus to ditch restraint and scream. However, the wild dynamics of the astonishing performance are always under the magisterial control of the Mingus bass.

The artistic discipline of *Pithecanthropus Erectus* was not matched by any self-control in its creator's life. The sexual adventures of this self-styled 'Chazzanova' were threatening his marriage, and his treatment of the members of his Jazz Workshop meant a constant turnover of personnel. Jackie McLean left in March, in typically inflamed circumstances. Sick of the commands and reprimands that kept issuing from his boss during public performances, and tired of being told, 'I don't want Charlie Parker, man, I want Jackie',[8] McLean handed in his notice. Mingus, surprised and angry, punched him in the mouth – a particularly damaging assault when the victim is a horn player. McLean retaliated with a knife, whereupon his notice took immediate effect.

When Mingus threatened to fire his agent for not drumming up enough business, wife Celia jumped to the man's defence. The problem, she said, was that Mingus was alienating New York's club owners by going on stage and denouncing the deficiencies of their premises. And if he deemed the audience to be noisy or inattentive, then they, too, would get it in the neck. *Down Beat* magazine reported an occasion on which he sarcastically advised the chattering nightclub crowd, 'We have a new audience participation number. Here's how it works. We play for four bars. Then you talk, laugh and break glasses for four bars. And then we play again.'

A different kind of Mingus incident, at a new club called the Pad, had an entirely beneficial consequence. Mingus counted in 'Cherokee' at a tempo so fast that drummer Willie Jones could not cope. As the performance fell apart, Mingus described to the audience his feelings about Jones's incompetence. An audience member then introduced Mingus to Danny Richmond, a novice drummer who, Mingus was told, could play at any speed he liked. This turned out to be true, and in the years ahead Richmond became indispensable to Mingus. Unlike the great Max Roach, here was a gifted subordinate happy to be part of a unit where the bass, rather than the drums, was the guiding force.

*

Amongst Mingus's powerful emotions, his contempt for Charlie Parker's imitators was matched by his love for the man and his music. On his next Atlantic album (*The Clown*, recorded in February 1957) he included 'Reincarnation of a Lovebird', a long, sad, wide-ranging melody, preceded by an introduction crammed with Parker memorabilia. Snatches of '52nd Street Theme', 'Dizzy Atmosphere' and 'Salt Peanuts' are there to evoke the era, while other fragments are lifted from specific Parker works, including 'Moose the Mooche', 'Relaxin' at Camarillo' and his inspired variation on 'Embraceable You'.

As well as Danny Richmond, the latest Jazz Workshop included another who would become a Mingus stalwart: trombonist Jimmy Knepper. Knepper was from California and a close friend of the legendary Parker stalker Dean Benedetti. On the West Coast back in 1945, when Mingus played briefly with a band of white youngsters led by Benedetti and featuring Knepper, their manic enthusiasm for Parker's music had forced him to start taking it seriously.

Mingus had planned a musical tribute to Bud Powell, to be included on the album alongside 'Reincarnation of a Lovebird', but this one did not materialize. However, the next time he recorded (in July) he was ready with a salute to another of the Massey Hall five. 'Dizzy Moods', based on Gillespie's 'Woody 'n You', was composed while driving to Tijuana with Danny Richmond. The rest of the album celebrates that extra-marital Mexican visit – in terms far more orgiastic than Aaron Copland could manage in his *El Salón México*. The most thrilling and evocative track is 'Ysabel's Table Dance', featuring the paso doble rhythm, with dancer Ysabel Morel shaking her castanets and Mingus strumming his bass like a flamenco guitarist.

The album (called *Tijuana Moods*) was financed by RCA, in part settlement of a claim Mingus brought against them for using Thad Jones when the trumpeter was under exclusive contract to Debut. But this did not help Debut itself. By the middle of 1957 production had stopped. Mingus said this was because the musicians' union withdrew the company's licence on the grounds of unpaid bills. So instead he launched another record company, called Jazz Workshop. The two important albums issued on this short-lived label were both filled with bootleg recordings of live performances by Charlie Parker. Those on *Bird at St Nick's* had been recorded by Jimmy Knepper in 1950 while Parker played for a dance at New York's St Nicholas Arena. *Bird on 52nd Street* consisted of Knepper's copies of tapes made at the Onyx club by Dean Benedetti.

*

In September 1957 America hit a constitutional crisis when Governor Orval Faubus of Arkansas defied a Supreme Court ruling and used the forces at his command to prevent nine black children from attending Central High School in Little Rock. At first President Eisenhower did nothing while the ugly scenes in the Arkansas state capital were beamed around the world. Shocked by the television pictures of Southern white racists jeering and spitting at a young black child, Louis Armstrong (whom Mingus had rejected as an Uncle Tom) issued a passionate denunciation of Faubus and Eisenhower, ending 'Because of the way they are treating my people in the South, the Government can go to hell.'[9]

Mingus's response to the events in Little Rock turned into a regular part of his nightclub act: a nagging, lurching piece of music, supporting anti-racist verses chanted by Danny Richmond and Mingus himself. Due to the nervousness of record company executives, no proper recording was made of 'Fables of Faubus' for three years.

On his next pair of albums – *East Coasting* and *Scenes in the City* – Mingus took stock of his situation as the artist from California who had carved a niche in New York. The title track of *East Coasting* is harmonically hectic in the bebop manner, and the same album's 'Conversations', with its winding theme and combative exchanges, aims to distil the art of Charlie Parker. The other album, *Scenes in the City*, was originally called *A Modern Jazz Symposium of Music and Poetry with Charles Mingus* – a title justified by the mixed-media character of the first and longest track. Here the music is programmed to integrate with a text describing the sensations of a young black man in New York, written with the help of the poet of negritude, Langston Hughes.

These two albums were made for the specialist Bethlehem label, with whom Mingus hoped to work again. But when sales turned out to be disappointing, Bethlehem dropped him. Meanwhile his rows with the club owners sometimes skidded into physical violence. According to Max Gordon, boss of the Village Vanguard, when insufficient cash was forthcoming at the end of one evening, Mingus smashed some bottles, grabbed a kitchen knife and made deadly threats.

He liked to boast he had links with gangsters and he constantly shook his fist at the world. Objecting one night to the high level of background noise when his band was playing at the Half Note Café, he abandoned the live music and operated a record-player instead, while his sidemen read their books or played games of cards.

In December 1957 Celia gave birth to their son, an event that put extra pressure on his earnings and did nothing for his peace of mind. He was vexed by the reluctance of RCA to release *Tijuana Moods*. RCA had stumbled on a gold mine called Elvis Presley. They left the Mingus item on the shelf for five years.

Even more devastating to his pride was the departure of Celia, who walked out on 2 April 1958, their seventh wedding anniversary. He tried and failed to find relief in psychoanalysis, then took the desperate step of presenting himself at the gates of Manhattan's Bellevue Hospital and insisting on admission. These walls had enclosed Charlie Parker in 1954 and Bud Powell on numerous occasions. Once inside, Mingus took fright. Other patients were seriously mentally disturbed, the staff were unsympathetic, he was placed in a locked ward and became convinced that he had been classed as just another of those troublesome black men requiring a lobotomy. He sent out an SOS and his friend Nat Hentoff organized his release.

Back in the world he quickly found a new girlfriend and formed a new band. The lady was the fair-haired Diane Dorr-Dorynek, who became his publicist and assistant, and took over the task of typing his copious auto-biography from the redoubtable Celia. The quintet, including the indispensable Danny Richmond and two new saxophonists, John Handy and Booker Ervin, gave a concert at the Nonagon Art Gallery in Manhattan on 16 January. And when Mingus came to record for Atlantic again, on 4 February, it formed the nucleus of the bigger unit he brought with him. In his sleeve note for the album they made (called *Blues and Roots*) he explains that his intention is to confound those critics who complain that he doesn't swing, by giving them 'a barrage of soul music: churchy, blues, swinging, earthy'.

He provided six new compositions but declined to write them down, insisting that the players learn their parts from him by ear. The result is six performances full of soul, earth and fire, the greatest of which is 'Wednesday Night Prayer Meeting'. This hair-raising, high-speed aggre-gation of 6/8, 6/4 and 4/4 time-signatures has Mingus as the preacher, inciting his players with screams and hollers, and at the same time using his mighty instrument to keep everyone in line.

Shortly after recording *Blues and Roots*, he was signed by the heavy-weight Columbia Records. His ally inside Columbia was Teo Macero, the saxophonist who had Debut to thank for his first chance to make a record as a leader. Now Macero was a staff producer, working on such hits for Columbia as Miles Davis's *Kind of Blue*. Having secured Mingus a contract, he piloted the two albums that followed.

The first of these (*Mingus Ah Um*, made in May 1959 with a septet) is designed to display the range of Mingus's talent to a wide public. The opening track, 'Better Git It in Your Soul', is closely related to 'Wednesday Night Prayer Meeting', but here the performance is less ferocious and more formulaic, and there's a catchy tune before we get down to the 6/4 blues. 'Fables of Faubus' is a surprise inclusion, but its power to offend has been neutered by the removal of the words. The outstanding new composition is 'Goodbye Pork Pie Hat', created by Mingus in response to the death in March of Lester Young. This slow 12-bar blues has a simple, intensely beautiful melody, arising from radically modified blues harmonies. The way the blues essence is preserved in spite of the chordal complications is reminiscent of Charlie Parker's 'Blues for Alice', and sure enough, the album also includes one of Mingus's Parker tributes. This time it's 'Bird Calls', a fiercely fast 18-bar theme preceded and followed by ornithological references. Excited twittering sounds form the introduction, and the coda is replete with simulated birdsong, ending in ethereal notes teased by Mingus from the recesses of his bass.

Six months later the second Columbia album, *Mingus Dynasty*, was recorded with a ten-piece ensemble. Mingus himself supplied the detailed sleeve notes, which begin by pondering the genius and the legacy of Charlie Parker. What matters most about the work of Parker, Mingus tells us, is the 'primitive, mystic, supra-mind communication' that it shares with Beethoven's late string quartets. The calamity is that 'sham copies have distorted Bird's beauty and greatness'.

Not surprisingly, the most exciting track on the album is 'Gunslinging Bird', subtitled 'If Charlie Parker Were a Gunslinger There'd Be a Whole Lot of Dead Copycats'. Faithful to the Mingus philosophy, the music has nothing blatantly derivative about it. It's a savage 6/4 blues with links to the 'Wednesday Night Prayer Meeting', but travelling much faster and switched from F to the key of C. Exploiting his nine sidemen to the full, Mingus creates powerful eddies and cross-currents, which sweep the listener away.

At the other end of the spectrum is 'Far Wells, Mill Valley': an elaborate tone poem, composed during Mingus's recent visit to Farwell Taylor, his Californian guru.

*

Mingus's one-year contract with Columbia was due to expire in the spring of 1960. The two albums had sold well and Columbia would have been happy to renew, but Mingus insisted that sales must have been far higher than the company would admit. The argument turned bitter and the relationship was terminated.

Next stop for Mingus was Mercury records. Their newly appointed jazz producer, Leonard Feather, was hoping to make his mark with a popular and economical album by a Mingus small group, but Mingus thought otherwise. He argued that the time was ripe for a review of his Californian juvenilia. The jewel in this retrospective crown was to be 'Half-Mast Inhibition', written when he was in his teens (around the same time as 'The Chill of Death') but never performed. Unfortunately for Feather's budget, this orchestral concert work required no less than twenty-two players, including woodwind, cello and tuba. These large forces were assembled on 24 May, and since 'Half-Mast Inhibition' was entirely notated, with multiple changes of mood and time-signature, Gunther Schuller was recruited to conduct.

The album's title, *Pre-Bird*, has an antediluvian air, but one piece on the disc was entirely new. 'Prayer for Passive Resistance' opens with chain-gang atmospherics: a thudding backbeat and cries of anguish from the brass. Out of these brutal beginnings arises a keening saxophone solo, played in 4/4 against the turbulent 12/8 laid down by Mingus.

Passive resistance had been a hot subject in America since 1 February, when four black teenagers in Greensboro, North Carolina, had the courage to sit down at a 'whites only' lunch counter.

Thrilled by the rise in black assertiveness, Mingus and Max Roach were planning a protest of their own. Their target was the Seventh Annual Jazz Festival at swanky Newport, Rhode Island. Their principal grievance against this supposedly non-profit event was the way fashionable stars (including some, like the Kingston Trio, with no jazz pedigree) were paid fat fees to attract a teenage mass audience, while artists like themselves were either overlooked or expected to play for a pittance. Their bold scheme was to hold an alternative festival just down the road.

The first requirement was a suitable site, and Mingus came up with the perfect spot. Cliff Walk Manor hotel at Newport belonged to Nick Cannarozzotti, a prosperous businessman alleged to have Mafia links. Mingus persuaded him to hire out the hotel grounds in exchange for a slice of the take. Mingus, Roach and their volunteer helpers built a band-stand and painted it fire-engine red, enclosed the huge lawn with fencing, hired 500 chairs, and organized ticketing and publicity. Most impressive of all was the quality of their cast list. Mingus and Roach led their own bands, of course. The new free jazz was spearheaded by Ornette Coleman; and the mainstream was personified by Jo Jones, Roy Eldridge and Coleman Hawkins. As well as playing in their set groups, all these musicians took part in free-wheeling jam sessions.

The main festival opened on 30 June, and the self-help venture ran alongside. On the third day divine providence smiled. The main festival was shut down after persistent violence and vandalism among 12,000 white teenagers fuelled on beer. So the Cliff Walk Manor alternative had the field to itself. This must have given Mingus particular satisfaction. Before the Festival started, when he presented himself at the Newport hotel where he had booked and confirmed a room by telephone, they had turned him away.

*

One week after the Newport triumph, Mingus and his quintet (with Eric Dolphy, Booker Ervin and Ted Curson) were in the South of France for the inaugural Antibes Jazz Festival. The concert they gave on 13 July was recorded by the French company Barclay, and issued eventually by Atlantic records. Much of the programme is made up of familiar Mingus compositions ('Wednesday Night Prayer Meeting', 'Prayer for Passive Resistance', 'Better Git It in Your Soul') but the pair of items at the centre of the concert are outstanding.

'What Love' (a meditation on Cole Porter's 'What Is This Thing Called Love?') includes a startling episode by Eric Dolphy on bass clarinet. His eloquence, freedom and intensely vocalized, sometimes savage, tone are just what Mingus sought – a language beyond Charlie Parker's, yet faithful to the Parker essence.

As if to confirm the continuity that underlies radical artistic change, Mingus follows 'What Love' by calling Bud Powell up to the stage to join the band. The number they choose to play together is a Powell favourite,

'I'll Remember April'. Showing him the respect due to his vast historical importance, Mingus's young hornmen hold back and allow him to improvise for six uninterrupted choruses. Then they come forward and make short contributions themselves, ending with a burst of collective improvisation. Contrary to the popular account, Powell did *not* leave the stage in disgust when the front-line fireworks started. His discreet comping can be clearly heard until the very end.

Back in New York City the Mingus band returned to its long residency at the Showplace, the club in Greenwich Village where its routines were developed and perfected. The chance to put these on record came in the autumn, when Nat Hentoff, jazz journalist and fierce Mingus advocate, was put in charge of production for the new Candid label. On 20 October 1960 Mingus brought his musicians to the studio, where Hentoff turned down the lights and encouraged him to replicate a typical Showplace evening, complete with announcements. The consequent album was entitled *Charles Mingus Presents Charles Mingus*.

In his preamble, Mingus reminds everyone that 'we don't applaud here at the Showplace. In fact, don't even take any drinks. I want no cash register ringing.'

The part of the programme that pleased Hentoff most was 'The Original Faubus Fables'. Having savoured the boldness of this satire as performed in jazz clubs, he had felt cheated by the wordless edition issued on Columbia. For the Candid version the verbal assault on the Governor of Arkansas was restored.

Hentoff enjoyed using his position for political as well as musical ends. Six weeks before the Mingus album, he had recorded Max Roach's blistering *Freedom Now Suite*. Shortly afterwards (at the beginning of November) he reassembled the musicians who had taken part in the alternative Newport Festival and made an album to mark their achievements, called *Newport Rebels*.

*

Before the Candid sessions were completed, Mingus had fallen out with the Showplace and quit. Other upheavals during 1960 included moving home, and replacing blonde-haired Diane Dorr-Dorynek with blonde-haired Judy Starkey. He married his new partner and before the end of the year she presented him with a baby daughter.

The following summer he spent seven weeks in London, England, playing himself in the ludicrous film *All Night Long* (loosely based on Shakespeare's *Othello*, but switched to a jazz milieu and fitted with a happy ending). His work on the project was discontinued after he broke down the hotel room door of the blonde press lady assigned to look after him.

Back in New York he revived the Jazz Workshop, teaming stalwarts like Danny Richmond and Jimmy Knepper with multi-instrumentalist Roland Kirk, whose speciality was playing three reed instruments at once. In November, when the group made the Atlantic album *Mingus Oh Yeah*, bassist Doug Watkins was brought in because Mingus wanted to concentrate on playing the piano and singing.

Oh Yeah is a relative of the earlier album *Blues and Roots*. From the deep blues of 'Devil Woman' through the churchiness of 'Ecclusiatics' to the Fats Waller-style fooling of 'Eat that Chicken', it revels in the black experience. The oddest track, 'Passions of a Man', is music theatre radio-phonically enhanced. While Kirk creates eerie atmospheres with flute, whistle and siren, the many voices of Mingus (overdubbed) converse and jest in fake African tongues.

In an interview with his Atlantic producer Nesuhi Ertegun, Mingus said 'Passions of a Man' 'is me trying to identify myself with something'. He considered calling it 'Passions of a Black Man', 'but the black people I have met made me feel I wasn't good enough to be black. My hair wasn't beautiful nappy like theirs was, my skin wasn't dark ebony black and beautiful.'[10] Several times during the interview he compares the album to 'my book', the sensational memoir of his identity search for which a publisher was being sought. Not long after *Oh Yeah* was released, a book deal was announced, with much brouhaha. Major publishers McGraw-Hill were allegedly paying an 'unprecedented' advance of $15,000 for this massive, 1,500-page 'autobiographical novel', which would be in the shops in 1963.

*

After her separation from Mingus, Celia had returned to San Francisco and taken up the offer of a job with Fantasy Records. Since he trusted her completely, Mingus was happy for Fantasy to take over the distribution of the Debut catalogue – including its crown jewels, the Massey Hall recordings. *Jazz at Massey Hall* remains a Fantasy best-seller.

In the spring of 1962 Mingus made a triumphant return to Toronto as guest of honour at the launch of the film *All Night Long*, to which he was chauffeured in an air-conditioned limousine.

Confirming the upswing in his fortunes, United Artists announced plans to record a concert at New York's Town Hall on 15 November, where his music would be performed by a thirty-piece orchestra. On top of that, United Artists wanted to record a very special album of music by Duke Ellington, performed by the composer at the piano, with Mingus on bass and Max Roach on drums. The session was scheduled for 17 September and at first Mingus said no, he could not manage it because he was overwhelmed by the writing of the music for his Town Hall concert.

In the end the temptation to record with his idol was irresistible, but things did not run smoothly, as Duke Ellington recalled in his autobiography:

> In the middle of that session Mingus started to pack up his bass, so I asked what the trouble was.
> 'Man, I can't play with that drummer,' he said.
> 'Why, what's wrong?' I asked.
> 'Duke, I have always loved you and what you're doing in music, but you'll have to get another bass player.'[11]

Mingus lugged his bass out to the elevator. Ellington followed, speaking soothingly. Before the elevator arrived he had persuaded Mingus to return, 'and we recorded very happily from then on until the album was completed'.

The title track of the album is 'Money Jungle'. Max Roach remembers the graphic technique Ellington used to explain to Mingus and himself how this minor-key blues should be played:

He said, 'Just picture a big city like New York, and all the skyscrapers are tree trunks, and coming out of the windows and the doorways is money. A forest. Streets of money. The serpents and animals that are crawling up and down on this money are our agents and guys who are taking advantage of us.'[12]

This description was guaranteed to arouse strong feelings in Mingus, who plays on 'Money Jungle' with teeth-gnashing fury.

The track that Ellington himself judged to be the most successful is 'La Fleurette Africaine'. In his autobiography he described how he motivated Mingus and Roach to deliver the performance he wanted:

'La Fleurette Africaine,' I explained, 'is a little African flower . . . growing miles away from human eyes in the central part of the jungle that is God-made and untouched.'[13]

Thus inspired, Roach softly enhanced the theme with rhythmic niceties, as if heard from afar; and Mingus invented a repeating, tremulous, exquisitely delicate phrase, like the petals of a flower unfolding. 'It was one of those mystic moments,' said Ellington, 'when our three muses were one.'

Mingus's edginess during the session must have been due in part to the pressure he was under to write an evening of music and have it ready for a concert recording by thirty players on 15 November. This pressure increased intolerably shortly afterwards when the concert date was brought forward to 12 October. Orchestrations were farmed out to friends and colleagues, and still he was left with too much to do. He summoned the faithful Jimmy Knepper (already immersed in chores for the project) and told him he needed him to write some backgrounds for the soloists. When Knepper demurred, Mingus punched him in the mouth and smashed a tooth, ruining the trombonist's embouchure.

So Knepper was missing from the final list of performers, which included Mingus's boyhood pals from the West Coast like Buddy Collette and Britt Woodman, plus the massed ranks of his present and former sidemen.

Music was still being written during the rehearsals, and on the night of the concert the recording engineer for United Artists was floundering. The audience at Town Hall objected to all the starting and stopping, and at midnight the stage hands closed the curtains before the programme was completed. For their LP of the concert United Artists managed to scrape together only thirty-six minutes of poorly reproduced material. Mingus brought a lawsuit against them, and Jimmy Knepper brought a criminal action against Mingus, who was convicted of assault and given a short suspended sentence.

*

In the three weeks before Christmas 1962 Mingus, whose artistic processes seemed to thrive on conflict, led an exciting 10-piece band at New York's Village Vanguard club. Their programmes mixed old favourites with excerpts from a major new work he was preparing and testing.

On 20 January 1963, having signed a contract with the Impulse label, he took the band to the studio and recorded the monumental finished article. Or rather, he recorded the raw material from which the finished article would emerge after hours of editing and overdubbing. Ever since his experimental enhancement of the Massey Hall tapes, he had been an enthusiastic exponent of post-production techniques. For this new album, *The Black Saint and the Sinner Lady*, he raised the infant science of tape-doctoring to a new level. According to Bob Thiele, the producer for Impulse, by the end of the main recording session Mingus had already planned fifty tape-splices. He also required an overdubbing session, where he added intricate embroidery from Charlie Mariano's alto saxophone. The end result is an integrated, richly textured work that lasts nearly thirty-eight minutes: school of Ellington rather Parker. In his sleeve-note Mingus described it as 'my living epitaph from birth till the day I first heard of Bird and Diz'. Then, giving the project a further twist, he handed over the remainder of the sleeve-note space to his analyst, Edmund Pollock, Ph.D., Clinical Psychologist. Here is the essence of what Dr Pollock has to say:

His sufferings as a person and a black man were surely enough to cause sour bitterness, hate, distortions and withdrawal. Yet Mr Mingus has never given up . . . He is painfully aware of his feelings and he wants desperately to heal them . . . Inarticulate in words, he is gifted in musical expression, which he constantly uses to articulate what he perceives, knows and feels . . . He is the Black Saint who suffers for his sins and those of mankind.[14]

*

Happy with the professionalism of *The Black Saint and the Sinner Lady*, the owners of Impulse responded positively when Mingus proposed that he should record a collection of solo piano pieces. The session took place on 30 July.

The first track on the album, 'Myself When I Am Real', is one of the best, a spontaneous yet structured expression of yearning. Another stand-out track, 'Old Portrait', reworks a sad song he wrote back in 1946, during the depression that followed the failure of his first marriage. The final and longest track is called 'Compositional Theme Story: Medleys, Anthems and Folklore'. Mingus described it as 'a mixture of all the things I've heard, known and felt about this country'.[15] The mood is sorrowful, and the plethora of familiar fragments includes 'What Am I Here For?', 'When Johnny Comes Marching Home' and 'Goin' Home', the ersatz Negro spiritual from Dvořák's *New World Symphony*.

Although sales of the Impulse albums were encouraging, when the time came to renew his contract the company declined to offer improved terms, so Mingus walked away. The year 1963 was ending badly. Fearful of libel actions, McGraw-Hill pulled out of publishing his memoirs. His young wife Judy was pregnant again and the marriage was collapsing. The assassination in November of President Kennedy looked like a victory for the enemies of racial equality.

At the end of January 1964 he began a two-month residency at the Five Spot Café in Greenwich Village, and used the opportunity to rehearse, fragment by fragment, a new, extended composition for a small group. The chance to perform this work in full, before a large audience, came on 4 April, when his sextet took part in a benefit concert at Town Hall for the NAACP (the National Association for the Advancement of Colored People). The philosophical basis for the piece had come from Eric Dolphy, as Mingus tried to make clear in his announcement to the receptive Town Hall crowd:

> Eric Dolphy explained to me that there was something similar to the concentration camps once in Germany now down South . . . and the only difference between the electric barbed wire is that they don't have gas chambers and hot stoves to cook us in yet. So I wrote a piece called 'Meditations' – as to how to get some wire cutters, before someone else gets some guns to us.[16]

As well as planting the seed for the piece, Dolphy, on both flute and bass clarinet, was crucial to its flowering. It begins with a lament played by Dolphy's flute and Mingus's bowed bass, then moves through a kaleidoscope of savage and sorrowful moods. During the turbulent passage representing the horrors of the slave ships and the slave auctions, Mingus abandons his bass and releases his pent-up feelings through the piano.

The week following the NAACP benefit the sextet travelled to Germany, where 'Meditations for a Pair of Wire Cutters' featured heavily in the concert programmes. Although Mingus scented racism in the German air, at the end of the tour Dolphy elected to stay behind. So it was a revamped group that came to play at the Jazz Workshop in San Francisco at the end of May. While they were here they recorded long versions of 'Meditations' and 'Fables of Faubus' for the Fantasy label, which was still enjoying the benefits of the Debut catalogue and the presence of Mingus's ex-wife Celia (now married to Fantasy boss Saul Zaentz).

Back in New York, Mingus went to work again at the Five Spot Café, with a sextet including trumpeter Lonnie Hillyer and alto saxophonist Charles McPherson. For the most dramatic part of the act, McPherson had to hide in the cloakroom and create the illusion that he was Charlie Parker's ghost.

At the end of June came the shock news that Eric Dolphy had died in Berlin. The effect on Mingus was devastating. His pianist at the time, Jaki

Byard, remembers him 'throwing his bass on the floor (it was a magnificent instrument he had bought in Milan) and literally stomping it to a
pulp'.[17] Dolphy was generally presumed to have died of a heart attack, but
Mingus disagreed. He recalled that after they had complained about the
service in a German hotel, Eric found a swastika daubed on his door. He
announced categorically that his dear friend had been murdered by the
Nazis.

At the end of August he was cheered by Bud Powell's triumphant
return to Birdland after years in exile, but Dolphy's death still weighed
heavily upon him. While on stage at the Monterey Festival on 20
September, he experienced a pain in his chest 'and the fear of the possi-
bility of my death surged through me'.[18] The outstanding musical event
at Monterey was an orchestral arrangement of 'Meditations'. After rave
reviews in *Time* and *Newsweek*, he decided the recording of the concert
should be issued by his new company, Charles Mingus Enterprises, the
produce of which could be obtained by mail order only.

*

Back in New York there was the pleasure of spending time with his
beloved Bud Powell, but the Beatles had invaded America and the commercial outlook for jazz was bleak. Mingus found intermittent work and
was able to keep his small group going until the autumn of 1965.

By the spring of 1966, separated from his wife Judy, he had come to
rest, with his piano, his double basses and the remainder of his effects, in
a loft apartment at 5 Great Jones Street in the heart of Greenwich Village.
Here he hoped to found a School of Arts, Music and Gymnastics.

In September he landed his first job in six months: sharing the bill at
the Village Gate club with the flautist Herbie Mann. The psychiatrist Dr
Luther Cloud was in the audience the night Mingus flipped:

> He threw a drum at Herbie Mann, because Herbie was trying to play
> African music, and he said, 'What does a Jew like you know about
> African music?' Then he busted up a microphone. He had a little pistol
> around his neck, as a charm, but it happened to be a Derringer with two
> bullets in it.[19]

He was booked to tour Europe in a heavyweight trio with Sonny Rollins and Max Roach, but at the last minute he pulled out, preferring to stay at home and be the subject of a documentary film by Thomas Reichman.

The resulting movie, called simply *Mingus*, catches a crisis in the life of a great artist and faltering human being. The action begins amongst the clutter inside the loft in Great Jones Street. 'It looks like junk,' Mingus tells the camera, 'but my whole life since I was a baby is in these boxes.' His agony is that he has been served with a notice to quit, for alleged lease violation. Tomorrow, 22 November 1966, the city marshals will be here to evict him and impound his possessions. He swears that when they come he will not surrender quietly, and to prove he's in deadly earnest he calls on Reichman to film him as he loads his rifle ('the kind that killed Kennedy') and fires a bullet into the ceiling.

Evidently by prior arrangement, Reichman directs him to stand before the camera and recite the pledge of allegiance to the American flag. This is the essence of his considered reply:

> When they say black, or Negro, it means you're not an American. I pledge allegiance to *your* flag . . . a prestige badge worn by a profitable minority. Yeah, I pledge allegiance to the United States of America. I pledge allegiance to see that some day they will live up to their promises to the victims that they call citizens.

The final scenes in this quintessentially American drama are played next morning, out on the chilly sidewalk, with a secondary cast of policemen and furniture-removers. When Mingus appears, journalists and TV crews pounce. The leader of the pack is a thrusting interviewer for NBC, who sticks out his microphone and wants to know how Mingus feels. Veering between aggression and tears, Mingus explains that he has been trying to establish a school, where distinguished artists like Buddy Collette and Max Roach could come and teach the new generation. This information stirs little interest.

The news hounds brighten when a Mingus associate, the glamorous blonde, Sue Graham, makes her entrance, but what sends them into ecstatic fits is their discovery that the police are arresting Mingus because they have found a box of hypodermic needles. 'Do you deny taking the heroin?' NBC's obnoxious representative demands to know as Mingus is put into a police car. Then a fight breaks out among the jostling cameramen and reporters. Intrigued, Mingus opens the car door and starts to get back out, but he is chided by his laughing escort, 'Sit down and behave yourself! You've got a million dollars' publicity.'

In the anticlimactic, unfilmed sequel Mingus was released after producing a permit for his gun and a doctor's prescription for his vitamin B injections. However, the episode did not have a happy ending. The trauma of the eviction clinched his perception that society's forces were ranged against him, and he went into serious decline. It would be five years before he came to the studio and made another album.

He holed up in a small apartment at the corner of East 5th Street and Avenue A – close to one of Charlie Parker's last addresses – and put boards on the barred windows and extra locks on the door. Steady payments from Fantasy records for the Debut catalogue helped him meet his bills. He ate and drank too much and grew extremely fat.

On a sunny autumn day in 1968 he called Judy and said he was coming to take Carolyn and Eric, their two small children, to play in Central Park. Judy came too, and was sitting watching when the game went seriously wrong. Mingus took off his clothes and began scattering his money to the wind. Unable to calm him, Judy called for help. Police and an ambulance arrived. Mingus was taken to Mt Sinai, the nearest hospital, where they subdued him with Mellaril. This powerful antipsychotic drug, sometimes known as the liquid cosh, is a close relative of Largactil, the pacifier that was dished out to Bud Powell in such generous quantities. Mingus continued to take Mellaril for several years.

He was discharged from hospital after a month and went back to East 5th Street. He stopped composing. He wheeled around Greenwich Village on his six-speed English bike. He worked as a photographer.

The Good Samaritan who reclaimed him for music was Duke Ellington. In September of 1969 the University of California at Berkeley staged a two-day event, honouring the Duke in the year of his seventieth birthday. Mingus was one of those invited to come and pay tribute. Ellington was aware of his disciple's depression and determined to lift him out of it. He sent for the score of Mingus's 1957 composition 'The Clown'. His orchestra would perform this difficult piece and he himself would speak the narration. Mingus was expected to conduct, but the occasion overwhelmed him and he hid in the top balcony while the maestro doubled as narrator and conductor. When Ellington called 'Is Mr Charles Mingus in the house?' he could not bring himself to take a bow, but after this joyful event he gingerly resumed his musical activities.

Sue Graham acted as his manager and took bookings for the band. She also found a new publisher for his memoirs. Regina Ryan at Knopf bought them for $5,500, and commissioned Nel King (who had worked on the screenplay for *All Night Long*) to edit the text. Compromises were made to avoid lawsuits, and the original 1000-plus pages were boiled down to 365. Still heavily dosed with Mellaril, Mingus did not complain. He had wanted to call the book *Half Yaller Nigger* or *Half Yaller Schitt-Colored Nigger*, but he accepted that these titles might give offence and offered something milder.[20]

Beneath the Underdog appeared in May 1971. Its sex scenes made it an immediate *succès de scandale*. Bookings for the band picked up, and at good prices. *Down Beat* readers elected Mingus to their Hall of Fame. The Guggenheim Foundation granted him money to write new music. Columbia took him up again.

When Columbia asked him what he would like to record, he insisted on 'The Chill of Death', the macabre words-and-music extravaganza he had written in 1939. He reminded them that they had already recorded it once – in Los Angeles back in 1947, when they refused to issue it. They promised to do better this time, and urged him to write more material for large forces to fill up the album. The arranger Sy Johnson helped by orchestrating a selection of Mingus material new and old.

Charlie Parker had been a fan of 'The Chill of Death', and the way Mingus presents it here is a touching acknowledgement of that fact. It comes in two consecutive versions: first with the orchestra in deep background, accompanying Mingus's spoken narration; then with the same orchestration pushed forward, to support a Parkerian rhapsody from the alto saxophone of Charles McPherson.

The title of this Columbia album was *Let My Children Hear Music*, and Mingus wrote a reflective essay to go with it, dwelling on the nature of creativity and rejecting the shapeless excesses of free jazz. For him there were two equally valuable kinds of composer. First, the 'pencil composers', like Bach, Beethoven and Brahms. Second, the spontaneous composers, amongst whom Charlie Parker was the greatest genius. Mingus offered himself as the bridge between the two traditions.[21]

On 4 February 1972 there was a grand celebration evening in New York's Philharmonic Hall. Billed as 'Charles Mingus and Friends', this sell-out event was designed both to promote the new album and consolidate his position as a jazz patriarch approaching fifty. Among the musicians taking part was Dizzy Gillespie, still recovering from a serious heart-scare, who contributed some gentle scat-singing on 'Ool-Ya-Koo'.

Sue Graham lined up a European tour that filled the summer of 1972. Dizzy Gillespie, now fully recovered, sat in with the band during the July festival in Nice. Mingus told an interviewer that while Gillespie was playing he stared at his back, thinking how important he was and hoping he'd live for ever. 'Suddenly Dizzy turned around and said, "Where's all this love coming from?" He looked at me. "You really do love me, don't you?" I felt like I was in heaven.'[22]

At the Chateauvallon festival in August, Mingus found himself on the same bill as Max Roach. This reunion was less warm. Roach offered to assault him when he heard him claiming all the credit for the achievements of Debut records. Gillespie intervened.

Back in New York, Mingus moved into Sue Graham's apartment.

In January 1973 his latest sextet gave a Carnegie Hall concert markedly retrospective in character. Gillespie was the guest star, and the programme included 'Wee' (or 'Allen's Alley' or 'Big Noise') and 'Woody 'n You', as well as 'Profiles of Dizzy', a tribute written by Mingus, incorporating some of the trumpeter's favourite licks.

Henceforth the Mingus schedule was a heavy one, mostly on the campus and festival circuits. With Danny Richmond as his trusty adjutant, he took to recruiting the rest of his bandsmen from among the new generation of players who could deliver the high energy his music needed. By the end of 1974, after considerable shuffling, he had hit upon his ideal team. Pianist Don Pullen was equally at home in rhythm-and-blues and the avant-garde. Tenor-saxophonist George Adams was grounded in the blues and entirely at ease with the latest trends. Trumpeter Jack Walrath was a graduate of the Berklee school and a Gillespie fan, whose work experience included cutting-edge jazz groups, the Motown Revue and the band of Ray Charles.

During the last days of December the quintet made a double album for Atlantic called *Changes One and Two*. At its heart was the outstanding new Mingus composition 'Sue's Changes', written in honour of his partner Sue Graham and her many moods. Over the course of seventy bars this piece constantly transforms itself, from slow to fast, tough to tender, and back again, before exploding into an avant-garde freak-out of unlimited duration. The eruption subsides and the whole sequence begins again, and keeps recurring while the soloists take it in turns to scale its temperamental range.

'Sue's Changes' became a part of the increasingly popular Mingus stage show, which found itself tapping into the hugely lucrative rock-music market. The repertoire made no crass compromises with current fashions, but the way the group looked did the box office no harm at all. Take the 1975 TV show made in Montreux, for example. At the back the weighty Mingus and his bass represent Moses and the tablets of stone. Out in front his handsome young messengers preach the word. George Adams (who is black) wears a dark velvet fez and jacket, decorated with sumptuous brocade. Jack Walrath (who is white) sports a flowery shirt, an Afro hairdo and a Marlborough-man moustache. Altogether a winning package.

Early in 1977 Mingus boasted to a friend that he had made more than a quarter of a million dollars in the previous year.[23] But he was having trouble with his legs and took to walking with the assistance of a cane. He complained to Danny Richmond that his fingers were failing him and reluctantly connected his bass to an amplifier. Sue blamed the problems on his colossal weight. Imagining that something was pressing on his nerves, she tried to discourage his mammoth eating binges. His debility advanced. On 23 November 1977 he went to the Columbia Presbyterian Neurological Institute for an examination. The diagnosis was devastating. He was suffering from amyotrophic lateral sclerosis, commonly known as Lou Gehrig's disease: an irreversible creeping paralysis. They told Sue he had three to six months to live.

In January 1978, when he came to the recording studio for the last time, he was confined to a wheelchair and wearing a neck brace. He said little and could play nothing. Atlantic had hired a large ensemble to perform arrangements of his music composed by others. Enough material was recorded to fill two LPs. The longest track was a jam session on a boppish 32-bar theme that Mingus called 'Something Like a Bird', his final salute to Charlie Parker.

On 18 June, complaining bitterly, he allowed himself to be transported to Washington, DC for a party thrown by President Jimmy Carter on the south lawn of the White House. Hundreds of musicians, including Dizzy Gillespie and Max Roach, attended this celebration of twenty-five years of the Newport Jazz Festival. Heading the guest list was George Wein, the Festival Director, against whose commercialism Mingus and Roach had rebelled nearly twenty years earlier. Wein called on President Carter to come and shake the helpless Mingus by the hand. Press photographers and TV crews gathered round the wheelchair. Carter embraced the stricken figure, and Mingus burst into tears.

Sue went over to Max Roach and told him that Mingus wanted to say hello. Roach, still smouldering after the flare-up, walked away.

Sue took Mingus to Mexico, following rumours that a healer there called Pachita possessed the power to cure his fatal disease. But Pachita's elaborate and lengthy ministrations were of no avail. Mingus sought to explain his affliction as part of a divine plan: 'God's got a funny soul. He plays like Charlie Parker. He may run some thunder on you, he may take the sun up and put it in the night time, the way it looks to me.'[24] He died on 5 January 1979.

Obedient to his command that there should be no absurd jazz funeral like Charlie Parker's, Sue travelled with his ashes to India, where she released them into the Ganges.

*

Ten years after his death, on 3 June 1989, an elaborate and loving tribute was paid to him at Alice Tully Hall in New York's Lincoln Center. In the course of cataloguing his papers a young musicologist called Andrew Homzy had discovered a bundle of manuscripts that Mingus had labelled 'Epitaph'. Gunther Schuller stitched the tapestry together and conducted the posthumous première of this two-hour orchestral magnum opus, in which young stars like Wynton Marsalis played alongside such Mingus stalwarts as Britt Woodman. Deeply missed was the galvanizing presence of the author: one of the twentieth century's greatest composer-performers.

ELEVEN

IT'S TIME

'We have proved we're masters of our instruments. Now we have to employ our skill to tell the story of our people and what we've been through.'
Max Roach[1]

TEN DAYS after returning to New York from Toronto, Max Roach again worked with Charlie Parker. The occasion was the vexatious recording session involving woodwinds and voices. Roach and Mingus put their shoulders to the propulsion of the cumbersome forces, then went into business mode and offered Norman Granz the Massey Hall tapes.

In July, Roach recorded with Parker for the very last time. This was a quartet session for Granz, with Al Haig and Percy Heath. Parker arrived two and a quarter hours late. In the forty-five minutes that remained he made four of his most glorious recordings, including two blues, 'Now's the Time' and 'Chi Chi' (the one he had jotted down three months earlier, sitting at Roach's kitchen table).

*

Financially Roach was in fine shape, thanks to the generosity of his high-earning girlfriend Margo Ferraci. As well as making sure Max wanted for nothing, Margo injected vital cash into Debut, so the company could keep going.

At the same time Miles Davis, semi-derelict and heavily drug-dependent, was roaming the New York streets. In his autobiography Miles recalls an incident outside Birdland in the summer of 1953: 'I was standing outside wearing some dirty old clothes when Max Roach walked up and told me I was looking good. Then he put a couple of $100 bills in my pocket.'[2]

In September, Roach made a radical career move, accepting an offer of six months work at the Lighthouse club, a seaside getaway in Hermosa Beach on the southern fringe of Los Angeles. Here he would drum for Howard Rumsey's Lighthouse All-Stars, a mainly white group, entertaining an exclusively white clientele.

Charles Mingus was an expert on Los Angeles. He advised Roach that the distance between the Lighthouse and any accommodation friendly to a black musician would be so vast that an automobile would be essential. So Roach should take his brand new Oldsmobile. Mingus would help him drive it there.

Breaking their journey in St Louis, they called on Miles Davis, who had returned home to his parents and was trying to beat his heroin habit. Miles rode with them to the West Coast. Here, according to his autobiography, Miles continued to use heroin, and caused trouble by hanging around the Lighthouse, where blacks were not welcome as customers.

*

A bonus for those employed at the Lighthouse was its popularity with executives from the Hollywood studios, who used it as a watering hole and a source of musicians for their projects. Not long before Roach arrived, Shorty Rogers had been plucked from here to provide the soundtrack for the Brando film *The Wild One*. And now the movie mogul Otto Preminger was gearing up to produce *Carmen Jones*, a Cinemascopic Americanization of Bizet's torrid opera.

All those appearing in *Carmen Jones* would be black, with most of the singing done by unseen operatic professionals. Only one member of the cast would sing as well as act. She was the black diva Pearl Bailey, and she was contracted to deliver a characteristically high-octane performance, based on Bizet's *Canzonet Bohemian*. For added frisson, Preminger decreed that the nightclub setting for this song should include a top team of dusky rhythm makers. And to lead the team, how about Max Roach from the Lighthouse? Without his thick spectacles (usually discarded for public performances), Roach's proud features are strongly photogenic. The scene where he appears is one of Preminger's most dynamic. It starts on the dance floor, where a compulsive drumbeat is galvanizing the throng, inciting them to holler 'Go Max! Go Max!' Cut to Roach in close shot: relaxed, smiling, in powder-blue tuxedo, beating a soft tattoo upon his tom-toms with downy mallets. Thus inspired, Pearl Bailey arises singing from the sea of dancers. 'Beat Out Dat Rhythm on a Drum!' is her eager refrain, while Max coolly drives the music forward. For the finale, Ms Bailey grabs a pair of drumsticks and plays a duet with the rhythm master.

It was not just the film-people who scouted at the Lighthouse. Record producer Gene Norman attended regularly, and he too was impressed by the Roach package of talent and charm. He urged Max to quit the Lighthouse All-Stars and form a group of his own. Reports of Roach's star quality reached Joe Glaser, Louis Armstrong's agent and the most formidable operator in the music business. He let it be known he wanted to represent Roach and his band. Max was being hauled into the vortex of the American success machine. Having scrupulously recruited Stan Levey as his Lighthouse replacement, he set about building his team. His first and crucial move was to send for trumpeter Clifford Brown.

*

Unassuming Clifford Brown was now twenty-three years old. He had grown up in Wilmington, Delaware. When he was nineteen, the Dizzy Gillespie Orchestra came to play in his home town and found themselves short of one trumpet player. The locals pushed Clifford forward. Gillespie employed him for the evening and was astounded by what he heard. He reported his findings to his friend Max. Then a serious road accident put Brown out of action for a year. Gillespie visited him in hospital and urged him to realize how important he was.

In the spring of 1951 Brown was well enough to take occasional work in Philadelphia. Here he was hired to play at the Club Harlem for a week, in a quintet led by Charlie Parker. In an interview for *Down Beat* magazine, Brown described that experience and the boost he received from Parker's good opinion: 'Bird helped my morale a great deal. One night he took me in a corner and said, "I don't believe it. I hear what you're saying, but I don't believe it."'[3]

So Brown had been doubly anointed, and by the two greatest horn men in the modern movement. By 1953 he was transfixing New York's jazz crowd and making wonder-discs for Blue Note that travelled the world. In March 1954 came the invitation to join Roach in California.

Nearly seven years Brown's senior, Roach treated the young maestro with affectionate respect. They set themselves up in an apartment that doubled as a rehearsal studio, hunted together for the right players to complete their intended quintet, and worked on ideas for the repertoire. During these halcyon days, according to Max, he awoke each new dawn to the bewitching sound of Clifford exploring the trumpet or the piano.

The big test came at the end of April. Gene Norman had fixed it for them to give a concert in the Pasadena Civic Auditorium, which he would record and issue on his own label. On the appointed evening a quintet was rehearsed and ready, and the drama of its launch on the world had been carefully prepared. First a cavernous, anonymous announcement: 'Presenting the outstanding exponents of the new jazz, led by Max Roach!' Whereupon Max, alone in the spotlight, sets a brisk tempo with his brushes, while delivering a short speech. He calls upon the band members to join him, and as he names them, each adds a strand to the ongoing 12-bar blues: 'George Bledsoe, our bass violinist ... Our pianist, Carl Perkins ... Teddy Edwards, our tenor saxophonist ... And the great Clifford Brown on trumpet.'

Gems from the concert include 'Tenderly', showcasing Brown's dramatic and gorgeous ballad style, and 'Clifford's Axe' (on the chords of 'The Man I Love'), where Brown and Roach take us on a roller coaster ride.

For Roach, playing with Brown was as rewarding as playing with Charlie Parker; it was part of the same intense, creative continuum. For Brown, the drumming of Roach was relentlessly inspirational. The insidious power of the master's cymbal strokes goaded him ever onwards, and sometimes, during the furnace of live performance, he felt the skin on his face was being scorched and his lips were melting.

Shortly after the Pasadena concert, the three other members of the quintet were replaced. The new tenor saxophonist, Harold Land, and the new bass player, George Morrow, won their positions after excelling in the locally famous jam sessions held in Eric Dolphy's family's garage. And by the happiest of coincidences the perfect candidate to fill the piano vacancy arrived at just this moment. He was Richie Powell, Bud's younger brother, and he'd come from New York to California as part of the short-lived Johnny Hodges band. Six years earlier Richie, unwilling to compete with Bud's keyboard genius, had been pestering Max for drum lessons. Max had sent him back to the piano, and now a distinctive style, with refreshing voicings, was evolving from Richie's moderate technique and innate musicality.

At the beginning of August 1954, after an intense stretch of rehearsals in the Dolphy garage and performances in clubs like the Tiffany (where Charlie Parker had recently foundered), the settled quintet made its first batch of studio recordings for the EmArcy label.

EmArcy netted a magnificent haul: thirteen tracks to flaunt the band's potency. Amongst the original compositions was a three-part fantasia for drums that Roach named *Mildama*: a triple acronym, embracing his wife Mildred and their children Daryl and Maxine. Of the several new pieces by Brown, 'Joy Spring' is perhaps the most ravishing. The title is apt not only for the uplifting theme, but also for its composer's blithe improvisation upon it. Like Mozart, Chopin and Charlie Parker, Brown had been blessed with the mysterious power of song. From some inner source, pure melody kept bubbling forth. And on 'Joy Spring' our delight is compounded by Roach's ecstatic, polyrhythmic brushwork.

At the end of August there was another live recording for Gene Norman. The revised quintet, introduced this time as 'The Max Roach

All-Stars with Clifford Brown', gave an ensemble display even more bril-liant than the one back in April. Their programme included several numbers they had already recorded for EmArcy, but here escalated to new peaks. For instance, 'Jor-du' (a sinuous theme by Duke Jordan, Max's old colleague in the Parker band) is rendered with unstoppable energy and swing. Fired by Roach, all parties excel. Harold Land's beguil-ing lines ride the beat with deceptive nonchalance. Richie Powell frisks and skitters happily at this medium tempo. Clifford Brown is masterful, with his broad, majestic tone and rich fund of ideas. Events unfold according to the quintet's favoured formula: introduction; theme; solos by the horns and piano; then four-bar exchanges between the front line and Max, leading to an extended drum solo before the reprise. The con-sequence of this plan is a steady crescendo of excitement.

The champagne item on the concert programme was 'Parisian Thoroughfare', Bud Powell's cunning evocation of the Gallic capital. This version is bumper fun, complete with simulated street sounds and flashes of the cancan, the Marseillaise and *An American in Paris*.

*

At the end of autumn 1954, having conquered the West Coast, the Roach–Brown quintet relocated itself in the East. Brown had recently married. He set up home with his bride in Philadelphia, close to friends and family in Wilmington and well positioned for the job opportunities in the New York megalopolis. Richie Powell and his wife also settled in Philadelphia. This was familiar ground for Richie. His mother's country home, to which brother Bud liked to retreat, was in the suburb of Willow Grove. Now Bud became a regular visitor to Richie's new apartment.

Before he left for California, Roach had bought a terraced house on Willoughby Avenue in Brooklyn, not far from where he grew up. Here lived Mildred and the children. And now Max was back, the premises also accommodated quintet members Harold Land and George Morrow.

The band followed an unremitting schedule of work and travel, jour-neying by road around a circuit that included New York, Boston, Pittsburgh, Philadelphia, Baltimore, Washington, DC, St Louis,

Cleveland, Detroit and Chicago. The commitments left Roach little time for other music-making. On a free day in December he took part in, but could not save, a sad recording session for Norman Granz by an extremely sick Bud Powell. And then on 21 January 1955 he made one of his increasingly rare contributions to the catalogue of Debut records.

While he had been in California, the reputation of Debut had been advancing on the back of its Massey Hall releases. Now Roach joined Mingus to record in a trio led by pianist Hazel Scott. Ms Scott's jazzing of the classics and twinkling personality had made her a star and the first black woman to host her own television show. She was married to Congressman Rev. Adam Clayton Powell, whose power base was the Abyssinian Baptist Church in Harlem. Bud Powell (no relation to Rev. Adam) adored Hazel. Whenever they met he insisted she play some Bach for him. Hazel referred to Bud as 'my baby' and promoted him as a genius. Roach and Mingus liked to tease her about her ladylike keyboard style, but welcomed the benefit of her name on the company roster. Debut captioned her LP *Relaxed Piano Moods*, and decorated the sleeve with a picture of her sweet face cupped in her elegantly gloved hands.

*

At the end of February 1955, in EmArcy's New York studios, the Roach–Brown quintet made its next set of recordings. These works of extreme brilliance included an outrageously fast 'Cherokee', several new pieces by Brown, a charming original by the blossoming Richie Powell, and a bone-shaking performance of 'The Blues Walk' that became a model for the emerging 'hard-bop' movement.

Two weeks after these recordings were made, while the quintet was in Detroit, the death of Charlie Parker was announced. Roach did not attend the funeral and the band did not interrupt its itinerary. From Detroit they went to Toronto, and from Toronto to Philadelphia, where, on 28 March at the Blue Note club, they played a benefit night for Parker's family.

On 6 May, while the quintet was working at the posh Basin Street club in midtown Manhattan, a starry concert was mounted at Carnegie Hall in Charlie Parker's memory. The Roach–Brown contribution to the evening was wildly received, consolidating the band's hot reputation.

The touring continued with scarcely a gap. In November, Harold Land, who had been away from his family in California for more than a year, felt compelled to quit and return home. He took his regretful leave while the group was doing a stint in Chicago. Extremely fortunately, the city at that moment was sheltering his ideal replacement.

Sonny Rollins was a gifted eighteen-year-old novice tenor saxophonist when Bud Powell chose him for a record date back in 1949. In the six years since then, he had matured into a considerable artist, especially renowned for his recordings with Miles Davis. He had also, despite stern warnings from his idol Charlie Parker, acquired a heroin habit. When Roach and Brown sought him out, he had withdrawn from the music scene and was staying at the Chicago YMCA, taking jobs loading trucks and concentrating on the defeat of his addiction. After a trial evening at Chicago's Bee Hive club, he accepted the musical challenge of playing regularly in the Roach–Brown quintet, and embraced the clean-living Brown as a model and an inspiration.

The band played gigs in Philadelphia, Washington, DC and Baltimore before its return engagement at the Basin Street club in New York, where it was the Christmas attraction.

On the evening of Friday 23 December, three nights after the Basin Street opening, Roach slipped away for a few hours and drove downtown to the Café Bohemia in Greenwich Village. Here the Charles Mingus Jazz Workshop was recording a set of 'live' performances for issue on the Debut label, and Roach felt he should support his business partner. He dislodged the Workshop's regular drummer and sat in for three numbers, including the moody 'Drums' and the dialectical 'Percussion Discussion'. Then he hurried back uptown to rejoin his quintet.

*

Impressed by New York's response to Roach–Brown in person, the producers at EmArcy wanted another album immediately. The quintet paid several visits to the EmArcy studios at the start of 1956, and the results were issued as an album entitled, slightly misleadingly, *Clifford Brown and Max Roach at Basin Street*. The superb quality of the sound recording brings home the subtle power of Roach's melodic drumming, the cathedral breadth of Brown's trumpet tone, and the urgently personal voice of new boy Rollins.

Three of the pieces they recorded were freshly composed by Richie Powell, including the zappy 'Gertrude's Bounce', in honour of the eye-catching ambulatory motion of his friend Gertrude Abercrombie. These were altogether super sessions for Powell. He also provided a fizzing arrangement of 'Love Is a Many Splendored Thing', during the performance of which he adds a chordal accompaniment to the Roach drum solo, providing a thrilling effect.

Also present in the studio was the composer Tadd Dameron (author of 'Hot House' and many more fine inventions). After two years in limbo with a drug problem, Dameron had been persuaded by Roach to return to New York. For the quintet he wrote 'The Scene is Clean', a sumptuously harmonized celebration of the Clifford Brown lifestyle.

The recordings for *Clifford Brown and Max Roach at Basin Street* were slotted between club engagements in Baltimore, Boston and Detroit. When the album was complete, the quintet went back again to Detroit and thence to Boston once more. Before the next gig, in Philadelphia, Roach took a short break at his New York home. Here he received word that Richie Powell and Sonny Rollins had been involved in a car crash. He raced to Philadelphia to be with them, and was sickened to find that racism in the city of America's founding fathers had blocked their admission to a hospital. Instead, they were nursed back to health by Pearl Powell, mother of Richie and Bud, at her home in Willow Grove.

*

Sonny Rollins' position in the quintet was complicated by his pre-existing contract with Prestige records. The company expected a new album from him, so he asked Roach and Brown if it could be done with the quintet, but under his name. They generously agreed, and *Sonny*

Rollins + 4 was recorded at Rudy Van Gelder's studio in Hackensack, New Jersey, on 22 March 1956.

The most talked-about track on the consistently excellent LP is the Rollins composition 'Valse Hot'. The inspiration for this rare foray into three-quarter time was an eccentric 1952 recording by Thelonious Monk of 'Carolina Moon'. Roach had been the drummer at that Monk session, and the giddy jazz waltzing had triumphed, thanks largely to his metric mastery. On 'Valse Hot' his firm foundation makes life easy for the others, and his teasing, polyrhythmic solo provides the high spot.

By the early summer of 1956 the quintet's expanding repertoire was being heard not just in the jazz meccas of the North East and the Middle West, but across the country, thanks to their live broadcasts from Basin Street over national radio. The network of venues interested in booking the band was spreading, and in June, Joe Glaser fixed for them to play at the Continental Restaurant in Norfolk, Virginia.

Roach faced the prospect with mixed feelings. The naval town of Norfolk is just a short drive from his birthplace in Dismal Swamp, so here was an opportunity to catch up with his extended family and child-hood friends. But this was the South, and the Continental Restaurant was a segregated club, for whites only. Before opening night he put it to the management that the band would not be happy to play unless his family could come in and listen. A compromise was reached: a special table was set up for a few of his relatives. They came to every show. 'And so in a little way,' Max told me, 'we broke the colour line at that time.'

That Norfolk engagement is full of happy memories for him. During the daytime he and the band were entertained in various Roach households. At night magnificent music was made, and captured on a private tape.

*

After Norfolk, the quintet had a short break before their next engagement in Chicago. Clifford Brown and Richie Powell went back to Philadelphia to rest. Sonny Rollins, however, was due to make another album for Prestige at the Van Gelder studio in Hackensack on 22 June. He persuaded Roach to join him in a quartet with pianist Tommy Flanagan and bassist

Doug Watkins. The resulting album, *Saxophone Colossus*, is an aptly named monument, wherein Rollins' stature is magnified by Roach's cool brilliance. On 'St Thomas', for instance, Roach serves up the calypso rhythm as a dainty, almost ethereal delight, then shadows Rollins' improvisation with uncanny empathy. And on 'Blue Seven' the grand architecture of the drum solo arises magically from the minimal theme – what in Liszt's day they were pleased to call 'thematic transformation'.

On Tuesday 26 June 1956 Roach set out from New York on the 800-mile drive to Chicago. Normally he would have picked up Clifford Brown in Philadelphia, but this time Clifford had called to say he would travel with Richie Powell and Richie's wife, because he had a meeting with a trumpet manufacturer en route.

When Roach arrived at the Chicago hotel on Wednesday afternoon, he found no Clifford, but there was a message to call Joe Glaser. Glaser told him that Brown, along with Powell and Powell's wife Nancy, had been killed in a car crash. It had happened at night in the rain on the Pennsylvania Turnpike. Nancy had been driving. She lost control in the slippery conditions. The car struck a guard-rail and plunged down a 75-foot embankment. All three occupants died instantly.

Glaser added that if Max wished, the gig could go ahead with a replacement trumpeter: he had established that Miles Davis and Roy Eldridge were both available. Max said no. He locked himself in his hotel room and shared a dark night of the soul with two bottles of cognac.

A year earlier, when informed that Charlie Parker's doomed chariot of fire had run its course, he had been saddened but not crushed. But the death of Clifford had nothing hubristic or self-inflicted about it. It was utterly senseless and cruel. And coupled with the death of Bud Powell's blossoming kid brother Richie, it was too much to bear. It seems likely that Max's near-ruinous relationship with alcohol dates from here.

*

His first, desperately sad, public duty – he became upset when telling me about it nearly thirty years later – was to attend the triple funeral service in Philadelphia for Clifford, Richie and Nancy.

Then there was the engagement book to consider. At the time of the deaths the quintet faced a pressing list of commitments. Roach could not yet bear to replace Powell and Brown, so he put it to expectant club owners that, if they wished, he would come and give memorial performances with just saxophone and bass. Some agreed. The consequence was a musical freedom and a sound to which Rollins would famously return.

In mid-September in New York, three months after the bereavement, Roach made another album for EmArcy. They called it *Max Roach + 4*. Pianist Ray Bryant was booked for the recording, and trumpeter Kenny Dorham joined the band on a permanent basis. Roach and Dorham had been friends for years. While in Paris in 1949 with Charlie Parker's group, they had made a set of Parker-less recordings with Max as leader.

Also present in the studio was a composer with whom Roach went back a long way. George Russell had gone to live with Max's family in Brooklyn back in 1944, when illness forced his retirement from playing. Max's mother had nursed George while he worked on his *Lydian Chromatic Concept of Tonal Organisation*, a key document in the advance of modal improvisation. Dizzy Gillespie had recognized Russell's gifts and employed him to write for his 1947 orchestra.

The Russell composition chosen by Roach for the latest album was 'Ezz-thetic' (named for the stylish boxer Ezzard Charles). This zigzagging drama based on the chords of 'Love for Sale' was not a new piece. Charlie Parker had played it with his strings; and in 1951 Roach had taken part in a recording by Lee Konitz and a below-par Miles Davis. The version of 'Ezz-thetic' that opens *Max Roach + 4* is authoritative and compelling, serving notice that grief and liquor have not dulled Max's artistic edge.

The last track on the LP, clinching the sense of historical continuity, is a revival of Dizzy Gillespie's 'Woody 'n You' (first recorded by its composer with Coleman Hawkins in 1944, with Roach as the drummer).

Three weeks later tradition was again asserted when Sonny Rollins turned his next album for Prestige into a tribute to Charlie Parker. *Rollins*

Plays for Bird includes a medley of tunes associated with the master, preceded by the immortal fanfare Bird used to launch 'Parker's Mood'. The personnel is the one that played on *Max Roach + 4*, except that pianist Ray Bryant has been replaced by Wade Legge – formerly Dizzy Gillespie's regular keyboard man.

*

In December, Roach unhitched himself temporarily from his band, and turned up as a sideman on an LP by a founding father of the modern movement. He had known Thelonious Monk since the early 1940s, and admired and loved him for his profound originality. He had recorded with Monk several times already, assisting with the delivery of some fiendishly complex creations. In 1952, as well as underpinning the waltzing 'Carolina Moon', mentioned earlier, his drums were integral to the vertiginous 'Trinkle Tinkle' and the whirlwind of difficulties lightly entitled 'Skippy'.

The new Monk album was named *Brilliant Corners*, after its most sensational track. This fresh composition placed huge demands upon the players. Its lurching phrases pile up into an asymmetrical whole, which is stated (and then improvised upon) twice: first at a medium pace and then, cruelly, at double speed. Roach's expertise knits the ensemble together, and when he comes to solo, he dissects Monk's design with a watchmaker's precision.

The delighted producer of this album for Riverside records was Orrin Keepnews. Nine months later Roach would return and ask him a favour. We shall come to Mr Keepnews. In the meantime, Roach's band was due to make another LP for EmArcy.

Impressed by the popular success of 'Valse Hot', the EmArcy management decreed that the new record should consist entirely of waltzes. So out came *Jazz in 3/4 Time*, an album dominated by a 'Valse Hot' remake, brisker and smoother than the original, and nearly twice the length. For the rest there are some lilting show tunes and two new Roach compositions: 'Blues Waltz' and 'Little Folks'. The last has the naive charm of a Sunday-school hymn. Max says it came to him while he was watching his young children Daryl and Maxine at play. However, by the autumn of 1957 a new lady had entered his life. She was the intensely beautiful singer Abbey Lincoln.

When Max and Abbey look back on it now, each remembers the other as representing salvation. Max told me that Abbey appeared 'when I was drinking myself into oblivion'. Ms Lincoln frequently credits Roach with rescuing her from the despised status of supper-club sex object.

Born Anna Marie Wooldridge, the tenth of twelve children, she grew up in rural Michigan. An agent discovered her while she was singing with a local dance band and set her on a course that ended in Hollywood. Here she starred in the glitzy revue *Ça C'est Paris*, met Max Roach, and landed a spot in a new Cinemascope production, *The Girl Can't Help It*. This cult rock 'n' roll movie of the mid-1950s had a daft story involving Jane Mansfield and seventeen numbers from top acts like Little Richard and Eddie Cochran. Abbey Lincoln's contribution was a gospel-tinged song called 'Spread the Word'. She delivered it with panache, her willowy form blatantly underscored by a slinky orange frock. According to the publicity, this was the garment worn by Marilyn Monroe in *Gentlemen Prefer Blondes*, so thereafter Ms Lincoln was 'the girl in the Marilyn Monroe dress'. This did not please her. Her hero was Billie Holiday, and she wanted to be recognized as a singer in the Holiday, not the Hollywood, tradition.

Max Roach believed in her talent and sought someone to record it. The obvious outlet would have been Debut, but by the middle of 1957 the company was in trouble, blocked from making any further recordings by the American Federation of Musicians, who said money was owing. Moreover, Roach and Mingus had fallen out. So Max went to Riverside boss Orrin Keepnews, the producer of *Brilliant Corners*. When Keepnews said no, he was not interested in recording singers, Max made him an irresistible offer. If he would record *this* singer, Max would provide an all-star band, including himself, Kenny Dorham and Sonny Rollins, which would play for minimum wages. The consequent album – called *That's Him* and packed with well-delivered standard songs – was the first of three by Lincoln for Riverside.

*

For his next album for EmArcy, Roach revisited some high spots from his playing days with Charlie Parker. Sonny Rollins had now left the band. His replacement was Hank Mobley, who had played on Max's first LP as leader back in 1953 (when they premièred Parker's 'Chi Chi'). Kenny Dorham stayed and Max dispensed with a pianist, so the group was renamed The Max Roach 4. Among the pieces chosen for the album were 'Confirmation' and 'Au Privave', two of Parker's finest (both immaculately served by Roach when the composer made his own recordings). The new versions were recorded in December 1957, and completion of the Parker album was deferred until the spring.

Meanwhile, Sonny Rollins recruited Max to play on the new album he was making for Orrin Keepnews. Since leaving Roach's band, Rollins had been leading a saxophone-bass-drums trio (the line-up favoured for a while by Roach after the deaths of Clifford Brown and Richie Powell). The bassist chosen for the Riverside adventure was Oscar Pettiford, a founder of the modern movement, who had played alongside Max at the Onyx club in Dizzy Gillespie's seminal quintet of 1943.

Having assembled this trio of heavyweights, Rollins spent the first session limbering up with lightweight material, including Harry Warren's 'Shadow Waltz' and Noel Coward's 'Some Day I'll Find You'. The second session produced a nineteen-minute masterwork. Rollins called it *The Freedom Suite*. His composition is built in three distinctive sections, linked by a churchy waltz. Its performance is a marvel of impassioned spontaneity, with each player a crucial partner in the creative act.

Unusually for the time, Rollins let it be known that the music carried a political sub-text, aimed at the racial prejudice within America. Here is an extract from what he wrote for *The Freedom Suite*'s sleeve-note: 'America is deeply rooted in Negro culture: its colloquialisms, its humor, its music. How ironic that the Negro . . . who has exemplified the humanities in his very existence, is being rewarded with inhumanity.'

Roach was impressed. One day he would follow this example of music put to a campaigning purpose. More immediately, on 11 April 1958, he returned to the studio to finish the *Plays Charlie Parker* album.

Three long tracks do the trick. One is the obligatory 'Parker's Mood', complete with fanfare. The other titles come from Parker's first recording session as leader, when Roach, Miles Davis and Dizzy Gillespie were the key supporting players. More than a decade later 'Billie's Bounce' has grown slicker, and 'Koko' has accelerated from an already mind-boggling metronome reading of 300 beats per minute to one closer to 400.

For this second instalment of the LP there was a new saxophone player, a twenty-three-year-old music student called George Coleman – the first of many youthful unknowns whom Roach would foster.

By the time his band recorded for EmArcy again (in Chicago in June) he had recruited a phenomenal new trumpeter. Booker Little was barely twenty years old. He had first come to Max's attention three years earlier, while he was rooming with Sonny Rollins at the Chicago YMCA. The new album, called *Max Roach + 4 on the Chicago Scene*, offers the love song 'My Old Flame' (famously recorded by Charlie Parker) as a showcase for Booker Little's precocious brilliance.

For this album only, Roach added the Chicago pianist Eddie Baker. Soon thereafter he conducted a radical experiment, replacing the piano with a tuba, played by seventeen-year-old Ray Draper. Following rehearsals *chez* Max in Brooklyn and a try-out at Small's Paradise in Harlem, the novel line-up was unveiled at the 1958 Newport Jazz Festival. EmArcy recorded the concert and issued it as *Max Roach + 4 at Newport*.

The programme – a mixture of hallowed items like 'A Night in Tunisia' and new material such as Booker Little's 'Minor Mode' – is unified by Roach's commanding musical personality. His shouts of instruction and encouragement can be clearly heard, but mainly this is bandleading through the drums: intricate, fingertip control over the improvised patterns of his young players.

The 'tuba band' went on to accumulate a large repertoire, and when EmArcy declined to record them again, Roach made albums for other labels: one for Riverside and one for Time, both fresh and varied. He did a lot of the writing himself, including a delicate arrangement of 'Milano' (the tune by his friend John Lewis), and an original essay called 'Pies of Quincy', exploiting the eloquence of his Zildjian cymbals.

Max loved the brassy tuba for the colour it brought to the ensemble voice, for its attack and for its historic link with the marching bands of New Orleans. But in spite of Ray Draper's virtuosity, the instrument struggled to sing. After six months it was dropped.

*

EmArcy next recorded Roach when he appeared as star soloist with the percussion section of the Boston Pops Orchestra. During a concert at the 1958 Lenox Summer School in New England, he added his improvisations to the ensemble's fixed arrangements. The album was issued as *Max Roach with the Boston Percussion Ensemble*.

Max believed passionately in the Lenox School of Jazz, where he came and taught for several summers in the late 1950s, together with fellow practitioners like George Russell, John Lewis and Dizzy Gillespie. Here he felt at peace, engaged in lively dialogue with the young students and encouraging their radical ideas. But his life at large was bedevilled by a stubborn problem. His addiction to alcohol was proving much harder to throw off than his short-lived heroin habit, and when he drank the consequences were dire. During a visit to Birdland one night, he abused everyone at the bar, friends and strangers alike, then fought his way on to the stage, seized the public address system and blitzed the audience with insults.

When he was sober he still played superbly, as evidenced by the set of recordings his band made at the end of January 1959. By now Ray Draper's tuba had been replaced by the flexible trombone of Julian Priester, and Booker Little was coming into his maturity. But the EmArcy jazz label had been shut down and Max's contract had passed to the parent company Mercury. They elected not to release this new album (called *The Many Sides of Max*) for five years.

A month after the recording session, while the band was in Pittsburgh, it was blown apart by an almighty row. Details are lost but drink was the likely villain. Booker Little, George Coleman and bassist Art Davis all walked out on Max during a club performance. Julian Priester offered this painful recollection:

> We were stranded in Pittsburgh, Max and I, when Booker and George and Art Davis left . . . We were fired from the club where we were performing. So Max put together a group with the Turrentine brothers, and we performed in the dining room of the hotel that we were staying at. And as a result we were able to pay our hotel bill and had enough money to get back to New York.[4]

The Turrentine brothers were Tommy (trumpet) and Stanley (tenor saxophone). Bassist Bob Boswell, their Pittsburgh colleague, completed the new quintet, which stayed together for more than a year.

Soon Mercury summoned Max to record again, although all the material needed for a Roach album was sitting on their shelves. It was not his new band they were interested in. The record industry's infatuation with the selling-power of stereophony was reaching its peak, and Mercury wanted a hi-fi battle between Roach and Buddy Rich, with the two drummers launching their bombardments from opposing loudspeakers. To rescue the project from vulgarity, Max insisted that his whole group be involved, playing specially commissioned arrangements. Even so, the album *Rich versus Roach* says more about marketing than it does about Max's art.

In July, grateful perhaps for the drum bonanza, Mercury invited Max to record again. This time he produced the album himself and called it *Quiet As It's Kept* – a dig at the lowly status of jazz in America's cultural hierarchy.

Among the LP's many beauties is 'As Long As You're Living', a blues that germinated in the hotel where Roach and Julian Priester were stranded after the Pittsburgh bust-up. According to Stanley Turrentine, the members of the new band would assemble in Max's room for briefings and rehearsals. Odd time-signatures were a favourite Roach topic, and one day they found him playing a 5/4 rhythm with his brushes on a chair. The horn players joined in with some riffs, then lit upon a catchy melody: certainly the first 12-bar blues, and probably the first jazz piece, in 5/4 time.

'As Long As You're Living' was already in the regular repertoire before the LP was made. Three months afterwards, when Abbey Lincoln made her third album for Riverside, she sang a version with words added by Oscar Brown, Jr. This was an ingenious and memorable arrangement, backed by Max and the band, but it was eclipsed commercially by 'Take Five', the colossal, bolt-from-the-blue hit in 5/4 time just scored by the Dave Brubeck quartet. Stanley Turrentine and Julian Priester challenged the justice of Brubeck's success. They remembered playing 'As Long As You're Living' at a festival in Detroit earlier in the year, when Dave Brubeck and his men showed an inordinate interest. They found it hard to accept the emergence of 'Take Five' as a coincidence. According to Stanley Turrentine, 'Max went crazy. He really got upset.'[5]

Roach's tangible response was another album for Mercury. This one, called *Moon-Faced and Starry-Eyed*, consisted entirely of love songs, with no drum solos at all. Abbey Lincoln sang on two of the tracks, meaningfully entitled 'I Concentrate On You' and 'Never Leave Me'. Max and Abbey had grown extremely close, but although she was sometimes able to mitigate the destructive effects of his drinking, she could not persuade him to give it up. In the late autumn of 1959, when all other remedies had failed, he consigned himself to Bellevue for a spell of aversion therapy on one of the segregated medical wards.

Charles Mingus had been a patient at Bellevue the previous year. So now four of the Massey Hall five had spent time within New York's most famous mental institution; it was a measure of the ferocity of the pressure felt by black artists in America.

*

Shortly after his release from Bellevue, Roach enjoyed the balm of a trip to Europe, where he and his band experienced the usual adulation. On their concert tour they shared the bill with a distinguished trio of Americans abroad, whom Max was delighted to see again: Kenny Clarke, Oscar Pettiford and Bud Powell. Whenever Max came to France, visiting Bud was a high priority.

During this 1960 trip the Roach quintet made copious recordings, official and unofficial, including a concert captured in Germany and a carefully organized session at the Barclay Studios in Paris. Much of the material for the latter was composed by Roach himself. The central work is *Parisian Sketches*: a set of five loosely-linked evocations. This light-hearted compendium hints at the more weighty suite that Roach was already constructing. And the last track on the French album, called 'Liberté', is linked to the new work more directly. Its boldly simple, heraldic theme, fired by Roach's eruptive drumming, will reappear in American dress with the title 'Freedom Day'.

*

Between the visit to Europe and the recording of the politically-charged magnum opus came the 1960 Newport Jazz Festival. After Roach's Bellevue incarceration, he and Mingus had become reconciled, and the two now conspired to create an alternative to Newport's main event, which they condemned as bloated and corrupt. Their self-help answer, located within earshot at Cliff Walk Manor, triumphed when George Wein's jazz extravaganza was cut short after rioting and tear gas. None of the alternative festival's concerts was recorded, but we know from reports that Roach acted as gracious MC, that trumpet prodigy Booker Little was back in his band, and that Abbey Lincoln played her part in the stage act.

Since meeting Max Roach, Abbey Lincoln had found herself. As she put it, 'My consciousness was opened. Max introduced me to museums and things, because I wasn't that kind. I didn't know anything about culture. I was really a simple country girl.'[6]

By 1959 Roach and Lincoln had become Civil Rights activists, with many friends in the black literary communities of New York and Chicago. In particular, Roach formed an association with the multi-talented Oscar Brown, Jr. They collaborated on an expansive stage work, intended for 1963: the centenary of the Emancipation Proclamation that officially ended slavery in America. By 1960 several sections of the work (words by Brown, music by Roach) were ready, and a performance of these parts was mounted in Philadelphia under the auspices of the National Association for the Advancement of Colored People.

Here ended Roach's association with the Mercury record company. Given the endorsement of the NAACP, one might have expected Mercury to invest in Max's bold new venture, but not a bit of it. The company recoiled from anything that might be construed as subversive. Fortunately, the maverick journalist-turned-producer Nat Hentoff attended the performance in Philadelphia. When he learned of Mercury's negative attitude, he invited Roach to record for his newly-formed, uncompromised Candid label.

The Candid album drew on material from the Brown–Roach collaboration, together with music Roach had composed for an agitprop ballet. To distinguish it from the *Freedom Suite* created by Sonny Rollins two years earlier, the new work acquired the urgent and comprehensive title *We Insist! Max Roach's Freedom Now Suite*. It was recorded at the end of August 1960, seven months after the heroic example of four young black students in Greensboro, North Carolina, set off a wave of sit-ins at whites-only lunch-counters across the American South. A press photo of one such gesture of dignified defiance dominates the album's stark black-and-white cover.

The suite has five movements – all with a part for Abbey Lincoln. In the first movement, 'Driva' Man', Oscar Brown's words describe the cruelty inflicted on America's plantation slaves by their ferocious overseers. The slow 5/4 metre of Roach's music achieves a hobbled effect, and the sense of anguish is intensified by the whiplash of Max's rim shot on every fifth beat. Members of his regular quintet fill in the ensemble background while, between the two sets of sung verses, no less a person than Coleman Hawkins delivers a gripping tenor saxophone solo. Max had first recorded with Hawkins back in 1944, when he was the hottest young drummer on 52nd Street and 'the Hawk' was already an institution. When invited to lend his authority to 'Driva' Man', Hawkins accepted the role at once. He loved new challenges, and here were two of them: a 5/4 time signature and a political thrust. Having delivered what 'Driva' Man' required, he stayed to witness the remainder of the session, marvelling at the quality and slant of the compositions.

The second movement, 'Freedom Day', describes the joyful reaction of the slaves to the 1863 Emancipation Proclamation. In its instrumental form it had already been recorded in Paris as 'Liberté'. Here, Abbey Lincoln revels in Brown's heady text, and there is a jubilant solo by Max himself.

The third movement (originally a ballet score) is entitled 'Triptych: Prayer/Protest/Peace'. This is a tour de force for Lincoln, with Roach's drums providing a lean but telling accompaniment. Part one, 'Prayer', is the wordless lament of a patient people in bondage. Part two, 'Protest', is where their patience explodes into rage against the pain inflicted by their oppressors. Putting her lovely voice at serious risk (because for her the issue transcends mere singing), Ms Lincoln unleashes a performance that astounds and terrifies: a sonata of primal screams, roars and howls, to exorcise the centuries of hurt and bitterness. Part three, 'Peace', hums and sighs with serene exhaustion after the cathartic violence.

The last two movements of the *Freedom Now Suite* are devoted to the independence struggle in Africa, a cause that black American activists had come to see as inseparable from their own. 'All Africa' is a hymn to pan-Africanism, with a text by Oscar Brown, Jr. extolling the African Beat, and a guest contribution from the Nigerian drummer Michael Olatunji. 'Tears for Johannesburg' is a throbbing, wordless threnody for the victims of the recent Sharpeville massacre, where sixty-nine unarmed black Africans, including women and children, were shot dead by the South African police.

The album attracted enormous interest and controversy, and the *Freedom Now Suite* became a regular Roach/Lincoln concert presentation. They took it around the world, and they took it on tour in the USA to raise funds for the NAACP.

Three months after the LP was made, they recorded for Hentoff's Candid label again, this time as part of the Newport Rebels – a group of the key contributors to the famous victory of the alternative Newport Festival. The idea was to resurrect in the studio the freewheeling spirit of the summer event at Cliff Walk Manor. So, for example, Charles Mingus was paired with Roy Eldridge; and Abbey Lincoln sang with a group including cutting-edge reedman Eric Dolphy and drumming monument Jo Jones, pillar of Count Basie's band in Kansas City during the 1930s. And Max enjoyed the privilege of having Jones play alongside him, as an extra member of the regular Roach quintet, on an exultant new Booker Little piece they called 'Cliff Walk'.

*

Of all the artists he recorded for his Candid label, Nat Hentoff saw Abbey Lincoln as the one most passionately committed to the cause of equality and justice for black people. 'She was very outspoken,' he said, 'very much in front. She had integrity that could cut your head off.'[7]

Ms Lincoln cropped her hair and adopted flowing, timeless garb. She formed the Cultural Association for Women of African Heritage, whose membership included the budding writers Rosa Guy and Maya Angelou. They monitored African current affairs and were thrilled when, in the summer of 1960, Patrice Lumumba, the first (and last) democratically elected prime minister of the newly independent Republic of the Congo, travelled to the US and addressed a gathering in Harlem. Malcolm X described Lumumba as the greatest black man who ever walked the African continent. White reporters demanded to know if he was a Communist. Within six months he had been murdered, the victim of a plot hatched by the Belgian government and encouraged by the CIA.

When news of the assassination reached New York, Abbey Lincoln's Cultural Association was moved to act. On 14 February 1961 they held a protest meeting in front of the United Nations building. Roach was there too.

Watching the TV news that night, Lincoln was horrified to hear it announced on NBC's influential Huntley-Brinkley Report that there had been ugly scenes at the United Nations, and that the rioters had been armed with bicycle chains and brass knuckles. In the wake of these broadcast lies, Max and Abbey were visited at home by a team from the FBI, who carefully noted the African sculptures and furnishings. 'One of the officers was black and the others were white,' Max remembered, 'and they were *thorough*. We had nothing to hide, of course. We didn't have any weapons or anything.'

A week after the demonstration at the UN, Lincoln made another album for Nat Hentoff, backed by a band of luminaries led by Roach. Several songs have words by the Harlem poet Langston Hughes. The title track, 'Straight Ahead', has lyrics by Abbey herself, complaining about the slow arrival of equal rights for American blacks, and it was this mix of music and politics that offended the critical establishment. In his review of the album, Ira Gitler decried the invasion of art by propaganda and denounced Lincoln for being 'a professional Negro'. Roach and Lincoln delivered a counter-blast, and *Down Beat* published the debate under the heading 'Racial Prejudice in Jazz'.[8]

The critics were not alone in having their attitudes challenged. Roach and Charles Mingus drew up a list of jazz clubs that expected musicians to work in filthy conditions. When the musicians' union failed to support action against these premises, the two rebels tore up their union membership cards.

Roach's next tactic was more debatable. On 19 May 1961 Miles Davis was to appear at Carnegie Hall, an unprecedented concert at which he would perform 'live' some of the famous music he had recorded with the Gil Evans orchestra. The proceeds would go to the African Research Foundation. Roach's African nationalist friends convinced him that this so-called Foundation had no philanthropic motive. It was a neo-colonialist racket. Instead of trying to alert Davis privately, Max chose to make a supremely public statement. While Miles was serenading the packed auditorium, he walked up the aisle and sat down on the stage, dressed in a white jacket and carrying a placard boldly inscribed: AFRICA FOR THE AFRICANS. FREEDOM NOW. Astounded, Miles stopped the music and walked off. The concert resumed after Max had been removed by security guards. When it was over he shouted through the stage door, 'Tell Miles I'm sorry. Tell him he was so great I was crying during the first half. Tell Miles I love him.'[9] Their close friendship survived.

*

During the early 1960s Roach and Lincoln stayed in the vanguard of black political dissent, and Max regularly insisted in interviews that he would never again play anything that lacked social significance. His next album, *Percussion Bitter Sweet*, remains a masterpiece in the arena of campaigning art. Recorded in August 1961 for the radically-minded Impulse label, it consists entirely of Roach compositions, played by one of the best of his post-Clifford Brown ensembles. In the front line along-side Booker Little and Julian Priester are tenor saxophonist Clifford Jordan, and Eric Dolphy, who plays flute, alto sax and bass clarinet. The pianist is Mal Waldron, who served Charles Mingus on such triumphs as *Pithecanthropus Erectus*. Abbey Lincoln sings on two tracks, including the opener, 'Garvey's Ghost', where her wordless contribution enhances the eerie texture.

In the 1920s Marcus Garvey, a charismatic, Harlem-based Jamaican, recruited members for his Universal Negro Improvement Association. With its slogan 'back to Africa' and its plan to resettle diaspora blacks in their ancestral homeland, the UNIA became the largest mass movement in African-American history. It established 700 branches in thirty-eight states of the USA before Garvey was arrested by the Federal government, imprisoned and deported back to Jamaica. He died in 1940, leaving a philosophy that inspired both the Rastafarian movement and the Nation of Islam. So 'Garvey's Ghost' is far from downcast. It jigs to a sprightly 6/8 beat, with Max in his element, flanked by a pair of Afro-Latin percussionists he has invited to join the celebrations.

The last track on the album switches the scene from Harlem to Cape Town. Expressing the frustrated potential of the black population, 'Man from South Africa' has an urgent 7/4 rhythmic undertow, from which the soloists rise to vent their feelings.

The central track, 'Tender Warriors' (written for the youngsters risking their lives in the civil rights struggle), is the most highly charged. After its bittersweet theme, where harsh chords claw at Dolphy's airy flute, it surges forward in a restless 6/8 rhythm. When Dolphy comes to solo, he switches from flute to bass clarinet. His outburst of rage and anguish is topped only by Roach's incandescent drumming.

Although 'Tender Warriors' paints a general picture of embattled youth, when he wrote it Max was still haunted by the deaths of Richie Powell and Clifford Brown. For him, the lethal amounts of driving required of black musicians trying to make a living were an indictment of America's skewed cultural hierarchy and its loaded system of rewards. So Powell and Brown also counted as martyred cadets. (Two years later, when a bomb planted by the Ku Klux Klan killed four Sunday school children in a Baptist church in Birmingham, Alabama, performances of 'Tender Warriors' were dedicated to those murdered little girls.)

On 5 October 1961, in his bruised and vulnerable state, Roach was dealt another dreadful blow. On that day his trumpeter Booker Little died of kidney failure at the age of just twenty-three. Max couldn't help tormenting himself with the thought that he was somehow putting a curse on young trumpet players, but his principal response was positive and creative – the composition of a large new work he called 'It's Time'.

Written for performance by his jazz group together with a chorus of sixteen trained voices, 'It's Time' combined three of Roach's current pre-occupations: complex metres, political engagement and the expressiveness of the human voice. For the recording he chose his singers with great care. They all had to be good at reading music (the polymetric vocal score is far from easy) and, just as importantly, they had to be capable of delivering what he called 'that black church *sound*'. To help him assemble the right sixteen, he enlisted Coleridge-Taylor Perkinson, who had been a classmate at the Manhattan School of Music. Perkinson (a black American named after the internationally-renowned black English composer Samuel Coleridge-Taylor) was a questing musician, keen to reconcile the African-American and European traditions. In the recording studio it would be his job to conduct the choir while Max led from the drums.

The first sessions took place in January 1962 and ended in failure. As with Charlie Parker's venture with voices back in 1953, the problem of containing both the jazz and the choral components seemed insuperable.

But unlike Norman Granz, who cut the Parker experiment short, the producer for Impulse, Bob Thiele, agreed to persevere. At three further sessions in February the *It's Time* album was recorded in its entirety.

The work is in six movements, with pointed titles like 'The Profit' and 'Living Room', although the voice parts are largely wordless. The chorus addresses its task with spirit, but it is Roach's peak-power drumming that gives this album its authority and edge.

The virtues are summed up in the title track, 'It's Time'. The riveting opening statement (an example of Max's 'mixed metre theory') can be heard either as ten bars of 4/4, or as eight bars divided as follows: two bars of 3/4, two of 4/4, two of 6/4 and two of 7/4. All at lightning speed. The fiery solos that follow, from tenorist Clifford Jordan and from Max himself, have their blaze stoked by jabbing choral interventions.

The title 'It's Time' refers of course to the metrical complexities, but it means more besides. Echoing Charlie Parker's 'Now's the Time', it's a call for racial equality and a just society.

*

In the autumn of 1962 United Artists records went to Duke Ellington with a bright idea. They proposed that the grand master of American music should make a piano trio album with two of its notorious rebels: Charles Mingus and Max Roach.

Mingus and Roach both idolized the Duke and both had played in his band, Mingus briefly and disastrously in 1953, and Roach briefly and nervously when he was still a schoolboy. The new adventure with Ellington as pianist began in the great man's office, where the Duke described the music he had composed but not written down.

The next time they met was at the recording session. 'He got to the studio early,' Max remembered, 'and when Mingus and I arrived he said, "Just think of me as a poor man's Bud Powell, fellas."'[10] News of this extraordinary summit meeting had spread, the studio was crammed with journalists, and the atmosphere was one of champagne celebration. According to Max, the quaffing throng unsettled Mingus, and this was why he walked out halfway through and had to be coaxed back.

In spite of (or perhaps because of) the turbulence, the piano trio album, called *Money Jungle*, is a thriller, hailed by critics as one of the greatest cross-generational get-togethers in jazz. When it came to be re-released on CD, four extra items were discovered in the vault. These include 'A Little Max', Duke's tribute to Roach, in which piano and bass make dainty background patterns, while Max flaunts his grace like a wing-heeled tap-dancer.

*

The Mingus/Roach friendship weathered the little storm at the Ellington session, but by then their business partnership was effectively over. Mingus had proposed that the Debut catalogue should be transferred to Fantasy records on the West Coast, and Roach had agreed. Both men were too active creatively to take care of Debut's affairs, and Fantasy was a well-run company, with Mingus's ex-wife Celia on board.

In October 1962, when the Max Roach Quartet was playing at the Jazz Workshop in San Francisco, Fantasy sent in a recording unit one evening and issued the result as a Debut/Fantasy LP.

The members of his quartet that evening – tenorist Clifford Jordan, pianist Mal Waldron and bassist Eddie Khan – all enjoyed unrestricted solo space, and just two extended performances fill the entire album.

The title track, 'Speak, Brother, Speak', was named by Max after the street-corner orators familiar to black communities across America. The form is the 12-bar blues, and over the course of twenty-five minutes each member has his lengthy say, spurred by shifting rhythms. Last to speak are the drums, whose irresistible rhetoric is delivered in 5/4 time.

The other track, called 'A Variation', is similarly expansive, but this time the starting point is a slow, prayerful theme, composed by Roach, which rests on simple, solemn modulations.

Speak, Brother, Speak furnishes a lively footnote to Roach's career as a Debut executive. He would make no more records in America for two years. The time was spent touring, at home and abroad. Some of the performances in Europe were recorded without his consent, resulting in a clutch of mislabelled LPs.

The next official album was for Atlantic, in 1964, in unexpected company. Hasaan Ibn Ali (formerly William Henry Langford, Jr.) was a formidable pianist from Philadelphia: a musicians' musician, in his mid-thirties, who had never made a record. Whenever he came to New York, the single-minded Hasaan would go from club to club, taking a turn on all the pianos, then head for the Roach apartment. Max told me, 'Four o'clock in the morning the doorbell would ring, and it's Hasaan. I'd let him in and go back to bed. He'd run to my piano and play and play and play.'

Sometimes the music was so beautiful that Roach would get up and turn on his tape recorder. Feeling bound to use his influence, he took the case of Hasaan Ibn Ali to Nesuhi Ertegun, boss of Atlantic records. Ertegun agreed to sponsor an album featuring this unknown artist, provided that Max Roach was the headline name. The compromise title was *The Max Roach Trio featuring the Legendary Hasaan*. (Art Davis, a Roach regular, played the bass.)

The album is made up entirely of Hasaan compositions, played with a torrential lyricism and shot through with traces of Thelonious Monk and Bud Powell. According to Hasaan himself, his prime influence was Powell's friend Elmo Hope, to whom he dedicated his poignant ballad 'Hope So Elmo'.

Reckless with his health, Hasaan died young. Roach had provided ideal support for this doomed young man on his only record. Bringing the best out of great but idiosyncratic pianists was a speciality of his. Thelonious Monk had been a beneficiary, and so too had Bud Powell, about whom Max never ceased to care.

He spent time with Powell whenever he visited Paris, and grew friendly with Bud's adoring protector Francis Paudras. When Paudras brought Powell back to New York in August 1964, Max was among those cheering on opening night at Birdland (although normally he avoided the place because he deplored the management). He came to see Paudras and Powell at their New York hotel, and when they told him that Bud was unhappy with the young drummer supplied by Oscar Goodstein, he put forward his protégé, J.C. Moses.

In December, a few days after the session with Hasaan, Roach and Abbey Lincoln threw a party at their apartment to celebrate Powell's return to his homeland. Of all the artists lined up to give Powell an embrace, the most startling was Sonny Rollins. Powell had known him as a quiet young lad. Now he was a maestro with a Mohican haircut, which he explained to Bud by saying he was following the practice of his ancestors. According to the awed account of Francis Paudras, when Max played the tape of his recordings with Hasaan, Rollins dropped to his knees and remained motionless throughout.[11]

*

The promoter George Wein, putting his Newport Festival humiliation behind him, tried persistently to fix a European tour for a supergroup consisting of Roach, Rollins and Charles Mingus. This monumental trio nearly materialized in 1966, but at the last minute Mingus pulled out, preferring to stay at home and star in a documentary film. Instead, Roach travelled to Europe with his regular group, along with Rollins. His role was to provide the concerts with a climactic finale in a trio with Roach and Roach's current bass player Jymie Merritt. One such concert was taped. Predictably exciting but poorly recorded, it was issued on a rogue LP misdated 1963.

The more significant album of 1966 is the one Roach recorded in the studio for Atlantic. The band was the one that went to Europe with him: James Spaulding (alto sax), Freddie Hubbard (trumpet), Ronnie Mathews (piano) and Jymie Merritt (bass). Max thought it one of his best: 'Everyone in it can create design and project feeling.'[12] Ensemble pleasures include 'Nommo' (Jymie Merritt's catchy composition in 7/4), but what makes this album special are the three pieces for drums alone. These represent design at its most exquisite. In 'The Drum Also Waltzes' delicate traceries grow from a gentle pulse in three-quarter time. 'For Big Sid' (Max's tribute to the swing drummer Sid Catlett) rings changes on a favourite rhythmic pattern. Known as *mop mop* because it lands firmly on two crotchets, this was the lick that engendered Charlie Parker's 'Red Cross'. Third and most impressive of the drum solos is the one that gave the album its title: 'Drums Unlimited'. Starting and ending with a sizzling hi-hat pattern, and frequently bursting into a funky dance rhythm, this is Roach showing what the complete jazz drummer can do. Every facet of his drums and cymbals is given resounding voice as he travels, in his words, 'to the limits of my limits'.[13]

'For Big Sid' and 'Drums Unlimited' both featured in the Roach stage shows of this period. So too did 'Prayer/Protest/Peace' from the *Freedom Now Suite*, with Abbey Lincoln in the spotlight, causing a sensation. But the Beatles had invaded America with their Anglo-Saxon rock and roll, and as the 1960s progressed, jazz lost much of its audience. The Atlantic record company signed some big-name rock bands, and urged its jazz artists to acknowledge the way of the world. Roach's answer, in June 1968, was the album *Members, Don't Git Weary*.

The cover photo shows Max modishly attired in dashiki and chunky beads, and the performances inside, with one exception, are sharply up-to-date. Alto saxophonist Gary Bartz and trumpeter Charles Tolliver form the youthful, thrusting front line. Stanley Cowell, another bright talent in his twenties, doubles on acoustic and electric pianos, and provides three compositions, including the Coltranesque 'Equipoise'. Running counter to the post-bop grain is the title track, 'Members, Don't Git Weary', a spiritual from slavery days, turned by Roach into a hymn for the Civil Rights movement. To sing it he recruited the rich-voiced Andy Bey, whose emotional reading takes us deep inside the poetic text. Members (i.e. black folks) are exhorted to remain steadfast, because 'all the work's most done'; and a vision is offered of the land ahead, across the River Jordan, where those who have been despised will feast on milk and honey and march with the tallest angels. Throughout this fervent recitation, the members of the ensemble extemporize a raw, polyphonic background, guided by Roach's imperious drumming.

Although the album has been re-released and is now in favour, it did not sell in rock and roll quantities and Atlantic did not rush to make a follow-up. Shortly after the recording, Roach (now a patriarch of forty-four) took his young band to work at Count Basie's club in Harlem. This was his first regular Harlem engagement for more than twenty years: a further indication, if one were needed, that jazz in America was losing its young white following.

Under the terms of his contract with Atlantic one more album was due. He told me about the meeting in 1970, where company executives offered their advice: 'They said the name of the game is making money, what they call "coat-tailing" or "piggy-backing". That means you ride on familiar material. So they gave me a list of things that were hits at the time.'

Max went home and reflected on that meeting. He felt entirely unqualified to make an album of Beatles songs, and decided that his best chance of popularity lay with being true to himself. He called Atlantic, 'and I said "I'm going to do Negro spirituals, 'cos everybody knows Negro spirituals." There was a loud silence on the end of the phone, and then the man said, "Well, OK, do what you will."'

The resulting album, *Lift Every Voice and Sing*, was a radical fusion of jazz and the music of the black church. To perform alongside his young players Roach engaged an established church choir, the J.C White Singers from the Bedford-Stuyvesant district of Brooklyn. The repertoire was chosen from the treasury of songs created by slaves as a coded commentary upon their condition, and each of the performances was dedicated to a hero of the liberation struggle. 'Troubled Waters', for example, was dedicated to Paul Robeson, and 'Let My People Go' was for Patrice Lumumba. One of the most famous sorrow songs, 'Motherless Child', was dedicated to Marcus Garvey, because, said Max, 'when you read between the lines, "mother" means the continent of Africa'.

The moving performance of 'Were You There When They Crucified My Lord?' is led by the ragged-edged tenor voice of J.C White himself. According to Max, the suppressed term of reference here is a Southern lynching. He dedicated the piece to Malcolm X, Martin Luther King, Medgar Evers and all the other freedom fighters murdered by the forces of reaction.

The album was issued in 1971 and was a commercial failure. Max blamed its untimeliness. Richard Nixon was in the White House and the Civil Rights movement was in retreat, its leaders dead. 'But I was still in the 60s.'

*

As Roach likes to point out, one benefit delivered by the uproar of the 1960s was a dramatic increase in black teaching staff at American universities. After demonstrations by students, black and white, against the overwhelming 'whiteness' of the courses on offer, black studies departments were hastily set up in colleges across the country.

Having rejected the comfortable option of jazz-rock, Roach saw no future for himself in the music business. When three universities approached him with offers of professorships, he chose the University of Massachusetts at Amherst and threw himself into campus politics. The hidebound Music Department at Amherst was still refusing to recognize jazz as a major degree subject, and he suspected they were using his presence merely as window dressing. Nevertheless, he fought to establish a course on the evolution of African-American music, which he would teach. To that end he lobbied successfully for a grant to spend the summer of 1974 in Ghana, studying the sources.

The most famous drummer in Ghana, known as Ghanaba, was an old friend of his. In the 1950s (when his name was Guy Warren) Ghanaba had worked in America, endearing himself to Charlie Parker and his circle, and recording the popular album *Africa Speaks, America Answers*. Back home in Accra he had taken the title 'Kofi Ghanaba the Divine Drummer'. By a satisfying twist, Roach was in Ghanaba's home, listening to the battery-powered radio, when the resignation speech of the disgraced President Nixon hit the airwaves. Before returning to what he hoped would be an improved America, Max travelled widely in Ghana, skimming the cultural riches. He invested in a course on the balafon (the traditional African xylophone) with one of the master musicians at Legon University. It was a humbling experience:

> They don't play hand and hand, like left-right, left-right. It's hand *against* hand, *all* of the time. The first lesson, two against three, was a breeze. Then it got a little bit more complex, the second lesson, and I

was stumbling. And finally the third lesson, he gave me an exercise and I was really having problems with it. So he looked at me, he says, 'Listen, I'm gonna go out, and I'll be back in about an hour.' I knew then it takes *years* to get to that third stage.[14]

Back at the University of Massachusetts, after marching students charged the Music Department with 'cultural discrimination', jazz was finally accepted as a major degree subject. Max settled into the life of a tenured professor. For the first time ever he had a regular salary and medical cover. His 1960s were categorically over, and his partnership with Abbey Lincoln had ended with that decade (they were married in 1962 and divorced in 1970). When his new wife Janus presented him with twin girls, he bought an airy mansion in Greenwich, Connecticut. Here in the generous basement he stored the vast array of materials needed for his pet music project, called M'Boom.

*

Inspired in part by the polyrhythmic musics of the Third World, M'Boom is the ultimate African-American drum orchestra. Max explained his ambition like this:

> I wanted to have a percussion ensemble that reflected what we call American music. Not like Stockhausen, but the way we deal with *our* music. So I assembled a group of wonderful jazz drummers, who were also composers, and could play all the mallet instruments. And I put it together in a democratic fashion. For me, jazz reflects the democratic principle. Somebody gives us a germ of an idea – what we call a 'head' – and all of us have an opportunity to make a statement on that 'head'. It's like we all get a vote on it, and the result is what the piece is about.

Although democratic in principle, M'Boom was an organizational tour de force: eight of America's top, jazz-familiar percussionists, plus Max himself, moving among more than a hundred different instruments of determinate and indeterminate pitch. Rehearsals *chez* Roach were a delight, but the economics of taking this unit on the road were horrendous.

To satisfy his need for expression as a performer, he used to take a small band on tour during the university vacations. A bonus of these trips was renewed contact with old comrades-in-arms. In Europe in the summer of 1972 his group travelled on the same circuit as those of Dizzy Gillespie and Charles Mingus. Meeting up with Dizzy was unalloyed joy, but the reunion with Mingus turned sour when he overheard his former business partner telling the press that he alone had created Debut records.

In Europe in 1976 the paths of Roach and Mingus crossed again. Both their bands, together with a third led by the avant-garde saxophonist Archie Shepp, were in Paris that September when news broke that Chairman Mao Tse-Tung had died. A delegation of Italian Young Communists pressed for a concert of revolutionary music to commemorate the Chairman's passing. And who better to supply it, they wanted to know, than those three notorious radicals: Shepp, Mingus and Roach? Would they please form themselves into a supertrio and come and give a concert in Rome, for which funds would be found? Roach and Shepp said yes, but Mingus said no.

So Roach and Shepp went to Rome and performed a marathon duet, so full of fervour that the French Socialists insisted they come back to Paris to do it again for a recording. The resulting double-LP was aptly titled *Force*. Three of its four sides are filled with a loosely arranged homage they named 'Sweet Mao'. Side four has another free-flowing improvisation, called 'Suid Afrika 76': a reminder of the slaughter of black students that had just taken place in Soweto. The French awarded the album their Grand Prix International du Disque. It was the first in a series of weighty duets Roach would record over the next few years.

The next time he met Mingus was in June 1978. The setting was the lawn of the White House and the circumstances were sad. While Roach and Dizzy Gillespie performed 'Salt Peanuts' with a game President Carter, Mingus, now sinking fast, looked on from his wheelchair. And when Mingus offered Max a gesture of reconciliation, Max turned it down. A refusal he would never cease to regret.

*

In 1979 Bruce Lundvall, president of CBS records, telephoned Roach to tell him jazz was making money again, and to ask whether he would like to record some albums. Doubts were voiced at CBS headquarters when Max insisted that his top priority was M'Boom, a collective of nine percussionists, including himself not as leader but as an equal member. Some said such a project was inappropriate for a major record label, but Lundvall was a long-time Roach fan and the objectors were overruled.

The percussion mountain was transported to the CBS studio in New York where, for three days in July, new digital technology recorded the adventures of Roach and his team. The resulting album is a delicately-balanced, richly-textured symphony of skins and metal and wood. Five of the team members, including Max, supplied the compositions upon which the improvisations are based. They range from fierce (Omar Clay's 'Rumble in the Jungle') to dainty (Roy Brooks's 'Twinkle Toes'), with every shade in between. Roach's contributions include the poignant 'January V': a heartfelt requiem, complete with tolling bells and a snare drum rolling like the distant sea, for Charles Mingus. It was on 5 January 1979 that Mingus died.

*

On 15 December 1979 an audience of musicians, critics, and fans squeezed in the McMillin Theatre at New York's Columbia University for an event billed and anticipated in the manner of a heavyweight prize fight. Max Roach, the towering drummer who broke through in the 1940s, was matched with Cecil Taylor, the tigerish pianist who dominated the avant-garde in the 1960s. 'The most melodic of drummers versus the most percussive of pianists' was another favourite tag for the forthcoming duel. Afterwards, sticking to the pugilistic metaphor, reviewers judged that two hours of magnificent combat had ended in a draw.

No one had been looking forward to the engagement more than the fifty-five-year-old Roach, and he was the one who made sure it was professionally recorded. (The astounding result – essential listening – was issued five years later on the Italian Soul Note label.) 'With Cecil it was war,' he told me, 'but a love war.' And after such an exhilarating physical and mental challenge, he found it impossible to resettle in the groves of Academe. He needed the regular adrenaline of public performance, so he slimmed down his commitment to the University of Massachusetts and became an occasional professor.

As well as retaking the American stage, he had become exceedingly busy in Europe. In September 1978 at the Ricordi Studios in Milan he recorded an album of duets with the multi-instrumental virtuoso Anthony Braxton. Twenty years his junior, Braxton had emerged from the ferment of experimentation in Chicago in the late 1960s and found common cause with the European avant-garde in the 1970s. It was his habit to ground his performances in mathematical formulae and diagrams, but for this session Max persuaded him to put all his papers away. The result is a performance of sustained inspiration from the masters young and old. In the wake of its success, Roach and Braxton recorded again the following summer, in front of a fired-up audience at the Willisau Festival in Switzerland. Also at the festival, Roach and Shepp were reunited for another marathon. This time they called it *The Long March*.

Roach's regular touring companions, both in Europe and Japan, were the young members of his latest quartet: tenor saxophonist Odean Pope, trumpeter Cecil Bridgewater and bassist Calvin Hill. These were tough and talented apprentices who thrived on the furious tempos set by their demanding master. The quartet made records in Tokyo, Rome, Amsterdam and Paris, before settling into a long association with the Milan-based Soul Note label.

The first Soul Note album, *Pictures in a Frame*, includes rare examples of Roach's unhurried piano style, and one track on which he sings. His voice is hoarse and soulful, and the song is solemn. Written for a theatre piece called *Black Picture Show*, it tells the surreal and cautionary tale of a man whose garden full of seed became a garden full of snow.

*

In the summer of 1980 CBS released the percussion album, simply enti-tled M'Boom. To launch it the ensemble gave a New York concert in the nave of the Cathedral Church of St John the Divine, the largest Gothic space on the planet. For Roach the setting had the proper resonance, physical and metaphorical. Originally financed by white millionaires, the huge edifice had been overtaken by the spread of Harlem.

M'Boom sold only moderately well, but preparations for a second CBS album went ahead. This was to be mainly a quartet LP, but with a startling beginning, revisiting a high peak of the 1960s. The plan was for Roach to add an improvised drum part to the 'I Have a Dream' speech delivered at the Lincoln Memorial in Washington, DC by Dr Martin Luther King. The permission of the late Dr King's family was sought and readily granted to the composer of the *Freedom Now Suite*.

Nothing else on the album quite matches the intensity of this opening sequence. Roach had grown up with the hypnotic oratory of black Baptist preachers. His drum commentary on the shattering speech by one of the greatest is a response not just to the power of its content, but to the musicality and rhythm of its delivery. At the end, as King holds out his tantalizing vision of freedom, the quartet bursts in with an impas-sioned account of Roach's fitting composition 'It's Time'.

*

Max's mother had died in 1973 with one of her fondest wishes unrealized. 'When,' she kept asking Max, 'are you going to make a record with your daughter?' Mrs Roach had seen her granddaughter Maxine graduate from Oberlin College and enter the music profession as a violist, but it took Max until the 1980s to hit on a family project.

He asked Maxine to form a string quartet to play alongside his jazz quartet, and promised to write some material for public performance. The string players should be trained in the European discipline but also conversant with the ways of jazz. Furthermore, to confound every expec-tation, all four should be young, female and black.

The piece he wrote, called 'A Little Booker', harked back to the late trumpeter Booker Little and Little's composition 'Cliff Walk' (recorded by the Newport Rebels twenty years earlier). What Max did was take Little's exuberant phraseology, designed for a jazz front line, and rearrange it as passage-work for the strings.

To expand the double-quartet repertoire, he called on his trumpeter, Cecil Bridgewater, who was also a gifted composer. Bridgewater's contribution was 'Bird Says', a homage to Charlie Parker using the chord sequence of 'Confirmation', and calling upon the strings to negotiate a Himalayan range of Parker's favourite licks.

When Parker himself performed with strings, the 'straight' players could easily read the parts put in front of them but missed the exquisite subtlety of Parker's staccato-legato phrasing. This time, working with his daughter, Roach explored the technique of short-bowing until the right degree of percussiveness was achieved. Then he proudly dubbed the young ladies that Maxine had assembled 'The Uptown String Quartet', and announced that his double quartet was ready for business.

The premières of 'A Little Booker' and 'Bird Says' took place in Avery Fisher Hall at the Lincoln Centre on 25 June 1982. I was there and can testify that the concept worked, but the reviews were cool. In spite of overwhelming evidence to the contrary, the critics continued to maintain that strings can't swing.

Another première at the same concert met similar indifference. This piece, for string quartet and Roach solo, was written by Max's old friend Peter Phillips (a white composer from the West Coast). His string writing is jagged and spare – full of holes large and small for Max to exploit. Max fondly described it as a unique essay 'in abstract stop-time'. Phillips called the piece 'Survivors', to honour those giants of the revolution who were still going strong – Dizzy Gillespie and Max Roach in particular.

*

Throughout the 1980s Roach toured and recorded at home and abroad, enjoying all of the contexts he had created for himself: duo, quartet, double quartet and M'Boom. In 1984 – the year he reached sixty – I filmed him in each of these settings, and also persuaded him to reveal to the television audience his consummate artistry as a soloist.

The first of his demonstration pieces told a scintillating story, full of drama and suspense, using no more than a pair of sticks and a pair of cymbals controlled by a foot pedal. Sometimes called 'Mr Hi Hat' and sometimes 'Papa Jo', this favourite concert encore is Max's tribute to the supreme cymbal master Jo Jones.

The second filmed solo, equally frugal, showed how steel wrists can make a pair of wire brushes dance on the head of a snare drum. Roach called this one 'The Sweeper'.

The third showpiece ranged over the whole kit: the full complement of drums and cymbals known in the trade as the trap set. To make it even more interesting for the camera, he also played on all the surfaces not designed for the purpose: the sides of the drums, the supporting stands and the nuts and bolts. It amused him to entitle this extra-dimensional extravaganza 'The Third Eye', which was the name of my film production company. I am pleased to report that 'The Third Eye' became a regular part of his repertoire.[15]

*

By the mid-1980s his marriage to Janus was over and he had returned to live in his old apartment on Manhattan's Upper West Side. Here the tributes poured in, including an invitation to travel to London in 1986 and receive a singular honour.

The municipal authority, the Greater London Council, was about to be abolished by the British Prime Minister Margaret Thatcher, who believed it to be far too liberal. Before it shut down, the GLC threw a series of defiant parties, including a grand concert on 16 March at the Royal Albert Hall, 'Celebrating Africa's Contribution to the World'. Top of the bill was Max Roach. Also on stage were a West African dance troupe, a choir, and Max's friend from Ghana, Kofi Ghanaba, who performed the Hallelujah Chorus from Handel's *Messiah* on his talking drums. Four days later Roach was chauffeured to a touching ceremony in the South London Borough of Lambeth, where a reclaimed piece of ground off the Brixton Road was named Max Roach Park.

Across the Channel in France, of course, black music had always been accorded the deepest respect. Many exiled players had made their homes here. It was no surprise then that jazz fans in Paris saw the year 1989 – the 200th anniversary of the French Revolution – as a fitting moment to honour the rebel creators of le bebop. Many of the heroes were dead, but the two most illustrious survivors – Roach and Dizzy Gillespie – agreed to come and celebrate. In March the duo occupied a Parisian stage for two hours, and drew on two lifetimes of African-American musical experience. Young trumpeters were astounded by the stamina and cunning of seventy-one-year-old Gillespie, and drummers marvelled at Roach's speed of reflex and range of ideas. Happily for students of the percussive art, the concert has been preserved in a pin-sharp recording that captures every nuance of Roach's vast vocabulary.

*

Back in America, his two CBS albums having flopped, he did not make his next record until 1991. This 2-CD package, *To the Max!*, which he produced himself, is a handy résumé of his creative preoccupations. M'Boom is here, playing two new pieces he has written for them. The quartet performs fresh arrangements of two from the 1960s: 'The Profit' (from *It's Time*) and 'Tears for Johannesburg' (from the *Freedom Now Suite*). The double quartet stretches out on 'A Little Booker'. The drum solos include a refashioning of his 1966 tour de force 'Drums Unlimited'. And heading the programme is a major new work, a composition called 'Ghost Dance'.

The Native American Ghost Dance was a ritual born of despair in the 1890s, when the Plains Indians created a choreography to summon their ancestors and ward off the invading white man. Dressed in their ghost shirts (believed to ward off bullets), the followers of Ghost Dance were rounded up at Wounded Knee creek and massacred for resisting arrest. Moved by the story, and by the knowledge that there were Native American ancestors on his mother's side of the family, Roach composed a tribute to the victims. He wrote it originally for drums and brass quintet, but for the new album he arranged it for chorus with jazz soloists. Over an urgent 4/4 jazz pulse, the African-American choir sings of another, vanished world – a pre-Columbian continent where man and nature enjoyed a mystic union.

Roach had come upon the Ghost Dance while composing the score for a theatre piece entitled *Strangers*, by Leo Shapiro. He enjoyed writing for the theatre and did it well. Back in 1985 his music for *Shepardsets* (three Sam Shepard plays directed by George Ferencz) won an Obie award for best off-Broadway score. Shortly before recording *To the Max!* he wrote the score for *The Life and Life of Bumpy Johnson*, a play by Amiri Baraka celebrating the exploits of the Harlem outlaw and folk hero. Roach and Baraka (the poet, playwright and black activist formerly known as LeRoy Jones) had been friends since the 1960s, when they pursued the same radical agenda. The new play opened in January 1991 at the San Diego Repertory Theatre, and later transferred, fittingly, to the Aaron Davis Theatre in Harlem.

By now Roach's achievements were being acknowledged even in his own country, where the establishment had taken to showering him with tokens of its approval. Among all the awards, guild memberships and honorary doctorates, one prize stood out: a $372,000 MacArthur Foundation Fellowship. Nothing was required from him in return. The committee was simply rewarding his genius with financial security.

Rather than take his ease, he kept on touring and recording, and invested some of his funds in high-tech office equipment, including several computers. The aim was to impose order on his vast store of memories and memorabilia and funnel them into an autobiography. To give the book a cutting edge, he invited Amiri Baraka to work on it with him. The project remains incomplete.

The autumn of 1991 brought a chill intimation of mortality. On 28 September Miles Davis died, snapping the bond forged when they slaved together for Charlie Parker. During Davis's silent years, between 1976 and 1980, Roach was one of the few friends (Gillespie was another) who constantly visited him and lightened his grim seclusion. In November 1981, after Miles rejoined the world, Max was best man at his wedding to Cicely Tyson.

Music at a memorial concert for Davis was provided by Roach with

the brass quintet for which he had written 'Ghost Dance'. The instru-
mentation – two trumpets, trombone, French horn and tuba – was one
he knew Miles would have appreciated. Henceforth he would perform
regularly with this group. It felt to him like a living memorial, and he
named it the So What Brass Quintet. ('So What' is the opening track of
Davis's most famous record, *Kind of Blue*.) Other classics in the quintet's
repertoire included Charlie Parker's 'Confirmation' and the Parker–Davis
'Donna Lee'.

In spite of the daunting logistics, he also persisted in arranging out-
ings for M'Boom. In 1992 he produced a live album by this resplendent
aggregation, recorded at SOBs, a club in Greenwich Village specializing
in exotic sounds.

In January 1993 his world became a lonelier place with the passing of
Dizzy Gillespie, one of his oldest and dearest friends.

*

Here on earth the show rolled on and grew even bigger. In 1994 at the
Lincoln Centre, Roach masterminded *Juju*, a multi-media show involving
M'Boom, the Donald Byrd Dance Group and video artist Kit Fitzgerald.
To add showbiz allure, the rock drummers Ginger Baker and Tony
Williams were made honorary members of M'Boom for the evening.

In 1995 Roach was back at the Lincoln Centre with a show called
Degga: a rich mixture of percussion, the dancing of Bill T. Jones and
words spoken by the novelist Toni Morrison.

In that same year, the National Academy of Recording Arts and
Sciences elected the Debut recording *Jazz at Massey Hall* to its Grammy
Hall of Fame. Roach accepted the honour on behalf of all those who had
taken part, then got back to work.

At the University of Paris he performed in concert with Toni
Morrison, and on 13 April 1996 he visited London with Archie Shepp. In
the morning they held a workshop for inner-city schoolchildren. Max
talked about his life, emphasizing the value of 'the conservatory of the
streets' and the importance of finding your own sound. Then he told the
youngsters a cautionary tale: the one about his youthful arrogance, and

the way Charlie Parker put him in his place by sitting at his drum set and playing it with ease. To everyone's delight he followed the story with a smooth demonstration of the intricate, four-limbed pattern that Parker had taught him.

In the evening, before a capacity audience in the Queen Elizabeth Hall, Roach and Shepp extemporized a dramatic performance. It began with Max alone in the spotlight, drumsticks held aloft, singing the hymn 'I'm singing with a sword in my hand', which made its way at last to John Coltrane's 'Giant Steps'. This was living history, from two guardians of tradition. (Shepp, like Roach, served on the teaching staff at the University of Massachusetts.)

Max took his part-time duties at UMass seriously. He had enormous respect for Frederick C. Tillis, the African-American director of the Fine Arts Centre, and this respect was mutual. Tillis composed a large-scale work for Roach to perform with symphony orchestra, a concerto in three movements that journeyed through multicultural America. Max recorded it in 1996 with the New Orchestra of Boston, and the recording was issued together with a version of 'Ghost Dance' by the So What Brass Quintet.

He felt invigorated by the young members of this quintet, and over the next few years he worked with them steadily, breaking off for the occasional special assignment. He drummed for modern dancers at New York's 92nd Street YMHA; and in the same location he shared a platform one evening with his contemporary Tito Puente, the Spanish Harlemite who had earned the title 'King of Latin Music'.

In January 1998 he travelled to Paris and London with the substantial forces needed for the project described as Max Roach's America. On stage with him in the two capitals were a gospel choir, conducted by John Motley, and a jazz sextet including French horn. The non-stop two-hour programme was drawn mainly from the historic albums *Freedom Now Suite*, *It's Time* and *Lift Every Voice and Sing*, but with a prominent place for the recent 'Ghost Dance'. Excerpts from Martin Luther King's 'I Have a Dream' speech were declaimed by Max's son Daryl, in a call-and-response passage with his father's drums.

These European concerts were intense occasions, with the emotion reaching its peak during Roach's arrangement of 'Motherless Child'. To sing the lead during the performance of this most moving of sorrow songs, Max had brought with him Melinda Hoskins, whom European reviewers hailed as the new Mahalia Jackson. What they did not know was that this young lady with the stupendous voice was a member of the Roach family down in Dismal Swamp, making her very first professional appearance.

Twelve months later, a fortnight after his seventy-fifth birthday, Roach was back in London. He had come for a rematch with his old adversary Cecil Taylor, witnessed by a capacity crowd at the Barbican and recorded by the BBC. This was the first time the two had been recorded in combat since their epic bout in 1979, and before the main event each of the protagonists, first Max and then Cecil, treated the audience to a solo display.

The duet itself turned out to be less savage and more chess-like than the war of twenty years earlier. For the best part of an hour Taylor attacked the piano with his customary explosive energy, and during all that time Roach never attempted to seize the initiative. Instead, he shadowed his foe with fastidious precision, relying not on strength, but on ancient cunning.

*

Kansas City, Missouri, closed the twentieth century with a fitting gesture: the unveiling of a monument in bronze to Charlie Parker. Roach was invited to play a central part during the three days of ceremonial. By now he had attained the status of talisman or high priest, called upon to give his blessing whenever the bebop movement was celebrated. But he declined the cosy option of living on his reputation and entered the new millennium at the head of yet another fresh project.

The story of the Beijing Trio began in May 1998, when Roach heard the Chinese-American pianist Jon Jang, recognized an original voice, and promised that one day they would record together. Later that summer he was in San Francisco, Jon Jang's home town, and some studio time was booked. Instead of formal rehearsals, Roach chose to prepare by deepening his friendship with Jang and wandering with him in San Francisco's Chinatown, absorbing sensations.

The duo became a trio at the first recording session, when Jiebing Chen, a musician trained in Shanghai, appeared in the studio asking if she could meet Mr Roach. Chen's instrument is the ehru (a traditional, two-stringed violin). As soon as Roach heard the plaintive, soaring beauty that she could draw from it, he insisted she join the Asian-American partnership. The enchanting album that resulted, called simply The Beijing Trio, visits the African-American, the Chinese-American and the Chinese musical traditions. Since it was made, the trio has given concerts across America and in Europe. In June 2001 it charmed the audience in London's Festival Hall. The genre-busting keyboard style of Jon Jang and the exotic lyricism of Jiebing Chen brought cheers, but what lingered in the mind was the sensitive teamwork of their snowy-haired senior partner. At the end of the programme the Chinese youngsters insisted on leaving Roach alone with his public. While his road manager set up his hi-hat at the front of the stage, he charmed the audience with a vague speech, tinged with knowing forgetfulness. Then, overcoming his evident frailty, he gave a careful performance of his expected encore showpiece, 'Papa Jo'.

—

NOTES

Unless otherwise noted, the quotations from Max Roach throughout the book come from interviews with the author.

Chapter One: Cosmic Rays

1. Reisner, Robert, *Bird: The Legend of Charlie Parker*, London: Quartet Books, 1974, p.194.
2. Ibid., p.67.
3. Interview with Michael Levin and John S. Wilson, *Down Beat*, September 1949.
4. From the sleevenote for Elektra Musician, K 52359.
5. Reisner, *Bird*, p.67.
6. Interview with Leonard Feather, *Metronome*, August 1947.
7. Russell, Ross, *Bird Lives! The High Life and Hard Times of Charlie 'Yardbird' Parker*, London: Quartet Books, 1973, p.93.
8. Gillespie, Dizzy with Al Frazer, *Dizzy: To Be or Not To Bop*, London: WH Allen, 1980, p.117.
9. Ibid., p.151.
10. Davis, Miles with Quincy Troupe, *Miles: The Autobiography*, London: Macmillan, 1990, p.v.
11. Reisner, *Bird*, p.51.
12. Davis/Troupe, *Miles*, p.vii.
13. Gillespie/Fraser, *Dizzy*, p.232.
14. Ibid., pp.248–9.
15. Russell, *Bird Lives!*, p.205.
16. Ibid., p.209.
17. Interview with Michael Levin and John S. Wilson, *Down Beat*, September 1949.
18. Gillespie/Fraser, *Dizzy*, p.312.
19. Gitler, Ira, *Swing to Bop*, New York: Oxford University Press, 1987, p.147.

20. Davis/Troupe, *Miles*, p.96.
21. Interview with the author, BBC, December 1970.
22. Reisner, *Bird*, p.126.
23. Davis/Troupe, *Miles*, p.110.
24. Gillespie/Fraser, *Dizzy*, p.264.
25. Interview with the author, BBC, December 1970.
26. Russell, *Bird Lives!*, p.267.
27. Reisner, *Bird*, p.71.
28. Ibid., p.80.
29. Interview with Alyn Shipton, BBC, February 1997.
30. Reisner, *Bird*, p.174.
31. Ibid., pp.57–61.
32. Ibid., p.56.
33. Parker, Chan, *My Life in E-Flat*, Columbia, South Carolina: University of South Carolina Press, 1993, p.36.
34. Davis/Troupe, *Miles*, p.151.
35. Owens, Thomas, *Bebop: The Music and Its Players*, New York: Oxford University Press, 1995, p.250.
36. Miller, Mark, *Cool Blues: Charlie Parker in Canada 1953*, London, Ontario: Nightwood, 1989, p.53.
37. Reisner, *Bird*, pp.154–5.

Chapter Two: Dizzy Atmosphere

Unless otherwise noted, the quotations in this chapter come from Gillespie/Fraser, *Dizzy*.

1. Blindfold Test, *Metronome*, August 1948.
2. *Max + Dizzy: Paris 1989*, A&M CD 6404.
3. Gitler, *Swing to Bop*, p.124.
4. Taylor, Arthur, *Notes and Tones: Musican-to-Musician Interviews*, New York: Da Capo, 1993, pp.192–3.
5. Davis/Troupe, *Miles*, p.54.
6. Reisner, *Bird*, p.94.
7. Harrison, Max, *Charlie Parker*, London: Cassell, 1960, p.34.

Chapter Three: Un Poco Loco

1. Gitler, *Swing to Bop*, p.102.
2. Blesh, Rudy and Harriet Janis, *They All Played Ragtime*, New York: Oak Publications, 1971, p.194.
3. Gitler, Ira, *Jazz Masters of the 40s*, New York: Macmillan, 1966, p.112.

4. Groves, Alan and Alyn Shipton, *The Glass Enclosure: The Life of Bud Powell*, Oxford: Bayou Press, 1993, p.10.
5. Paudras, Francis, translated by Rubye Monet, *Dance of the Infidels: A Portrait of Bud Powell*, New York: Da Capo, 1998, p.282.
6. Ibid., p.144.
7. Gitler, *Swing to Bop*, pp.102–3.
8. Dance, Stanley, *The World of Duke Ellington*, London: Macmillan, 1971, p.105.
9. Gillespie/Fraser, *Dizzy*, p.231.
10. *The Complete Bud Powell on Verve*, Verve 314 521 669-2, Booklet p.41.
11. Spellman, A.B., *Four Lives in the Bebop Business*, New York: Limelight, 1994, p.189.
12. *The Complete Bud Powell on Verve*, Verve 314 521 669-2, Booklet p.65.
13. Ibid.
14. Ibid., p.66.
15. Gitler, *Jazz Masters of the 40s*, p.110.
16. Ibid., p.116
17. Ibid., p.120.
18. *The Complete Bud Powell Blue Note Recordings*, Mosaic MR5-116, Booklet.
19. Ibid.
20. Ibid.
21. *The Complete Bud Powell on Verve*, Verve 314 521 669-2, Booklet pp.72–73.

Chapter Four: Weird Nightmare

1. Mingus, Charles, *Beneath the Underdog*, London: Weidenfeld and Nicolson, 1971, p.66.
2. Interview with Ira Gitler, *Down Beat*, July 1960.
3. Interview with Mike Dean, BBC, August 1972.
4. Mingus, *Beneath the Underdog*, p.92.
5. Santoro, Gene, *Myself When I Am Real: The Life and Music of Charles Mingus*, New York: Oxford University Press, 2000, p.43.
6. Davis/Troupe, *Miles*, p.76.
7. Ibid., p.85.
8. Mingus, *Beneath the Underdog*, p.321.
9. Interview with Mike Dean, BBC, August 1972.
10. Essay enclosed with the album *Let My Children Hear Music*, Columbia 31039.
11. Reisner, Robert, *The Jazz Titans*, New York: Doubleday, 1960, p.56.
12. *Triumph of the Underdog*, directed by Don McGlynn, Academy Video CAV 057, 1997.
13. Mingus, *Beneath the Underdog*, pp.324–5.

14. There is a theory (floated by Mingus's friend Bill Coss, when he wrote the sleevenote for the Debut 12-inch LP DEB-124) that Parker and Gillespie caught a later flight not because Parker had disappeared, but because Oscar Goodstein and Celia Mingus had taken the last two seats.

Chapter Five: Maximum

1. Gillespie/Fraser, *Dizzy*, p.205.
2. Interview with Charles Fox, BBC, December 1989.
3. Gitler, *Swing to Bop*, pp.76–7.
4. Gillespie/Fraser, *Dizzy*, p.235.
5. Ibid., p.234.
6. Davis/Troupe, *Miles*, p.91.

Chapter Six: Jazz at Massey Hall

1. Miller, *Cool Blues*, p.71.
2. Correspondence with the author, September 2000.
3. Miller, *Cool Blues*, p.72.
4. Ibid., p.74.
5. In other accounts, the recording machinery was handled by Massey Hall's regular sound man or (least likely) by an engineer who travelled up from New York.
6. Miller, *Cool Blues*, p. 93.

Chapter Seven: Now's the Time

1. Interview with Nat Hentoff, *Down Beat*, January 1953.
2. Reisner, *Bird*, pp.229–30.
3. Ibid., p.207.
4. Gillespie/Fraser, *Dizzy*, p.366.
5. Parker, *My Life in E-Flat*, p.50.
6. Reisner, *Bird*, p.71.
7. Ibid., p.15.
8. Ibid., p.40.
9. Ibid., p.94.
10. Ibid., p.152.
11. Ibid., p.81.
12. Ibid.
13. Priestley, Brian, *Mingus: A Critical Biography*, New York: Da Capo, 1984, p.61.
14. Reisner, *Bird*, p.134.

Chapter Eight: To Be or Not To Bop

Unless otherwise noted, the quotations in this chapter come from Gillespie/Fraser, *Dizzy*.

1. Ron Riddle, 'A look back at Lenox', *Jazz 1*, 1958, pp.30–1.
2. Sleevenote for *Dizzy on the French Riviera*, Philips PSK 3159.
3. Interview with Charles Fox, BBC, December 1989.

Chapter Nine: Glass Enclosure

1. Taylor, *Notes and Tones*, p.225.
2. Reisner, *Bird*, p.225.
3. Groves/Shipton, *The Glass Enclosure*, p.60.
4. Sleevenote for *The Bud Powell Trio*, Columbia 33SX 1575.
5. Groves/Shipton, *The Glass Enclosure*, p.62.
6. Ibid., p.63.
7. Paudras, *Dance of the Infidels*, p.22.
8. Ibid., p.24.
9. Ibid., p.28.
10. Ibid., p.59.
11. Ibid., p.120.
12. Ibid., p.318.
13. Gitler, *Jazz Masters of the 40s*, p.129.

Chapter Ten: Meditations for a Pair of Wire Cutters

1. *Triumph of the Underdog*, directed by Don McGlynn.
2. Priestley, *Mingus*, p.53.
3. Davis/Troupe, *Miles*, p.155.
4. Essay enclosed with *Let My Children Hear Music*, Columbia 31039.
5. Reisner, *Bird*, p.152.
6. *Charles Mingus: The Complete Debut Recordings*, Debut 12-DCD-4402-2, Booklet p.32.
7. Sleevenote for *Mingus at the Bohemia*, Debut DEB-123.
8. Spellman, *Four Lives in the Bebop Business*, p.216.
9. Feather, Leonard, *From Satchmo to Miles*, New York: Da Capo, 1984, p.30.
10. *Mingus Oh Yeah*, Atlantic 790 667-2, CD bonus track.
11. Ellington, Duke, *Music is my Mistress*, London: WH Allen, 1974, p.243.
12. Interview with Charles Fox, BBC, December 1989.
13. Ellington, *Music is my Mistress*, p.243.
14. Sleevenote for *The Black Saint and the Sinner Lady*, Impulse IMP 11742.
15. Sleevenote for *Mingus Plays Piano*, Impulse IMP 12172.

16. *Charles Mingus: Portrait*, Prestige P 24092.
17. Ibid., sleevenote.
18. Quoted in Priestley, *Mingus*, p.162.
19. Interview with Russell Davies, BBC, August 1981.
20. Coleman, Janet and Al Young, *Mingus/Mingus: Two Memoirs*, New York: Limelight, 1994, p.4.
21. Essay enclosed with *Let My Children Hear Music*, Columbia 31039.
22. Quoted in Santoro, *Myself When I Am Real*, p.311.
23. Ibid., p.353.
24. *Triumph of the Underdog*, directed by Don McGlynn.

Chapter Eleven: It's Time

1. Quoted in Gitler, *Jazz Masters of the 40s*, p.197.
2. Davis/Troupe, *Miles*, p.154.
3. Interview with Nat Hentoff, *Down Beat*, 7 April 1954.
4. *The Complete Mercury Max Roach Plus Four Sessions*, Mosaic MD7-201, Booklet pp.20–1.
5. Ibid., p.21.
6. Interview with Jezz Nelson, Jazz FM, March 1997.
7. Interview with Jezz Nelson, BBC, November 2001.
8. *Down Beat*, 15 March 1962.
9. *New York Post*, 21 May 1961.
10. Interview with Charles Fox, BBC, December 1989.
11. Paudras, *Dance of the Infidels*, pp.273–4.
12. Note for *Max Roach: Drums Unlimited*, Atlantic 7567-81361-2.
13. Ibid.
14. Interview with Charles Fox, BBC, December 1989.
15. The film *Sit Down and Listen: The Story of Max Roach* (part of the *Repercussions* series) was issued on video by Home Vision Entertainment, VHS 833-9052.

SELECT BIBLIOGRAPHY

Bacon, Tony and Dave Gelly, Brian Priestley, Paul Trynka, *The Sax and Brass Book*, London: Balafon, 1998

Baldwin, James, *Notes of a Native Son*, London: Penguin, 1995

Balliett, Whitney, *Dinosaurs in the Morning*, London: Phoenix House, 1964

Blesh, Rudy and Harriet Janis, *They All Played Ragtime*, New York: Oak Publications, 1971

Carr, Ian, *Miles Davis: The Definitive Biography*, London: HarperCollins, 1999

Catalano, Nick, *Clifford Brown*, New York: Oxford University Press, 2000

Christie's Catalogue, *Bird – The Chan Parker Collection*, London: Christie's South Kensington, 8 September 1994

Coleman, Janet and Al Young, *Mingus/Mingus: Two Memoirs*, New York: Limelight, 1994

Dance, Stanley, *The World of Duke Ellington*, London: Macmillan, 1971

Davis, Miles with Quincy Troupe, *Miles: The Autobiography*, London: Macmillan, 1990

Ellington, Duke, *Music is my Mistress*, London: WH Allen, 1974

Feather, Leonard, *Inside Be-Bop*, New York: JJ Robbins, 1949

Feather, Leonard, *From Satchmo to Miles*, New York: Da Capo, 1984

Giddins, Gary, *Celebrating Bird: The Triumph of Charlie Parker*, London: Hodder and Stoughton, 1987

Gillespie, Dizzy with Al Fraser, *Dizzy: To Be or Not To Bop*, London: WH Allen, 1980.

Gitler, Ira, *Jazz Masters of the 40s*, New York: Macmillan, 1966

Gitler, Ira, *Swing to Bop*, New York: Oxford University Press, 1987

Gleason, Ralph J, *Jam Session: An Anthology of Jazz*, London: Peter Davies, 1958

Groves, Alan and Alyn Shipton, *The Glass Enclosure: The Life of Bud Powell*, Oxford: Bayou Press, 1993

Harrison, Max, *Charlie Parker*, London: Cassell, 1960

Harrison, Max, *A Jazz Retrospect*, London: Quartet Books, 1991

Haydon, Geoffrey and Dennis Marks (eds), *Repercussions: A Celebration of African-American Music*, London: Channel Four Books/Century, 1985

Hentoff, Nat, *The Jazz Life*, London: Panther, 1964

Hentoff, Nat, *Jazz Is*, London: WH Allen, 1978

Kilbourn, William, *Intimate Grandeur: One Hundred Years at Massey Hall*, Toronto: Stoddart Publishing, 1993

Miller, Mark, *Cool Blues: Charlie Parker in Canada 1953*, London, Ontario: Nightwood, 1989

Mingus, Charles, *Beneath the Underdog*, London: Weidenfeld and Nicolson, 1971

Mingus, Sue (ed.), *Charles Mingus: More than a Fake Book*, New York: Jazz Workshop/Hal Leonard, 1991

Owens, Thomas, *Bebop: The Music and Its Players*, New York: Oxford University Press, 1995

Parker, Chan, *My Life in E-flat*, Columbia, South Carolina: University of South Carolina Press, 1993

Paudras, Francis, translated by Rubye Monet, *Dance of the Infidels: A Portrait of Bud Powell*, New York: Da Capo, 1998

Priestley, Brian, *Mingus: A Critical Biography*, New York: Da Capo, 1984

Priestley, Brian, *Charlie Parker*, Tunbridge Wells: Spellmount, 1984

Reisner, Robert, *Bird: The Legend of Charlie Parker*, London: Quartet Books, 1974

Reisner, Robert, *The Jazz Titans*, New York: Doubleday, 1960

Russell, Ross, *Bird Lives! The High Life and Hard Times of Charlie 'Yardbird' Parker*, London: Quartet Books, 1973

Santoro, Gene, *Myself When I Am Real: The Life and Music of Charles Mingus*, New York: Oxford University Press, 2000

Shapiro, Nat and Nat Hentoff (eds), *Hear Me Talkin' To Ya*, New York: Dover, 1966

Shaw, Arnold, *The Street that Never Slept*, New York: Coward, McCann & Geoghegan, 1971

Shipton, Alyn, *Groovin' High: The Life of Dizzy Gillespie*, New York: Oxford University Press, 1999

Spellman, A.B., *Four Lives in the Bebop Business*, New York: Limelight, 1994

Taylor, Billy, *Jazz Piano: a Jazz History*, Dubuque, Iowa: Wm. C. Brown, 1983

Taylor, Arthur, *Notes and Tones: Musician-to-Musician Interviews*, New York: Da Capo, 1993

Vail, Ken, *Bird's Diary: The Life of Charlie Parker 1945–1955*, Chessington, Surrey: Castle Communications, 1996

Vail, Ken, *Dizzy Gillespie: The Bebop Years 1937–1952*, Cambridge: Vail Publishing, 2000

Weiler, Uwe, *The Debut Label: a Discography*, Norderstedt, Germany: private edition, 1994

Woideck, Carl, *Charlie Parker: His Music and Life*, Michigan: University of Michigan, 1998

Woideck, Carl (ed.), *The Charlie Parker Companion*, New York: Schirmer Books, 1998

SELECT DISCOGRAPHY

Jazz at Massey Hall. Debut OJC20 044-2.

CHARLIE PARKER

1. *The Complete Birth of the Bebop.* Stash ST-CD-535
2. *Early Bird.* Spotlite SPJ 220-CD
3. *Blues from Kansas City.* Decca GRD-614
4. *Complete Savoy Sessions.* Definitive DRCD 11148 (4CD)
5. *Red Norvo and his Selected Sextet.* Spotlite SPJ 127-CD
6. *The Complete Charlie Parker on Verve.* PolyGram 837 141-2 (10CD)
7. *Charlie Parker on Dial: the Complete Sessions.* Spotlite SPJ-CD4 101 (4CD).
8. *The Complete Dean Benedetti Recordings of Charlie Parker.* Mosaic MD7-129 (7CD)
9. *Complete Savoy Live Recordings.* Definitive DRCD 11153 (4CD)
10. *Bird in Paris.* Stateside ITJ-7005 (LP)
11. *Bird & Fats Live at Birdland 1950.* Cool & Blue. C&B-CD 103
12. *Summit Meeting at Birdland.* CBS 82291 (LP)
13. *The Complete Legendary Rockland Palace Concert.* Jazz Classics CD-JZCL-5014 (2CD)
14. *Charlie Parker Boston 1952.* Uptown UPCD 2742
15. *Charlie Parker Montreal 1953.* Uptown UPCD 2736
16. *The Washington Concerts.* Blue Note 22626
17. *Charlie Parker at Storyville.* Blue Note 85108
18. *Bird Meets Birks.* Zu-Zazz ZZ 1003 (LP)
19. *Rara Avis (Rare Bird).* Stash ST-CD-21

DIZZY GILLESPIE

1. *Masters of Jazz: Dizzy Gillespie. Volume 1.* Media 7 MJCD 31
2. *Masters of Jazz: Dizzy Gillespie. Volume 3.* Media 7 MJCD 45

3. *Masters of Jazz: Dizzy Gillespie. Volume 4*. Media 7 MJCD 86
4. *Masters of Jazz: Dizzy Gillespie. Volume 5*. Media 7 MJCD 110
5. *The Dizzy Gillespie Story 1939-1950*. Proper Records Properbox 30 (4CD)
6. *The Complete RCA Victor Recordings*. 07863 66528 2 (2CD)
7. *Lullaby in Rhythm*. Spotlite 107 (LP)
8. *Diz 'n Bird at Carnegie Hall*. Roost 7243 8 57061 2 7
9. *Dizzy Gillespie Pleyel Jazz Concert 1948 & Max Roach Quintet 1949*. BMG 74321409412
10. *Dizzy Gillespie and his Big Band in Pasadena*. GNP Crescendo GNPD-23
11. *School Days*. Savoy SV 0157
12. *The Champ*. Savoy SV 0170
13. *Pleyel Concert 1953*. Vogue 74321 154662
14. *Diz and Getz*. Verve 833 559-2
15. *Diz and Roy*. Verve VE-2-2524 (2LP)
16. *The Best of the Dizzy Gillespie Big Bands*. Verve VLP 9076 (LP)
17. *Dizzy Gillespie at Newport*. Verve 513754-2
18. *For Musicians Only*. Verve 837 435-2
19. *The Greatest Trumpet of them All*. Verve 2304 382 (LP)
20. *Sonny Side Up*. Verve 825674-2
21. *Gillespiana and Carnegie Hall Concert*. Verve 519 809-2
22. *Dizzy on the French Riviera*. Philips PSK 3159 (LP)
23. *Dizzy Gillespie & the Double Six of Paris*. Philips 830 224-2
24. *The Dizzy Gillespie Reunion Big Band*. MPS 533-550-2
25. *Oscar Peterson & Dizzy Gillespie*. Pablo PACD-2310-740-2
26. *Max + Dizzy: Paris 1989*. A&M CD 6404 (2CD)

BUD POWELL

1. *Bud Powell: Tempus Fugue-It*. Proper Records Properbox 22 (4CD)
2. *Swing Sessions 10*. EMI Pathé CO54-16030 (LP)
3. *The Complete Blue Note and Roost Recordings*. Blue Note CDP 7243 8 30083 2 2 (4CD)
4. *The Complete Bud Powell on Verve*. Verve 314 521 669-2 (5CD)
5. *New York All Star Sessions*. Bandstand BDCD 1507
6. *Lover Come Back to Me*. Magic Music 30009-CD
7. *In March with Mingus*. Magic Music 30005-CD
8. *Inner Fires: The Genius of Bud Powell*. Elektra 1046-71007-2
9. *Summer Sessions*. Magic Music 30006-CD
10. *Swingin' with Bud*. RCA Victor 74321 13041 2
11. *Paris Jam Session*. Universal 832692
12. *The Complete Essen Jazz Festival Concert*. Black Lion BLCD 760105
13. *A Portrait of Thelonious*. Sony 65187

14. *At the Golden Circle Volume 1.* Steeplechase SCCD 36001
15. *Bud Powell in Paris.* Reprise 6098 (LP)
16. *Our Man in Paris: Dexter Gordon.* Blue Note CDP 0777 7 46394 2 2
17. *Bud Powell: Salt Peanuts.* Black Lion BLCD 760121
18. *Return to Birdland 64.* Mythic Sound MS 6009
19. *The Return of Bud Powell.* Fresh Sound FSR-CD 27

CHARLES MINGUS

1. *Complete 1945–1949 West Coast Recordings.* The Jazz Factory. JFCD 22825
2. *Hamp: The Legendary Decca Recordings of Lionel Hampton.* Decca GRD-2-652
3. *The Red Norvo Trio: The Savoy Sessions.* Savoy SV-0267
4. *Charles Mingus: The Complete Debut Recordings.* Debut 12-DCD-4402-2 (12CD)
5. *Bird Box Vols. 10-12.* Jazz Up JUTB 3010/11/12 (3CD)
6. *Jazz Composers Workshop.* Savoy SV 0171
7. *Charles Mingus: Passions of a Man.* Rhino-Atlantic R 2 72871 (6CD)
8. *New Tijuana Moods.* RCA ND 85644
9. *East Coasting.* Affinity AFF86 (LP)
10. *Scenes in the City.* Affinity AFF 105 (LP)
11. *The Complete 1959 Columbia Recordings.* Columbia C3K 065145 (3CD)
12. *Mingus Revisited* (aka *Pre-Bird*). Verve 826 496-2
13. *Charles Mingus presents Charles Mingus.* Candid CCD 79005
14. *Newport Rebels.* Candid CCD 79022
15. *Money Jungle.* Blue Note CDP 7 46398 2
16. *The Complete Town Hall Concert.* Blue Note CDP 8283532
17. *The Black Saint and the Sinner Lady.* Impulse IMP 11742
18. *Mingus Plays Piano.* Impulse IMP 12172
19. *Charles Mingus: Portrait.* Prestige P 24092 (2LP)
20. *Let My Children Hear Music.* Columbia 31039 (LP)
21. *Charles Mingus and Friends.* Columbia C2K 64975 (2CD)
22. *Changes One.* Rhino-Atlantic 8122-71403-2
23. *Changes Two.* Rhino-Atlantic 8122-71404 2
24. *Me Myself An Eye / Something Like a Bird.* Atlantic CCL 68402 (2CD)

MAX ROACH

1. *Max Roach Quartet featuring Hank Mobley.* Original Jazz Classics OJC 202
2. *The Best of Max Roach and Clifford Brown in Concert.* GNP Crescendo GNPD 18

3. *The Complete EmArcy Recordings of Clifford Brown.* EmArcy 838 306-2 (10CD)
4. *Sonny Rollins + 4.* Original Jazz Classics OJCCD-243-2
5. *Sonny Rollins: Saxophone Colossus.* Original Jazz Classics OJC 202912
6. *The Complete Mercury Max Roach Plus Four Sessions.* Mosaic MD7-201 (7CD)
7. *Thelonious Monk: Brilliant Corners.* Original Jazz Classics OJC 200262
8. *Sonny Rollins: Freedom Suite.* Original Jazz Classics OJCCD 0672
9. *We Insist! Max Roach's Freedom Now Suite.* Candid CCD 9002
10. *Percussion Bitter Sweet.* Impulse GRD-122
11. *It's Time: Max Roach His Chorus and Orchestra.* Impulse IMP 11852
12. *Speak, Brother, Speak.* Original Jazz Classics OJC 646
13. *The Max Roach Trio Featuring the Legendary Hassan.* Atlantic 7 82273-2
14. *Drums Unlimited.* Atlantic 7567-81361-2
15. *Members, Don't Git Weary.* Koch KOC-CD-8514
16. *Lift Every Voice and Sing.* Atlantic 7567-80798-2
17. *Max Roach and Archie Shepp: Force.* Uniteledis UNI 289 76 (2LP)
18. *Max Roach and Cecil Taylor: Historic Concerts.* Soul Note SN 121100/1 (2CD)
19. *Max Roach and Anthony Braxton: Birth and Rebirth.* Black Saint BS 120024
20. *Pictures in a Frame.* Soul Note SN 121003
21. *M'Boom.* Columbia 57886
22. *Chattahoochee Red.* Columbia 37376 (LP)
23. *Max Roach Double Quartet: Easy Winners.* Soul Note SN 121109
24. *Survivors.* Soul Note SN 121093
25. *To the Max!* Blue Moon/MR R2 79164 (2CD)
26. *The Beijing Trio.* Asian Improv Records

INDEX